Project Management for Book Publishers

Project Management for Book Publishers provides readers with a solid understanding of efficient processes and workflows for content creation, product development, and the marketing and distribution of both physical and digital products.

Digital has brought more data, more training, and more accountability to the publishing process. But it has also shone light on how systems designed initially around print-first publications are ill-equipped to support an industry of now would-be digital media companies. This book addresses some of the major challenges for publishing houses facing this reality, including how to create a digital-aware workflow, implementing quality assurance procedures, and using different management systems to develop an efficient workflow. Beginning by explaining project and product management practices used throughout technology and media companies, it then delves into when and how these principles can be applied to the publishing workflow. Topics covered include Waterfall and Agile Project Management, Scrum methodology, Kanban framework, ebook and audio formats, metadata, quality assurance, crowdfunding, in-app monetization, ONIX, and accessibility. Readers will consider not just how to contend with online platforms that allow authors to publish with the click of a button, and audiences accustomed to accessing content across multiple platforms and formats, but also challenges arising from factors such as the data-driven acquisitions model in libraries, the downward spiral of sales in college bookstores, the call for accessibility, and the need for fluid content systems that can work with different publishing databases and software.

Written for publishing professionals at all levels, this book will also help advanced students of Publishing and Book Studies navigate best practices for project management in the modern publishing landscape.

John Rodzvilla is Assistant Professor of Digital Publishing in the Department of Writing, Literature and Publishing at Emerson College, Boston. He was previously the Graduate Program Director for the Master of Arts Degree in Publishing and Writing and the Senior Electronic Publisher-in-Residence at Emerson College.

Project Management for Book Publishers
The Programs and Workflows Behind Making Books and Digital Products

John Rodzvilla

LONDON AND NEW YORK

Designed cover image: sebastian-julian / E+ via Getty Images

First published 2025
by Routledge
4 Park Square, Milton Park, Abingdon, Oxon OX14 4RN

and by Routledge
605 Third Avenue, New York, NY 10158

Routledge is an imprint of the Taylor & Francis Group, an informa business

© 2025 John Rodzvilla

The right of John Rodzvilla to be identified as author of this work has been asserted in accordance with sections 77 and 78 of the Copyright, Designs and Patents Act 1988.

All rights reserved. No part of this book may be reprinted or reproduced or utilised in any form or by any electronic, mechanical, or other means, now known or hereafter invented, including photocopying and recording, or in any information storage or retrieval system, without permission in writing from the publishers.

Trademark notice: Product or corporate names may be trademarks or registered trademarks, and are used only for identification and explanation without intent to infringe.

Access the Support Material: https://www.routledge.com/9781032516721

British Library Cataloguing-in-Publication Data
A catalogue record for this book is available from the British Library

Library of Congress Cataloging-in-Publication Data
Names: Rodzvilla, John, author.
Title: Project management for book publishers : the programs and workflows behind making books and digital products / John Rodzvilla.
Description: Abingdon, Oxon ; New York, NY : Routledge, 2024. | Includes bibliographical references and index.
Identifiers: LCCN 2023055792 (print) | LCCN 2023055793 (ebook) | ISBN 9781032516738 (hardback) | ISBN 9781032516721 (paperback) | ISBN 9781003403395 (ebook)
Subjects: LCSH: Publishers and publishing–Management. | Book industries and trade–Management. | Electronic publishing–Management. | Project management.
Classification: LCC Z278 .R59 2024 (print) | LCC Z278 (ebook) | DDC 070.5068/4–dc23/eng/20240323
LC record available at https://lccn.loc.gov/2023055792
LC ebook record available at https://lccn.loc.gov/2023055793

ISBN: 978-1-032-51673-8 (hbk)
ISBN: 978-1-032-51672-1 (pbk)
ISBN: 978-1-003-40339-5 (ebk)

DOI: 10.4324/9781003403395

Typeset in Galliard
by Taylor & Francis Books

Contents

List of Illustrations   vi

Introduction   1

PART I
Workflow and Project Management Theory   9

1. Modern Publishing Operations   11
2. Publishing Workflows   24
3. Project Management   50
4. The Linear Project Life Cycle   62
5. The Iterative Project Life Cycle   78

PART II
Project Management in the Three Areas of Publishing   97

6. Content Creation Project Management   99
7. Content Production Project Management   117
8. Content Distribution Project Management   137

Conclusion: Final Note   167

Index   169

Illustrations

Figures

1.1 Robert Darnton's publishing communications circuit outlines the relationships between those involved in book publishing. From *The Case for Books* by Robert Darnton, copyright © 2009. Reprinted by permission of PublicAffairs, an imprint of Hachette Book Group, Inc.   17
1.2 Padmini Ray Murray and Claire Squires updated the communications circuit to reflect the changes caused by digital publishing and distribution. [TheDigitalPublishingCommunicationsCircuit.pdf] © 2013 Intellect Ltd. The definitive, peer reviewed and edited version of this article is published in *Book 2.0*, 3(1), 3–24, 2013. https://doi.org/10.1386/btwo.3.1.3_1.   18
1.3 The actors identified in the communications circuits from Darnton and Ray Murray and Squires can be grouped into clear work spheres focused on their work to give a better sense of the flow of work.   20
2.1 The level of detail between a top level, or handoff, diagram and a process level, or service diagram, provides two ways of looking at a process. In this example of printing a book, the handoff diagram shows when work moves between roles at a printing plant while the service diagram outlines the steps each role needs to complete to move the work to the next role. Please note, this image has been included for the visual overview; a higher resolution version can be downloaded at https://www.routledge.com/9781032516721.   36
2.2 Example of swim lane diagrams for high-level editing processes. This swim lane follows a final manuscript from the author through different editors from receipt to copy edit.   39
2.3 A comparison of randomized sticky notes recording tasks and organized sticky notes that show what tasks are part of a process or subprocess.   40
2.4 When systems are necessary for a process, they should be treated as actors and have a swim lane for their part of a process.   43
3.1 The three constraints of project management in their iron triangle format.   56

3.2 The high-level work breakdown structure for a book project shows the divisions of labor needed to move from idea to book. 58
3.3 The network diagram identifies the critical path of work in the tasks outlined in the work breakdown. 58
4.1 A linear project life cycle with six stages represents the major work needed for a standard book project. 64
4.2 A Gantt chart showing the length of time for content production. The chart shows the time a process will take in a sequence or if it can be completed simultaneously with another process. Please note, this image has been included for the visual overview; a higher resolution version can be downloaded at https://www.routledge.com/9781032516721. 70
5.1 Unlike the linear model where processes are visualized as steps from initiation to release, the Agile model is better visualized as a cycle where once one development cycle ends, the next one begins. 82
5.2 A Kanban board can provide a quick visualization of what work is completed and what work needs to be done. The board can use rows in a way similar to swim lanes to identify different team members, while the columns indicate if the work is yet to be worked on, is in process, or is completed. 87
5.3 The cards or sticky notes that are placed on a Kanban board will have the user story or task at the top of the card. The cards may also include an indication of the time needed to complete the task (hours or points) and the priority of the task (MoSCoW). This card indicates the user story will take twenty-four hours and has the priority of "should" complete in the MoSCoW terminology. 88
5.4 This example of a burndown chart shows the actual work that is completed as compared to the expected completion rate over time. The y-axis shows number of tasks and the x-axis the number of project weeks. 91
5.5 A velocity chart will measure the work completed against the work scheduled across multiple sprints. This will give the team a sense of how quickly they are completing tasks compared to their initial estimate. In this example, the team is having to complete work beyond the timebox allotted. 91

Tables

2.1 Example of risk matrix. Severity and probability are based on a scale of 1 (low) to 3 (high). Any risk that has an S*P greater than 4 requires the creation of a contingency plan. 32
2.2 Example of SWOT analysis on expanding international rights department. 33
6.1 A template for evaluation of and task recording for potential titles. 104

8.1 Different sales reps within a publishing house will need a variety of material for their clients. Reps selling to domestic bookstores may only need marketing material and information about the forthcoming book, while those who license a translation may need proposals and typescripts from the editorial department. 152

Boxes

2.1	Organizing Work: Function Versus Process	28
2.2	Interview Questions for Process/Activity Discovery	37
4.1	Sample Ebook QA Guidelines	73
5.1	Twelve Core Principles for Agile Project Development	80
6.1	List Development	103
7.1	Basic Steps Towards Accessibility in the Production Process	133

Introduction

Writers often portray the book publishing industry as a secretive club of elitist gatekeepers. In books like Pamela Redmond's *Younger* (2005), Alessandro Gallenzi's *Bestseller* (2010), Paul Fournel's *La Liseuse* (2012), Stephanie Johnson's *The Writers' Festival* (2015), and Zakiya Dalila Harris's *The Other Black Girl* (2021), publishing houses are portrayed as locations that are either mysterious to the writer or even dangerous to writer and editor alike. These books may not be as dramatic in their portrayal of publishing as the movie *Wolf* (1994) where Jack Nicholson and James Spader play publishing managers who are literal wolves, but they do reflect how writers and, through their work, the larger culture understand book publishing as a place where power isn't in the words themselves but hidden in an executive suite. For those who encounter the book publishing industry in fiction, the ordinary world of the office is often just a front that hides the machinations that decide who gets published and becomes a best-selling author. It is this sense of the author's powerlessness that R.F. Kuang captures throughout *Yellowface*, her novel about writing and publishing:

> [T]his is how things are. Publishing crawls. Gatekeepers sit on manuscripts for months, and meetings happen behind closed doors while you're dying from anticipation on the outside. Publishing means no news for weeks, until you're standing in line at Starbucks or waiting for the bus, and your phone pings with the email that will change your life.
>
> (2023, 131)

Throughout the novel publishing houses are portrayed as distant forces that hold power over an author's life. June Hayward, the novel's protagonist, is ignored by her first editor post publication of her debut novel and she only communicates with her new publishing house over phone, email, or Zoom, relying on her literary agent as liaison and interpreter of her editor's silences. Kuang offers a perfect representation of how the author sees the black box of publishing: a space where a manuscript submission is met with long silences, boilerplate rejections, or, if they are lucky, random revision requests that may start a book deal. In an effort to offer some transparency on the inner workings of book publishing, this book will approach the art of book publishing through the lens of project management theory.

DOI: 10.4324/9781003403395-1

Book publishing has always been about project management. After a commissioning editor negotiates the contractual terms with an author, a series of activities begin in different departments to plan for the eventual creation and publication of a book based on the proposal. Those activities may include: the development of a marketing plan and budget; the pitching on the proposal by a subsidiary rights department for translations, serializations, and audiobook licenses; and preliminary production schedules. Upon delivery of a manuscript the developmental editor works with the author to revise their text to become book-worthy before sending it deeper into the publishing house for legal reads, copy editing, interior layout, proofreads, and so on, before the house releases finished products.

Production departments have long viewed books as projects and have developed methodologies similar to the formalized practice of project management or have invested in project management training for their staff. But the importance of project management throughout the whole of the publishing house is rarely discussed when talking about book publishing. Books on publishing often only mention the term in passing when covering aspects related to book production. In the rare instances where the practice is discussed more fully—*Inside Book Publishing* (2022) by Giles Clark and Angus Phillips, *The Business of Digital Publishing* (2022) by Frania Hall, and Joe Biel's *A People's Guide to Publishing* (2018) are three such examples—the theory is discussed as being a key component to modern book publishing but is still relegated to chapters focused on production or organizational structure. The book that has covered project management for book publishing in the most detail is Adrian Bullock's *Book Production* (2012), which makes its focus clear in the title. There is little available for those publishing professionals looking to get certified as a project manager to advance in their job or those students in publishing programs searching for more information on how project management works in book publishing. The body of literature includes white papers (Beebe and Meyers 2000, BISG Workflow Committee 2019) or case studies on digitization (Schwartz 1999), ebook development (Borgstrom 2013), XML (Kleinfeld 2013), and print-on-demand (POD) requirements (Sip 2016). Turning to project management literature, one finds massive texts on the theory and practice designed as study guides for certification, a time intensive and expensive process that culminates in a lengthy online test. But the main focus of project management for book publishing—the creation of budgets and schedules dependent on the cost and availability of resources such as paper and persons to create and market a book—is the foundation for every functioning publishing house. This book will attempt to broaden the literature on book publishing to include a view of the book as a project that has a life cycle similar to other digital media products.

This book intends to show that the modern process of turning a manuscript into a book and getting that book into a reader's hands is just project management. I would even argue that it is necessary for book publishers to treat their work as project management if they hope to succeed in the twenty-first century's larger media marketplace. In an article, from 2 September 2022 for *Publishers Weekly*, Rachel Deahl asks, "is the publishing industry broken?" and outlines reasons for burnout in the publishing industry including the loss of a work-life balance within the industry due to the consolidations of houses and the digitization of work. Several executives in the article note that the burnout may be because new professionals come into the industry thinking book publishing is all about finding the next great novel but find that the work is correspondence, scheduling, and data entry. They also point out this has always been the case for book publishing. In other words, young professionals are coming into the industry without being equipped with the right tools for the job, including those of project management, become frustrated, and then leave. In addition to a workforce without proper training, most publishing houses have not done the needed work to reassess their resources in relation to the changes brought about by digitization and remain structured around outdated publishing roles.

Publishing is, and always has been, a technology-based business. The main points of contact with the general public, the editors and finished books, appear as aspects of creative work, but everything that takes place between those two points has always relied on technology to improve the work done. Adriaan van der Weel reminds us that

> printing is the first example of modern industrial production. After an initial capital investment in the means of production (a printing press and movable type) a series of identical copies of a product—a particular text—could be manufactured. It was an industrial process which involved a clear division of labor and resulted in a workflow efficiency that compared very favorably with manuscript production, even with the already efficient pecia system.
>
> (2011, 79–80)

Areas of book publishing may present themselves as a creative industry, but it is also an industry that has responded to technological developments. The industry no longer uses Gutenberg's modified winepress or hot type to create books; today's printers use computer-to-plate (CTP) machines to etch lithographic plates in a manner similar to an office copier or home printer. Books are now available as digital files of both text and audio or can be printed and bound on demand, all improvements brought about through adoption of technology that require a clear series of steps to complete.

Publishing Technologies: Desktop Publishing and Markup Languages

Before delving into project management theory and its place in book publishing, there are two technologies that need to be acknowledged as the main drivers for the evolution of book publishing from a print-based industry to a digital one: desktop publishing and the use of markup languages in composition and design. Both of these technologies have changed book publishing from an industry focused on the creation of a print product into one that focuses work around the creation, management, and storage of content as digital files. Both technologies developed over the last decades of the twentieth century and allowed the multinational corporate publishers the ability to grow seasonal lists from a few dozen titles a year to ones with new titles in the triple digits that are released in multiple formats. The technology also allowed small publishers and individual authors the ability to compete with those publishers in the marketplace by offering the means to print and distribute titles quickly and inexpensively, creating an opportunity to publish niche titles that, in an analog model, had made little economic sense.

The closest thing the book industry has to a universal publishing tool is Adobe's Creative Cloud, specifically InDesign, a "page design and layout toolset" available on both desktop and mobile devices to create and publish printed and digital material, including ebooks. The program was originally introduced as PageMaker in 1985 that competed with QuarkXPress for the professional market. In 2000, Adobe released InDesign, a revamped version of PageMaker and soon bundled it with other creative software like Photoshop and Illustrator on a disk and called the product the Creative Suite. Eventually that suite would become an online service now called the Creative Cloud. While some smaller publishing houses still rely on Quark for their book layout and the largest academic and professional publishers create books and articles using the LaTeX typesetting system for its ability to deal with formula and scientific notations, InDesign has become the leading layout program for book publishing as it allows book files to be shared across the company and with third-party entities like book packagers and freelancers who can work on their own system and share editable files back to the publisher.

While desktop publishing changed the workflow process of a publisher's production department, there was a parallel development going on outside publishing that would have a much bigger impact on the dissemination of information. When computers became part of our daily life, our relationship to text changed. Up to that point, text was contained. There were limits to its reach: limits such as an octavo-sized (152.4 × 228.6 mm) book with 25mm margins on all sides of the text block on the page. The paper that contained text had physical dimensions and defined borders. The web broke those borders and with them our relationship to text. Text now had interactive and referential properties that requires programming to provide semantically meaningful tags. By the start of the twenty-first century, text was no longer defined by its display format but by its markup which allowed for it to be repurposed and reused across different media. It also allowed for desktop publishing software to offer an interactive interface while hiding the document's structure and metadata in its code.

This ability to provide an internal structure to text changed how publishers could manage text. Texts were no longer stored on sheets of film that were not editable. Content could now be restructured and reused: articles were free from their sections; sections were free from their chapters; chapters were free from their books. The lack of a physical structure for content meant that publishers needed a richer system of metadata for the identification of content and new means of storage for the digital content.

These two technologies were key drivers in changing the internal working of a publishing house and moving it from an industry that had developed a way of working, centered around the creation and distribution of a print project to a modern media industry that relies on the practice of content management. The content a publisher creates is digital content that is stored digitally and transmitted to online retailers and printers. Anyone who hopes to understand how publishing works will need to also comprehend the digital processes by which a house manages a book project, not just the ways the house creates its product. That's what the rest of this book will explore.

This book has tried to construct itself in a way similar to other titles that address project management for a particular industry (Agro 2019, Badiru 2023, Buser, Massis, and Pollack 2014, Feist 2013, Ginevri and Trilling 2017). It introduces pertinent general theories from the field of project management and ties those theories to relevant examples for that particular industry. For this exploration within the book publishing industry, the book will be split into two parts: theory and practice. The book's first five chapters provide an overview on the theory on workflows and project management as they apply to the book publishing industry. Each chapter is designed to introduce the reader to the major concepts on book publishing, organizational structure, workflow analysis, and project management and how those concepts are integrated within a modern publishing house. Each of the last three chapters will apply the principles of project management, discussed in part one, to a different area of publishing. These chapters are focused on how publishing professionals within different departments engage with a book project and other departments throughout the life cycle of a project.

The focus on the book project is meant to provide a way to discuss project management without generalizing the work done by publishing professionals in all types of publishing houses. Unlike most books on project management that focus on generic life cycle models where the reader must do the work of converting the ideas about developing, planning, executing, and closing to their own work, I have tried to modify the models to reflect the needs of book publishers. The book rests on the premise that most book publishers are focused on turning a textual manuscript, developed by an author outside the organization, into a print and/or digital book that is distributed by the publishing house. My definition of a book for these chapters is a self-contained product that is primarily textual in nature and is to be considered complete. While I mention apps and serialized content in the sections on iterative project management, the product from each iteration should be considered a complete and finished product.

Outline of Part I: Workflow and Project Management Theory

The first chapter approaches book publishing as a series of operations that create and distribute content. I approach the industry as one where media moves between different actors (authors, editors, marketers, booksellers, readers) who are engaged in specific activities in a book project. In this chapter, I define the work in terms of a framework of content creation, content production, and content distribution. This model is then compared to the established communications circuit for print and digital publishing to reveal the ways that relationships within publishing are tied to the function of the role in that communications circuit.

Chapter two addresses how work is structured in a publishing house and how to capture a picture of that work through swim lane diagrams and how to use those diagrams to analyze and improve workflows within a publishing house. The process of discovering and recording a publishing house's work is approached through the Business Process Management (BPM) model which uses steps focused on framing, mapping, and evaluation as a means for workflow discovery. The development of workflow maps creates a visual outline that captures the actual work being done. The chapter ends with a section on the process of evaluating and revising work so that it aligns with a publisher's goals and strategic plans.

The third chapter introduces the main theories of project management as they pertain to book publishers. The chapter defines the parameters and constraints of a project that will frame the creation of the linear and iterative project life cycles that are addressed in the next two chapters. The chapter concludes with a brief introduction to the phases of beginning the project, planning, and organizing the project, executing the project, and the project's close.

When discussing project management and publishing there is a need to understand the history of book publishing as one that reflects the history of linear project management. The process of identifying a book proposal for publication and the process of converting the resulting manuscript into a book follows a linear project life cycle. This chapter (Chapter four) introduces a six-phase model that reflects the work done with a book publisher on a book project. The chapter will trace the process for how publishers evaluate proposals for publication and release a finished book through a life cycle that involves the initiation, planning, development, testing, release, and maintenance of a book project. Each phase of the project is outlined with explanations on the different documents publishers should expect to produce to ensure a successful project.

The complement to the life cycle of a linear project is that of the iterative project, often framed as an Agile project. This fifth chapter focuses on how the iterative project life cycle is different from the linear one and what this means in terms of publishing. Book projects from a publishing house will be linear in nature, but certain projects such as apps or databases may not have the predetermined outcome that dictates how a product needs to be developed. The development of these projects will take place through several release cycles that respond to user feedback. Agile projects are discussed in detail with special attention to Kanban boards and the Scrum methodology.

Outline of Part 2: Project Management in the Three Areas of Publishing

The book's second half will apply the theories of workflows and project management in terms of linear and iterative project life cycles to the publishing by focusing specifically on content creation, content production, and content distribution. Each chapter will explore the relevant processes in a book project as they apply to each of these three areas of publishing. Instead of focusing on the book as a product, these chapters will frame the work that goes into turning a manuscript into a multi-format book that gets distributed through physical and online retailers in terms of a project life cycle.

Chapter six frames the ideas about workflow and project management outlined in previous chapters in terms of content creation within a publishing house. The chapter's main focus is the work done by various roles in the editorial department and how those processes can be seen in the different phases of project management. An editor's work of acquisition and list management is seen as work done in the initiation and planning phases of a book project. The chapter also discusses version control and digital asset management. The chapter ends with an outline of the work of content creation in an Agile publishing project and how the emerging technologies of community publishing platforms and algorithmic creation are changing the nature of content creation.

Chapter seven traces how a book project moves from those involved in content creation to the content production workers who turn the typescript into a book. The production work to turn a typescript into a book is addressed as an aspect of production workflow and project management. Production's responsibility for the planning of the budget and schedules is addressed as is the work of a production department in the development phase of a book project. The chapter also outlines quality control measures for both print and digital products. The chapter ends with a section on the issues in adding accessibility to digital book products.

The last chapter frames the ideas about workflow and project management outlined in previous chapters and applies them to the work of content distribution within a publishing house. The chapter traces the work done by marketing, promotion, and sales departments on a book project and how those processes are tied to different phases of project management. The chapter discusses book returns and metadata as it applies to book sales. The chapter also examines how those involved with content distribution provide an essential means to gather user feedback in an Agile environment. The chapter ends with an examination of crowdfunding and subscriptions as alternatives to the bookstore model of book distribution.

References

Agro, Chuck. 2019. *Fine Art Movement and Storage: Project Management for the Visual Arts*. Lanham, MD: Rowman & Littlefield.

Badiru, Adedeji Bodunde. 2023. *Project Management for Scholarly Researchers: Systems Innovation and Technologies*. Boca Raton: CRC Press.

Beebe, Linda and Barbara Meyers. 2000. "Reprint: Digital Workflow: Managing the Process Electronically." *Journal of Electronic Publishing*, 5(4). https://doi.org/10.3998/3336451.0005.403.

BISG Workflow Committee. 2019. *Fixing the Flux: Challenges and Opportunities in Publishing Workflows*. New York: The Book Industry Study Group.

Borgstrom, Liam. 2013. "Simplifying E-book and Print Production." *Learned Publishing*, 26, 115–122. https://doi.org/10.1087/20130207.

Buser, Robin, Bruce E. Massis, and Miriam Pollack. 2014. *Project Management for Libraries: A Practical Approach*. Jefferson: McFarland & Company.

Deahl, Rachel. 2022, September 2. "Is the Publishing Industry Broken?" *Publishers Weekly*. https://www.publishersweekly.com/pw/by-topic/industry-news/publisher-news/article/90242-is-the-publishing-industry-broken.html. Accessed September 12, 2023.

Feist, Jonathan. 2013. *Project Management for Musicians: Recordings Concerts Tours Studios and More*. Boston, MA: Berklee Press.

Ginevri, Walter and Bernie Trilling. 2017. *Project Management for Education: The Bridge to 21st Century Learning*. Newtown Square, PA: Project Management Institute.

Kleinfeld, Sanders. 2013. *The Case for Authoring and Producing Books in (X)HTML5*. Presented at Balisage: The Markup Conference 2013, Montréal, Canada, 6–9 August 2013. In Proceedings of Balisage: The Markup Conference 2013. Balisage Series on Markup Technologies, vol. 10. https://doi.org/10.4242/BalisageVol10.Kleinfeld01.

Kuang R.F. 2023. *Yellowface*. New York, NY: William Morrow, an imprint of HarperCollins.

Sip, Roman. 2016. "Workflow of the Management in Printing Production in Condition of Print on-Demand," *International Journal of Management Science and Business Administration*, 2(10), 23–33.

Schwartz, Lysa. 1999. "Must Change, Will Change: Process Re-engineering in Publishing." *Publishing Research Quarterly*, 15, 100–109. https://doi.org/10.1007/s12109-999-0016-0.

Weel, Adriaan van der. 2011. *Changing Our Textual Minds: Towards a Digital Order of Knowledge*. Manchester: Manchester University Press.

Part I
Workflow and Project Management Theory

1 Modern Publishing Operations

Book publishing is not about printing books. Nor is it about audiobooks, ebooks, or even mobile apps. All these are only the formats that a publisher creates to distribute through bookstores, online retailers, author events, or through their own website. Modern book publishing is about the complex series of operations that makes the creation and distribution of those formats happen. A publisher needs a way to evaluate and transform an idea that arrives in the form of a manuscript into a book product. That product then needs to find its intended audience and meet a certain standard of quality expected by that audience. In order to create and distribute a book the publisher may engage in activities that include the editing of content according to rules of grammar and style and the designing of a template for the pages that is based on the principles of graphic design. It will also include functions such as marketing, printing, warehousing, and the financial management of income received from the sale of those products.

Those who work in modern book publishing do so with the understanding of who the audience for their products are, the marketplace where these products will be sold, and how they will be marketed and sold in those marketplaces to the right audiences. To get to a viable finished product requires publishing professionals to have discussions on not only the acquisition of the product in the first place but what ancillary products or licenses can be sold, how long it will take to make the book, the best time to release the book, which formats should be available on release, and even when a revision might be needed.

When a consumer holds a print book or opens an ebook on their handheld device, they are holding the result of hundreds of hours of work from several people—full-time employees as well as freelancers—that work together to create a digital document of text and images that can be output into a format for the reader to consume as a book. This book does not need to be a bound volume that sits upon a shelf. It could be printed and gathered but not bound as exemplified by Anne Carson's *Nox* or *Float*. It could be an ebook. It could even be an audiobook. As long as the container frames content that is limited in scope, non-performative in nature and is text-based,[1] it will be considered a book in the context of our focus on book project management. And yet, for the attention paid to how format defines the book, acknowledgement of the transformational work done within a publishing house rarely gets noted in the book. Movies, video games, and television shows have end credits that list everyone

DOI: 10.4324/9781003403395-3

from screenwriter to the catering company that was involved in its making, but a book may, at best, offer an acknowledgements page where the author thanks an editor and possibly a publicist alongside teachers, family, and friends. But what about the press operator who proofs the alignment of lithographic plates in a four-color process or the employee who processes payments on books sold and to make the semi-annual royalty payments to an author? Some presses, including Dialogue Books in the United Kingdom and Avid Reader, a division of Simon & Schuster US, have begun to include a credits page that names workers across a number of departments including editorial, marketing, production, and design, but this work remains unacknowledged in the book and often unknown not only to the author but also those working at the publishing house.

This is one reason why books carry a sense of magic: readers have little sense of what goes into the actual process of creating a book. There's a lack of awareness of publishing roles outside the author-facing ones. That lack of acknowledgement of the full labor that goes into the making of a book mixed with the jargon used by publishing professionals to describe their work results in an industry that can look like a group of wizards performing magic spells that result in sell sheets, digital advanced reading copies, and bound typeset pages on a bookstore shelf. For those who work in the industry, the magic is created through countless meetings, managing the flow of work, and the use of project management theory.

This book will outline best practices and standard methods for doing the work of creating and selling a book as a project with the caveat that every publisher will need to do the work to figure out how work is best structured in their company and develop their own processes accordingly. When I use the phrase "book publishing industry" in this book, I am talking about houses like Routledge, the publisher of this book, that has offices in several countries and hundreds of employees, as well as the small independent publisher that may have five employees and contracts with freelancers and service providers to do the needed work in terms of editing, design, and distribution. Book publishers of all sizes do the same work. The difference is in the scale of that work. That difference in scale dictates how publishers manage the work that determines their sustainability in an industry with small margins and the ever present threat of returns from retailers. It is this management that I will focus on throughout this book.

In addition to thinking about how the company's size affects how projects are managed, the work done within a company will also depend on what part of the industry the publisher is in. The book industry is really several different specialized industries that all happen to have a history of producing their information in the same format. How they get from an idea to a product in a reader's hand or screen will follow radically different workflows. For example, a trade book publisher may acquire a completed fiction manuscript from a book packager that can be on bookshelves in a matter of months, while an academic press may need eighteen months for a completed manuscript to go through rounds of peer review and a lengthy revisions process to create a variety of digital products that respond to the needs of libraries, Open Access policies, and various textbook rental markets as well as the normal retail channels.

That's not to say that there is no common ground between the different types of book publishers. Looking at the biggest and most general picture of book publishing reveals that these companies are working towards the goal of finding a manuscript to turn into a product that can be sold or distributed in the marketplace. The finished product could be a print book, digital content in a library database, an audiobook, or even serialized content from a subscription service. All publishers are working towards what Gretchen Peck described as the "publish once, output many" concept (2017, 29) that has influenced several modern publishers discussed throughout this book to revise their creation and production processes.

The Book Publishing Process: Creation, Production, Distribution

As a way to move away from the "print book" thinking that tends to dominate the way the industry visualizes its processes, I will adapt the threefold frame that Clayton Childress uses to describe the life cycle of a book in his study, *Under the Cover*. Childress presents a single case study that traces the journey of an author's idea from manuscript to finished book to the audience response at author readings and book club discussions. Childress's title expands upon the idea of a book's life cycle, the release-to-remainder journey, to include how an author develops ideas and readers respond. The three stages to the life defined by Childress are:

- The creation process,
- The production process, and
- Public reception.

Childress's book follows the development and publication of Cornelia Nixon's novel, *Jarrettsville* as a representative book for what Nixon's publisher calls a "typical publishing story" (2009, 12). Childress notes that he focuses on *Jarrettsville* because the whole publishing story

> requires finding an author who is willing to let an outsider into her creative process. It means interviewing her many times over, and pouring over the notes, drafts, emails, and communications she generated while writing.... To tell a typical publishing story also means to know why publishers that rejected the novel did reject it, and why the publisher that published it did so too.
> (Childress 2019, 12)

In doing this work, Childress has created a unique biography of a book that reveals the skills needed to pull off the magic trick of publishing a book and in doing so, he offers a way of understanding publishing that pertains to all book projects. Unfortunately, in Childress's model the publishing company appears as a secondary character. While literary agents, publisher Charlie Winston, and Nixon's editors appear throughout the book, the work of others in the publishing house only shines in the production section. *Project Management for Book Publishing* will show how the work done inside the walls of a publishing house mirrors the larger process described in Childress's book. Instead of focusing on the author's development of an idea into a manuscript, this book will focus on the other side of content creation: the editor's work of evaluation and development of a manuscript. This book will also approach audience reception from the publisher's point of view and group it with the sales process as the bridge that connects the creative act of making a book to its readership. What Childress defines as reception—a term used to focus on the reader's response to Nixon's text as well as the cover design and placement in bookstores—I will replace with the broader term, distribution. Distribution moves the focus of the last stage from audience response to what takes place within a publishing house to get the book on a retailer's bookshelf and make readers aware of its existence. Any work from a publisher that goes into the creation of a book project will be considered as being part of either:

- Content creation,
- Content production, or
- Content distribution.

Reframing the life of a book project this way allows for the work by the major departments within a publisher to become visible in the creation of a book. It also acknowledges a large part of the work that goes into the publication process including the warehousing, rights management, and returns that take place upon release of the title.

By reframing the book as a project, the industry can move away from the narrow focus that limits publishers into thinking in a precious format-driven mindset. By uncoupling the work from the finished product, the industry can better understand what it means to work in publishing in the twenty-first century. This is already happening at the global publishers Pearson and Wiley. These two companies no longer refer to themselves as publishers even though they continue to create what most people would consider books. In fact, Pearson's web page on company strategy does not mention publishing at all. It defines the company as one that creates "vibrant and enriching learning experiences designed for real-life impact" and goes on to list six key performance indicators (KPI) focused on digital growth, consumer engagement, product effectiveness, talent, diversity, and sustainability (2023). Pearson is still involved with both digital and book publishing, but this house also understands the shifts that have taken place in its markets. The textbook publisher that once relied on a captive student population to purchase course material from the campus bookstore now needs to develop multimedia content that works with different online learning systems or is available as textbook rentals from services such as Chegg and Vital Source. Wiley's focus on the about page of its website is about research and education. Wiley makes some mention of print, but similar to Pearson, its focus is on products and users over formats (2023). Wiley has also introduced a textbook rental option on their site, an initiative that reflects how the company is becoming more flexible in dealing with their marketplaces. This agility has been helped through their move away from the functional organizational model of most book publishers towards a matrix model that includes a project management office (PMO) that supports initiatives that use Agile methodologies for some of their academic and professional resources. Wiley has also been a company that has hired certified project managers as part of their workforce (Siegman 2018).

And these two companies are not alone. Directors and managers at multinational publishers spend a significant part of their year thinking about how to make their processes more efficient in and develop ways to be more responsive to a marketplace that continues to be disrupted by new technologies. Over the years this has included everything from redesigning book project workflows around tagged typescripts that were part of the "Start with XML" movement (O'Leary 2009) to publishing processes adapted from the tech sector such as Peter Armstrong's Lean Publishing Manifesto (2010) that treated the publishing process as analogous to that of software development where every book can be seen as an app and every editor, an angel investor. Even if these concepts were never adopted beyond the publishers who proposed them, the influence of project management and the tech industry on media companies has changed how professionals think about book publishing. One need only search as far as the former CEO of Penguin Random House Markus Dohle's testimony on Bertelsmann's bid for Simon & Schuster where he described the role of publishers as similar to "angel" investors, that is people who take a risk in financially supporting an idea in its infancy and then influencing the production and marketing of the product once it has been proven to be viable in order to make a profit.

For those professionals who may be working in a local office for a global company like Penguin Random House, they will need to understand how this investor mentality fits with the advances expected by authors as well as how that translates into the sales estimates for the finished book. The skills to manage the translation from manuscript to finished book may be listed as part of a job description, but the details hidden within the bulleted list may be part of a workflow diagram the publishing company has created to trace how each department operates. It is these diagrams that offer the professional a real sense of the work they will be doing.

Likewise for those authors and editors who want to start their own small publishing house, little is available on how to manage the needed processes in the manner of the large corporate publishers. Titles such as Thomas Woll's *Publishing for Profit* (2014) provide primers on the economic aspects of running a house but the actual processes tend to be vague when not relevant to the balance sheet. This book aims to fill in this gap and provide information on both the theory and practice of workflow and project management and the practice of project management within the three areas of work: creation, production, and distribution.

These categories focus on the main areas of work done within book publishing as well as their effect on the publishing house's finances. Some of the work includes the creating and shaping of textual content, the tagging of the content for storage in a company's digital asset system, and the creation of files to create sellable formats.. This is followed by the actual content distribution in different formats to an intended audience. This category not only includes the steps needed to move physical copies from a warehouse to retailer or customer, but also the management of digital access and the work done in the sales, marketing, and publicity departments to raise awareness of the publication by its intended audience.

The processes of content creation, production, and distribution are part of a much larger network of cultural production that involves authors and consumers, neither of whom will be addressed in this book. The focus here is within the publishing house and the work done between the delivery of a book project or completed manuscript to a commissioning editor to the delivery of a print copy to a bookstore or a retailer's warehouse or the uploading of a digital file to an online retailer. This book will not talk about the creative process for authors and how they navigate what to write and when. Those interested in understanding the writing process should read Jane Friedman's writing at janefriedman.com and in her book, *The Business of Being a Writer* (2018). I also won't focus on audience and the increased role readers have come to play in the word-of-mouth marketing of how the retail landscape for books has changed how publishers think about selling books. The topic of the reader's role is covered in Simone Murray's *The Digital Literary Sphere* (2018). A history of the role bookstores play in the distribution process is covered in Laura Miller's *Reluctant Capitalists* (2006).

A Process-Oriented Framework

In order to understand why the sequence of the book publishing processes is structured as it is, it is helpful to think through the publishing process in terms of relationships. By looking at the relationships that exist between publishers, the authors, and readers as well as the relationships between the different segments of the industry, the flow of work will often reveal itself in those relationships. For example, knowing how and when different editors are engaged with an author over edits will inform the promotion and marketing departments on when that author might be available for content marketing opportunities that include opinion pieces for print and online publications. Likewise, knowing when the final typescript has been delivered to the production department will define when the marketing department can create advanced reading copies (ARC) to send out for review and create hype among potential readers. An understanding of the relationships in publishing and their importance at different stages in the transformation of manuscript to book brings clarity to what work needs to be done within each department as well as in what sequence the work is carried out and who needs to know when it is complete and why.

When addressing publishing relationships, it is helpful to turn to the work done on the publishing communications circuit by Robert Darnton (1982) and Padmini Ray Murray and Claire Squires (2013). Robert Darnton's circuit, proposed in a 1982 *Daedalus* article, was meant as a visual explanation of the European book trade in the eighteenth century. It also turned out to be an accurate reflection of how different actors within the publishing process relied on one another to create, distribute, and promote print through to the end of the twentieth century. In addition to Darnton's communications circuit, the work done by Padmini Ray Murray and Claire Squires in 2013, to update Darnton's work to reflect the changes brought upon the relationships with the original communications circuit by the industry's adoption of digital technology, provides another view on how relationships have changed to include digital products, their workflows, and the increased access readers received with the introduction of the Internet.

In his diagram on the book trade in Europe, Darnton places the author and publisher at the top of the illustration with a double-headed arrow showing one of only two back and forth communications.[2] The diagram provides a simple visualization of how the different areas of publishing developed in relation to one another for both communication and the flow of work that was needed (van der Weel 2011, 105). In Darnton's diagram the publisher communicates with the author and printer bridging the author's creative work with the physical labor of the printing press. Publishers needed to communicate to both parties as part of their role in transforming the written manuscript into printed book. The printers in turn not only communicate with the publisher but also with their suppliers of resources, labor, and the shippers who were responsible for distribution, legal or otherwise, to a bookseller. The booksellers also connect with the readers, who in turn complete the circuit by communicating back to the author.

While this diagram was originally meant to provide a sense of how publisher and reader were able to skirt governmental control in Europe around the Enlightenment, it illustrates the relationship between the different types of workers within the book publishing process. For example, the printing process for books still involves the publishers and shippers as the publishers supply the files to the printers to print and the shippers are the ones who carry the books away from the press to a warehouse. As I will show when talking about content production, the management of the process of creating a book product does not require input from all parts of the publishing house or the retailers, it only requires input from those designing, composing, and coding the files for printing and distribution.

Ray Murray and Squires first proposed a revised version of Darnton's publishing communications circuit in 2012. This update added literary agents as a node that

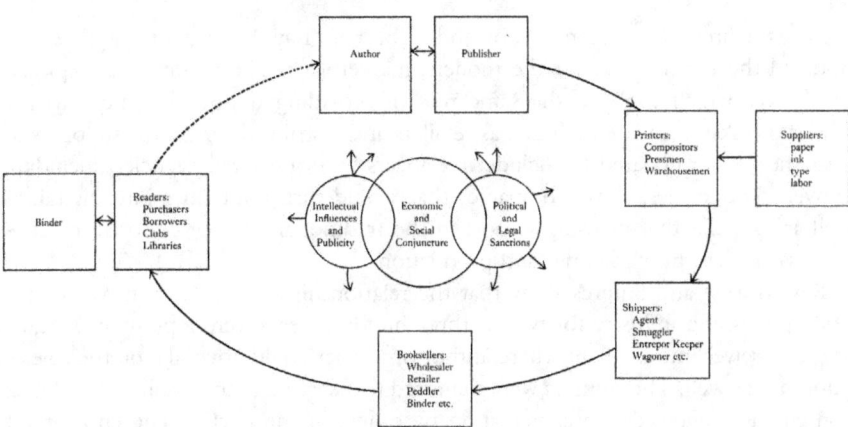

Figure 1.1 Robert Darnton's publishing communications circuit outlines the relationships between those involved in book publishing. From *The Case for Books* by Robert Darnton, copyright © 2009. Reprinted by permission of PublicAffairs, an imprint of Hachette Book Group, Inc.

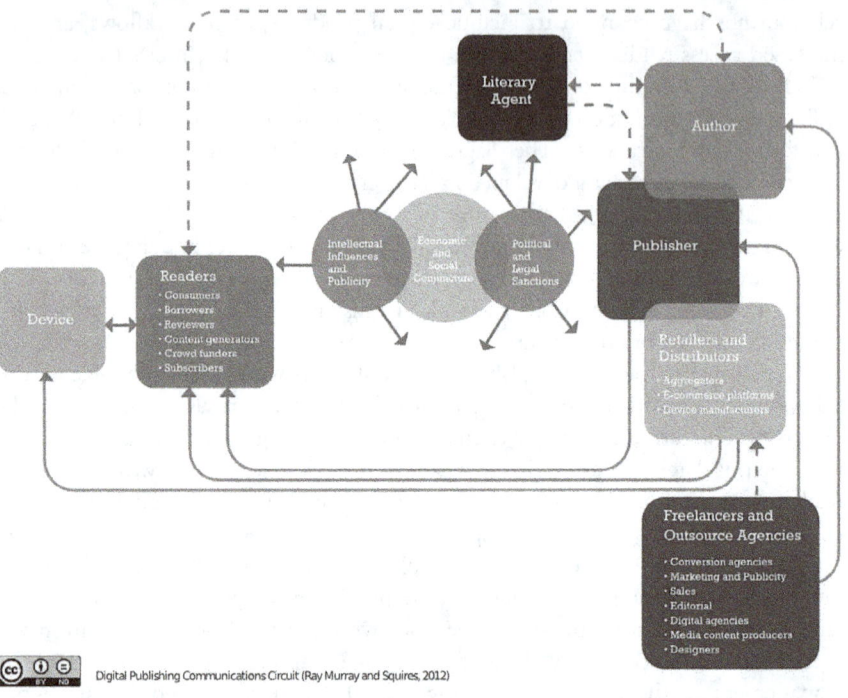

Figure 1.2 Padmini Ray Murray and Claire Squires updated the communications circuit to reflect the changes caused by digital publishing and distribution. [TheDigitalPublishingCommunicationsCircuit.pdf] © 2013 Intellect Ltd. The definitive, peer reviewed and edited version of this article is published in *Book 2.0*, 3(1), 3–24, 2013. https://doi.org/10.1386/btwo.3.1.3_1.

acted as a firewall between author and publisher. Ray Murray and Squires also updated the terminology for the modern marketplace. The bindery was replaced by devices which took on the same role of providing unbound content to the reader. Bookstores were reframed as retailers and distributors. And the suppliers to publishers were updated to include freelancers and outsource agencies, including conversion agencies, those companies that would turn print titles into digital, as well as agencies that provide support in the traditional areas of editorial, promotion, sales, design, marketing, and production.

Ray Murray and Squires show that the relationships that had been part of the book publishing industry for two to three hundred years were rapidly reconfiguring themselves into a circuit where author or retailer could now take on the role of publisher as well. The printers were demoted to a service to the publisher as digital content now allowed content creation by others in the circuit. The entire right side of Darnton's communications circuit appeared to collapse on itself as the traditional roles became more fluid in the digital space.

Squires and Ray Murray were primarily interested in what the communications circuit looked like for digital products, but as ebooks became another format within the industry the disappearance of the differentiation between author and publisher that occurred in the digital space also influenced the centuries-old print space as well. An argument could be made that once all publishing became digital publishing, the relationships in Darnton's original communications reoriented themselves according to a shift in responsibility between roles. As authors took on the activities of publishers, they needed to manage relationships with booksellers and printing services. Squires and Ray Murray's update revealed how the communications in much of publishing centered mostly around the work being done from the time the author pitched an idea to when that book was available for sale.

In the intervening years since Ray Murray and Squires introduced their update, the specialization of formats that has been taking place within publishing has introduced even more specialized aspects to the circuit. For example, Iben Have and Birgitte Stougaard Pedersen modified the digital publishing circuit model to visualize the audiobook creation and distribution system in Denmark. Audiobooks, which replace written text with audio, fit well with Ray Murray and Squires's model where author/publisher hire freelancers, including vocal and production talent before distributing the files to library services and online retailers. Services like Audible allow authors to use their ACX service to find vocal talent and audio producers who can help to create an audiobook of the title for the author. These audiobooks then appear on Audible, Amazon, and Apple's iTunes.

This fluidity in communication roles thanks to changes to the marketplace means that the work that needs to be done to move a book project through the publishing process can now be done by various workers. We can see this in the editing work that literary agents often perform on their clients' manuscripts. As the functions within publishing are no longer a good indication of what work gets done by whom, the industry needs a model to give shape to this labor. The individual activities involved in publishing have been well covered in titles like Adrian Bullock's *Book Production* (2012), Peter Ginna's *What Editors Do* (2017), Marshall Lee's *Bookmaking* (2004), Lynette Owen's *Selling Rights* (2024), and *Inside Book Publishing* (2019) from Giles Clark and Angus Phillips. In almost all these titles the focus is still on function and the work associated with those functions. What is helpful is that the work of publishing almost always centers around a deliverable. It is easy to start separating work from function by identifying deliverables such as:

- The profit and loss (P&L) statement,
- The manuscript,
- The author's contract,
- Licensing contracts,
- The advance info (AI) or title info (TI) sheet,
- The Marketing one-sheet,
- Co-op (Co-operative marketing with bookstores),
- Cover designs,
- Interior designs,
- Production files, and
- Bound books.

Once the deliverables are identified, connecting them to the previously defined communications circuit reveals a map of how work takes place in a publishing process, a map that can be used to frame a house's workflows and processes. A house is not able to begin to understand what they do as a series of activities and processes focused on the creation of book projects or the management of operations that support those projects. These activities can include editorial evaluations, peer review (for academic titles), the creation of the publishing proposal form, editorial pitch meetings, contract negotiations, developmental edits, page and cover designs, sales conferences, marketing plans, printing schedules, warehousing, and returns. When workflow is mentioned, it is often within the confines of the production process as those who work in production are always handling several projects at once and need documented workflows to ensure they can make the milestones for different projects and stay on schedule. Production departments are no longer the only place in the publishing house to think about workflows. Workflows are necessary for every department in a house.

To connect this work done in a publishing house with the circuit models outlined above, I offer a high-level visualization of the work that is carried out in book publishing centered around creation, production, and distribution.

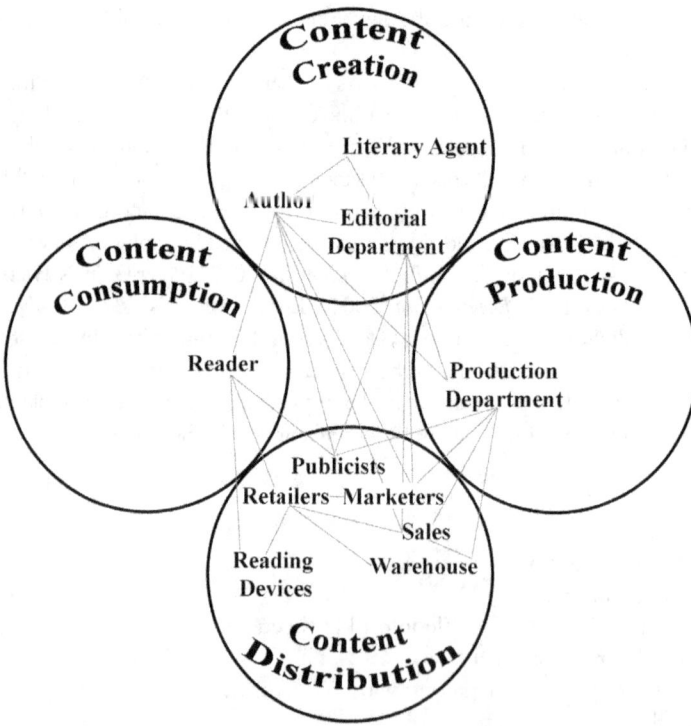

Figure 1.3 The actors identified in the communications circuits from Darnton and Ray Murray and Squires can be grouped into clear work spheres focused on their work to give a better sense of the flow of work.

Aligning author, literary agent, and editorial department as content creators, allows for the work needed to bind the content together for a book project. This diagram on publishing work focuses on roles as the locus for the work. In order to understand work, the publisher needs to be clear on how content is created. New book ideation comes from both inside and outside the house; commissioning editors generate ideas as well as reviewing authors' proposals. Creation work will include the developmental edits that are now carried out within multiple locations including the editorial department, the literary agency, book packagers, and book coaches. Readers may be involved as a beta reader for early drafts, or a sensitivity reader to check the manuscript for content that includes unintentionally inaccurate, biased, or stereotypical characterization, or as a peer reviewer, specialized work that is performed within content creation. While it is clear that readers have always had some say in the creation of an author's work—we can see their influence on both Dickens and Doyle to resurrect the dead in their work (Aig 1991)— the reader's role when viewed from a publishing communication perspective has been seen as an endpoint and not as an active participant in a book's creation. In modern publishing where authors have manuscripts already revised in response to comments from MFA writing workshops and public comments on social writing platforms and beta readers the author found through social media, a part of the readership for the book is now engaged with it before a bookstore offers it for sale.

In terms of the two communications circuits outlined by Darnton and Ray Murray and Squires, the big nexus that dominates the right side of their diagrams is that of publisher. Here dozens of positions that perform specialized work are thrown into the box simply labeled "publisher." Unlike every other node, the publisher node is the most complex piece of the puzzle. It's not as if the same person or group within that node is dealing with the author and distributor. And there is a lot of work that takes place within that block that, with the advent of digital publishing, has become more clearly separated. The idea of the holistic publisher also acts to hide the true scope of the work done to create, produce, and sell a seasonal list of book titles. It has only been in the reorganizations within publishing houses over the last thirty years that the industry has come to understand that the house is a collection of departments formed around specific tasks. Therefore, I have split it into the main departments that have been distributed to the spheres based on the work they do instead of their function to one another.

This move away from function allows for us to ignore the differences between an employee who does the work and the freelancer who is hired to do the work. There are financial implications in outsourcing work, but it won't be addressed in this book. I am more interested in the work itself and how it integrates within a publishing work process. The focus here is on the process. The person and department aren't as important as how the work gets done and its relationship to other work. The layout for a book can be done by a freelancer or someone on staff depending on the available time and resources, but the layout needs to be done between the creation of a typescript and a proofread.

The bottom of the work diagram covers content distribution. This area of work moves the results of the production work towards readers and retailers. The roles and workflows for print distribution are still tied to one of the most expensive parts of publishing: warehousing printed copies. When talking about the logistics of moving pallets and cartons of printed books from a printer to a retailer the warehouse becomes paramount to the distribution processes for traditionally printed books. Book publishers must also deal with the processes that center around digital files that are either ebooks or the source for print-on-demand copies.

Both the creative process of authors and the distribution process for retailers fall outside the scope of this book as both are processes that take place outside the publishing house. They are mentioned here to complete the picture of the work necessary to move from idea to execution of a manuscript to the creation and distribution of a finished book. The work done in retail will be addressed only as it integrates with the three processes defined above.

The part of distribution work that has grown since the Ray Murray and Squires circuit in 2012 is the influencing work of social media as a tool for both visibility and discoverability. This social influence includes both social media mentions (BookTube, Bookstagram, Book Twitter, and BookTok) as well as older methods such as reviews, awards, book clubs, and media appearances of the author that create the epitexts, or elements of text developed outside the text itself to connect the text to the larger culture. This social aspect has been part of the publishing process but, in terms of communication, it is seen as an influence on the communication between parties rather than an actual part of the circuit. In our understanding of the work done, the social influence constitutes a significant amount of cost and energy for the publishing company. In terms of pre-publications, it's a short-run print job before the book is officially published. In terms of an author tour, it is the scheduling and management of an author over several days and weeks. Any discussion of a publicity workflow needs to include the negotiations the publicists have with radio stations, podcasts, and talk shows where authors might appear to promote their new book. When evaluating book publishing as a work process the interaction with the media an author does for a book needs to be seen as concrete and actionable publicity work that adds value to a title.

As for the reader, it would be easy to see them as a node that is only acted upon by content distributors, but as noted previously, their relationships with publishing have also changed. At the same time that the reader can be more involved in the development of content through beta reading, their relationship to retailing has become more distant. Online bookstores and e-reading devices have changed the relationship between reader and retailer. The process of online visibility has changed the relationship of reader to author, publisher, and retailer. The way the reader discovers books is outside the scope of this book. Instead, I will focus on how marketing, publicity, and sales help increase the visibility and discoverability of a title in a chapter on content distribution. Marketing and sales can see how the events they organized can influence daily or monthly sales of a title, even if they cannot control the BookTok users' responses to the publisher's campaign.

While publishers can see workflow as the sum of these three components in whatever size and shape they may take within the organization, and the context each of the three components has within the organization, it's also important to realize they are interdependent.

Notes

1 There is an argument to be made that audiobooks are performative, but more often than not the audiobook is a straightforward reading of the text. George Saunders's audiobook for *Lincoln in the Bardo*, where over one hundred actors participate in the reading of the book, strains this definition, but there will always be exceptions to any proposed definition of a book. I need only point to Mark Danielewski's *The Familiar* series as something that challenges our ideas of scope and Max Ernst's *Une Semaine De Bonte* as a title that stretches the idea of content to understand no definition of a "book" can be comprehensive.
2 The other dual communication is between readers and their binders. A relationship that was required when publishers only sold book blocks to readers who were responsible for binding them.

References

Aig, Marlene. 1991, June 1. "Conan Doyle Had No Clue of Holmes' Popularity." *Los Angeles Times*. https://www.latimes.com/archives/la-xpm-1991-06-02-mn-339-story.html. Accessed 5 April 2023.

Armstrong, Peter. 2010. "The Lean Publishing Manifesto." *Leanpub.com*. https://leanpub.com/manifesto2010#a-book-is-a-startup-four-parallels. Accessed 5 April 2023.

Childress, Clayton. 2019. *Under the Cover: The Creation Production and Reception of a Novel*. Princeton: Princeton University Press.

Darnton, Robert. 1982. "What is the History of Books?" *Daedalus* (Summer 1982), 65–83.

Have, Iben and B. Stougaard Pedersen. 2020. "The Audiobook Circuit in Digital Publishing: Voicing the Silent Revolution." *New Media & Society*, 22(3), 409–428. DOI: doi:10.1177/1461444819863407.

Nixon, Cornelia. 2009. *Jarrettsville: A Novel*. Berkeley: Counterpoint.

O'Leary, Brian. 2009. "Start with XML." *Tech Forum, Book Net Canada*. https://www.youtube.com/watch?v=tGd-Q-wlhUc/. Accessed 5 April 2023.

Pearson. 2023. "Our Strategy." https://plc.pearson.com/en-GB/purpose/strategy. Accessed 13 February 2024.

Peck, Gretchen. 2017. "The Seamless Workflow of the Future: Publishers Get a Few Steps Closer to the 'Publish-Once, Output-Many' Model." *Editor & Publisher* (February 2017), 28–33.

Phillips, Angus and Michael Bhaskar. 2019. *The Oxford Handbook of Publishing* First ed. Oxford, UK: Oxford University Press.

Publishers Lunch. 2022. *The Trial: The DOJ's Suit to Block Penguin Random House's Acquisition of Simon & Schuster: Nearly Complete Transcripts and Comprehensive Coverage*. Bronxville, NY: Publishers Lunch.

Siegman, Tzviya. 2018. Personal interview.

Squires Claire and Padmini Ray Murray. 2013. "The Digital Publishing Communications Circuit." *Book 2.0*, 3(1), 3–24. https://doi.org/10.1386/btwo.3.1.3_1.

van der Weel, Adrian. 2011. *Changing Our Textual Minds: Towards a Digital Order of Knowledge*. Manchester: Manchester University Press.

Wiley. 2023. https://www.wiley.com/en-us. Accessed 5 April 2023.

2 Publishing Workflows

The Book Industry Standards Group released a white paper to address the growing concern within the book publishing industry that print-driven content development workflows ignore the work involved in digital and platform-agnostic distribution (BISG Workflow Committee 2019). This white paper stands as one of the few publicly available documents that deals directly with how publishers need to think about workflows as part of their business practices. Recording and revising workflows may be standard practice within corporate publishing houses where the documentation is needed for the management of resources across different imprints and companies accrued through acquisition and consolidation, but this practice of mapping the work that happens in the book creation process can also help midlist and small independent companies who struggle to maintain pace with changing format requirements and new digital marketplaces or startup publishers looking for a better way to control their costs. As Mary Hoffman of Greystones Press advises:

> Don't plan your publications before you have found out how much it is going to cost you to produce each book. Then work out your publicity, marketing and sales strategies and set yourself a period of time within which you must be making a profit.
>
> (Masson 2017, 84)

This idea of tracing how work gets done in a house allows managers to understand the daily work of the press as it relates to larger processes and to be more flexible in responding to major changes in book publishing like the growth of digital formats, new working arrangements including work-from-home and hybrid workspaces, and disruptions to supply chains that delayed delivery of both the raw goods that printers need to make books as well as the finished books themselves. Changes that all occurred in the five-year period from 2016 to 2021 when:

- Digital audiobooks replaced ebooks as the fastest growing segment of the industry;
- The COVID-19 pandemic caused global lockdowns forcing the publishing industry to a work-from-home model;

DOI: 10.4324/9781003403395-4

- Publishing companies adjusted their expectations for the 2020 holiday season due to pandemic-related delays for several books;
- All of which followed by global supply chain delays, including the six days when the *Ever Given* container ship blocked the Suez Canal in March 2021.

One method that businesses can use to identify and modify the work being done within their organization is the Business Process Management (BPM) model. BPM is a discipline centered on how to discover, model, analyze, measure, improve, optimize, and automate business processes (Jeston 2022, 3–6). It provides a system for understanding how people within an organization work and communicate with one another. This chapter will briefly outline how publishing houses can record, analyze, and revise their workflows to improve efficiency or as a precursor to instituting a larger project management process.

The definition of workflows that the BISG provides in their white paper is "the combined impact of decisions made about process, tools, and organizational structure" (2019, 3). It is a useful working definition to start the exploration of the publishing workflow, but in order for a publisher to identify the real work being done, that process identified in the definition needs to be delineated into the tasks, events, and interactions that happen within it to see how book work moves through a house. This discovery and modeling of the work being done can be outlined by the BPM model, which provides guidance on how to accurately capture the work within the process being evaluated. Engaging in workflow analysis through a model like BPM also means evaluating the organizational structure in relation to the tools and activities. This does not mean looking at the processes and tools as a result of decisions from a hierarchical structure of managers and vice presidents within the corporate publishing organizations but it does mean those doing the work need to consider that structure on the same level as the processes and tools used. The management-heavy model that worked for analog publishing might be the wrong management structure for companies dealing with digital workflows and rapid changes in the marketplace. When addressing the size of an editorial department and how that department handles title management, the workflow will depend on the quantity of work and efficiency of the tools over who is in the department. It is far more important to identify how many developmental and line edits are needed for each title and how many titles are produced a year than it is to focus on who works in the department. It is impossible for a house with only two developmental editors to complete seventy edits a year with each edit lasting approximately three weeks without outsourcing the work. Likewise, when defining the time it takes for a developmental edit, the department might be focused on the normal time it takes to edit an author who understands house style and writes cleanly and not the more involved developmental edit that occurs over multiple revisions that will also require an extensive copy edit to ensure the text adheres to the house style. Both are "developmental edits" in terms of an editorial process, but they are not the same in terms of time, resources, and cost. Understanding that there may need to be variations of an "intense" developmental edit, a "standard" developmental edit, and a "light" developmental edit can help clarify the work done in the department and provide a better idea of the cost of different types of book projects that are part of a department's workflow.

Publishers can also use BPM modeling to record the specialized work being done by employees within a house and trace how the work relates to other in-house processes to create a map of the way work moves through the house. The work maps produced in the BPM method are both a training tool for new employees and the foundation for future studies on the efficiency within the press and how that work can adapt to new demands.

Workflows are a necessary part of artisan and craft work but are more often taught through the mentorship of a master craftsperson. By the time of the Industrial Revolution the locus of information on process moved from master craftsperson to the organization, allowing a company to be the keeper of knowledge and disassemble the work into component parts which could then be handled by untrained workers instead of relying on guilds people. This change would find its fullest demonstration in Henry Ford's mass production assembly line. The managerial class would eventually take this idea that all work can be measured and develop metrics on work that could be used to reflect the value of a company and start to apply it to all parts of the company, not only the areas that produced things. By the 1950s the idea of "workflow" emerged as part of the language of office management systems where it would become integral to the nature of white-collar work. At the turn of the twenty-first century information technologies reconceptualized work as a set of processes that could be bundled together similar to how data management framed their work in terms of object-oriented programming (OOP).

The reimagining of creative work as a programmatic process similar to the way a computer runs a program began to influence the book publishing industry in the mid-1980s when the industry began to incorporate computers into its production processes and used Standard Generalized Markup Language (SGML) to aid in the printing of books. By the end of the first decade of the twenty-first century this sense of intellectual and physical work around a book has become completely digital. Editing, design, scheduling, typesetting, and printing are now done on screens removed from any physical process.

This means today's publishing company is a very different organization than what it may have been one hundred, fifty, or even twenty years ago. Those in publishing are no longer involved in the whole book-making process. The modern publisher is still focused on the turning of manuscripts into books, but the steps in that process have either been automated or are no longer managed in-house. Publishing houses rarely maintain the printing and binding equipment needed for the physical creation of the book. Likewise, houses rarely own the buildings where they work and cannot dedicate the street level to a storefront selling their titles directly to customers. Publishers today have narrowed their responsibilities down to the development of book files and the management of the marketing and distribution of the products of those files.

It's not only the printing and selling that have been removed from the publisher's office. The outsourcing of copy editing to freelancers provided a model to managers on a way to compartmentalize and offshore all aspects of the publishing process. Literary agents and freelance editors can now do editorial work that was once handled internally. Freelance designers can create the templates and bespoke layouts the publisher sends to a printer to print a book. Freelance marketing firms and publicity agencies are available to handle the promotion and marketing of big titles that might need more attention than what a publisher can provide. The list goes on, book packagers, ebook developers, literary scouts, and other types of professionals now offer publishing houses their specialized skills for every step of a book's creation and publication. This increase in outsourcing and specialization within the industry means that organizations looking to understand the work done at a publishing house will need to include the processes they no longer control but still add a cost to the creation of a book.

Parallel to the increase in specialization has been a push by executives to continually revise how work gets done in order to increase the overall annual production of a company. For book publishers this has meant that their industry which produced a few thousand titles annually throughout the 1980s is now one where publishers in the United Kingdom, the United States, Germany, and China alone produce over 800,000 traditionally published titles annually (Federation of European Publishers 2022, Börsenverein des Deutschen Buchhandels 2023). From the scientific management theory developed by Frederick Taylor up through Total Quality Management, management has experimented with different methods to control work with the goal of making it more efficient and departments leaner. The specialization of work along with the cycle of annual strategic plans has created a situation where departments may no longer understand the whole process of making a book and therefore have no sense of how the changes made in their department impact other processes.

Business Process Management

The demystification of work through deconstructing complex work structures into individual processes is the goal of the BPM approach. Each process becomes a unique segment of work that begins with a trigger and ends with a singular result. In the BPM approach, a process such as "creation of ebook files" would be broken down into the individual tasks: interior design, coding, addition of multimedia features, addition of accessibility features, versioning for different retailers, validation, testing, uploading, and archiving. By focusing on the creation of a book in terms of processes over departments or other function-based groups, BPM allows managers to trace the work as it actually moves throughout a house without debates on functional responsibilities or job descriptions. For example, a commissioning editor may say that they hand off a manuscript to an assigned production editor, but they may, in fact, give a manuscript to their assistant who checks it for completeness and adds production tags that adhere to production department specifications before sending it to a freelance designer who will send the finished files for review by the production editor. The commissioning editor is thinking in terms of function not the actual work done. The difference in the number of people who touch that manuscript and the time it takes each person to complete their work will impact the time and cost it takes to move the said manuscript through the publishing house.

Another way to frame BPM is as a "back to basics" focus on work. Tracing a publishing process is about answering the core questions of information gathering: who, what, when, where, why, and how. It should identify what starts the process, who needs to do work in that process, who is the next person who needs to be part of the work (when and where in terms of a sequence), how they interact with the systems and each other, and the result of the process (the why).

Identifying and modeling business processes is a lengthy process in and of itself that requires a lot of prep work before a company can begin to identify the current processes much less begin the revising work. Books such as Paul Harmon's *Business Process Change* (2019) or Alec Sharp and Patrick McDermott's *Workflow Modeling* (2008) provide a much more thorough outline on the procedure, but I hope this chapter provides a basic understanding on process modeling for book publishers looking to start mapping their work.

Box 2.1 Organizing Work: Function Versus Process

Before diving into how a publisher can start to identify their business processes, a note on the structure of publishing and the cross-functional nature of business processes. The industry has a long history of orienting its employees around functions: commissioning books, editing books, selling to bookstores, selling to non-bookstore retailers, print book production, and so on. This is in opposition to process orientation where employees from different departments work together in teams around a specific project. Publishing's functional business orientation is dependent on departments that only focus on the work they need to do and have little interaction with the work undertaken in previous steps or the work that needs to be done next. While a functional business orientation has previously been an efficient orientation to make books, it limits how people within the publishing house understand the complete process. In other words, a commissioning editor might not know what work is needed to go into the design of the book they are working on, and a production editor might not have any sense of what material is most effective for a sales representative. They only know their step in the process and trust that someone else handles everything before and after their work.

Current exceptions to this focus on function over process are the multinational publishers like Pearson, Wiley, and HarperCollins, who have spent the last decade or more moving from a functional business orientation towards a matrix structure where employees are both in departments and teams and often report to several managers depending on the work that needs to be done. There are also newer publishing ventures such as Canelo that approach book publishing with an entrepreneurial mindset focused on workflows and data (Pickup 2020). This move away from thinking about work in terms of function allows for new ways of thinking about how to modify workflows and, as will be shown in the next few chapters, allows these organizations to successfully introduce certain aspects of project management that cannot rely on management by a specific department.

Workflow Modeling

The basic methodology for modeling an organization's workflow has three steps:

1. Frame the process,
2. Map the current as-is process, and
3. Assessment and redesign.

Framing the process requires a publishing house to define the goals and objectives associated with the areas of work in question and what the organization hopes to learn about the work being done. For example, if a team is mapping the work processes that take place between delivery of the typescript to a production editor and the proofing of book files, they would want to identify each step in the process including the actual work of creating interior designs for that book project. When addressing the actual work, the team needs to understand who is involved and why. In the case of a book design, the team will need to investigate different ways a book gets designed. They will potentially need to focus on a bespoke design handled by a freelance designer and the in-house creation from a template if the publisher designs books through both methods. This framing will help guide the team with the diagramming of the work that happens next. Mapping of these workflows will focus on one process at a time and trace the work from a trigger or input to a result or output. The final part of the methodology is to review the mapped processes and identify those that need to be revised to align with the objectives and goals that were defined in the framing process.

It is important to note that this technique is not meant to record all work being done by a publishing house in one pass. Once the framing, mapping, and revising is complete for one area, the publisher can move on to another set of processes to frame, map, and revise. Once the processes have gone through the evaluation the framing, mapping, and revision can begin anew as the team focuses on the newly instituted processes that came out of their evaluation. Workflow modeling should be considered an iterative undertaking for a publisher, especially if a publisher's business plan changes radically from year to year. When done correctly, this process will inform the publisher of the cost of the work in terms of both resources and time. It will also illustrate what qualitative measurements or indicators might provide insight into a publisher's core business plan and critical success factors (CSFs), those aspects of a process that need to be of the highest quality to ensure that the process's objectives are met. Different publishers will have different CSFs due to the mission and culture of each house. If the publisher is primarily focused on selling copies of the book, a CSF might be getting thousands of copies of the hardcover into the large bookstores and supermarkets. For a small poetry publisher, it may mean getting a small print run of a chapbook printed in time for their author's appearance at a literary festival.

Framing the Process

The first step in modeling work processes for a publishing house is to create a set of initiating documents that outline the goals and objectives for the mapping being done. This team should be able to gather this information from the publisher's annual reports, job descriptions, and previous workflow documentation. From these documents the team should be able to find or create the following information that will help them map and evaluate the work in the next steps:

- The mission statement for the publisher,
- The current strategic plan,
- A description of the culture of the publishing house,
- A scope statement that includes constraints, list of stakeholders and stakeholder assumptions, and
- A risk assessment.

Mission Statement, Strategic Plan, and Culture of the Publishing House

An outline of both the mission statement and strategic plan will provide the guiding principles for the reasons a publisher publishes what they publish and how they publish those books. If a company's strategic plan is to stay lean, it often means a reliance on automating or offshoring most of the work involved in creating a book. These two documents will help the team to evaluate the processes so that those processes align with the culture of the publishing house. While the mission statement and strategic plan reflect the organization's values, it's also important to consider the culture of the house as the culture reflects the values of the people working on the books.

When the culture and strategic plan are misaligned, processes will often appear in conflict when mapped and assessed. It's not uncommon for projects and processes that were aligned with a company's mission to move away from that mission over several iterations as employees focus on refining and improving a function or product. A good example of this could be a division of a textbook publisher that was focused on developing apps that aligned with textbooks. Over time the app team began to develop standalone apps with original content. The team is now creating only standalone apps that have no connection to the textbooks they publish, but their work is still treated as part of the production process for digital textbooks. The mapping process reveals that app development is now on the same level and not ancillary to textbook production and that work needs to be repositioned within the organization. The mission and strategic plan provide a reference at hand when questions arise later in the process as the team tries to understand why work sequences are structured in a certain way or who does that work. They will also help the team to create or refine the goals and scope for the modeling work.

Scope Statement

A good scope statement should provide not only context on the business strategy of the publisher but should also provide information on the constraints to the process being evaluated, what stakeholders are involved, and any assumptions the stakeholder or workers might have about the process (Moore 2014). The list of constraints should address the time, cost, quality, and resources needed for the work. The identification of the duration of a work process as well as the expected cost and quality for that work will define the boundaries for what processes need to be examined and what resources are part of those processes. For most publishers clarifying the triggers and outputs will define the constraints. If a team is tracing the production process for a title and the scope of that process is constrained to only the first year of a book's publication, the team will not need to include revision or paperback reprint processes as part of the current review.

The second part of the scope statement would be an identification of the stakeholders, that is those who either trigger, engage with, or need the results of a specific process and those who sponsor or manage the work. Taking the time to identify stakeholders and outlining their assumptions about the work being done will help guide the team to the right people to interview when the time comes to start gathering information on the work being mapped. Knowing who the stakeholders are within an organization should provide a sense of the scale of the work being modeled. If a process involves employees in five different departments who have five different managers, the process will be more resource-intensive than one that has six employees who all work in the same department and report to the same manager.

During the identification of the stakeholders, the team should also gather any assumptions that those stakeholders may have about others. Common assumptions within publishing are often ideas such as "production editors only care about deadlines" or "another publisher distributes our books, so our titles will be secondary to those from the other publisher, therefore, we don't need to put as much work into our advance information (AI) sheets as the salespeople won't read them." Identifying the assumptions within a house provides the modeling team with information on where their work may be impeded by the way people doing the work consider how their work is received by others. As noted above functional organizations often keep employees siloed from one another and those employees will come to their own conclusions on how other departments function and those assumptions often influence how they view their work.

Risk Assessment

The final part of the preliminary work on a work process should be a risk assessment. This assessment will reveal not only what might go wrong but the steps that would then be taken to address that risk. One only needs to look at the shutdowns due to COVID-19 in the Spring of 2020 to understand why identifying risks on reduction of person hours or a disruption to publishing's supply chains should be part of the framing of work. While COVID could be seen as what Nassim Nicholas Taleb calls a "black swan" event—that is a rare and unpredictable event that has an extreme impact—supply chain disruptions and human resource issues are not uncommon risks in book publishing. The scale may have been off, but the reasons should not have been surprising to an industry that relies on shipments of paper via cargo ships and has experimented with work-from-home arrangements long before March 2020.

There are several ways to perform a risk assessment. One method is to create a simple risk matrix that identifies all potential risks and assigns a numeric value for severity, probability, and severity x probability. The goal of this method is to list all potential risks and rate them in terms of how likely they are to occur and what kind of impact they would have when they are to occur. When completed, this matrix will assign a value to each risk based on both the severity and probability of the risk occurring. The matrix should include those risks that are low-severity and low-probability up to the high-severity, high-probability risks. After the values have been calculated, the risks that have a higher severity and higher probability can be identified and contingency plans drawn up.

For example, a publisher might include in their list risks such as "typo in table of contents," "author doesn't deliver manuscript by the due date" and "losing full shipment of books between printer and warehouse." The severity of the first risk is low but highly probable. A contingency shouldn't be necessary for this risk, but it might be relevant later in this process if one of the areas of focus is the editing process. The second example has high severity but medium probability. Compare that to the third example which also has high severity but a low probability. In the latter two cases, both result in a lack of a book to sell, but an author missing a deadline is much more probable than a shipment of books being lost. Therefore, it probably makes sense to include a contingency plan that states "Offer bonus advance for delivery before due date."

Table 2.1 Example of risk matrix. Severity and probability are based on a scale of 1 (low) to 3 (high). Any risk that has an S*P greater than 4 requires the creation of a contingency plan.

Identified Risk	Severity	Probability	Severity * Probability	Contingency
Typo in table of contents.	1	3	3	
Author late in manuscript delivery.	3	2	6	Offer bonus advance for delivery before due date.
Shippers lose shipment of books between printer and warehouse.	3	1	3	

The purpose of a risk matrix is not to identify everything that could go wrong and figure out every contingency. Only those risks that have high severity and high probability will need contingency plans. In the example above, typos might not be considered if the publishing processes being reviewed are for the distribution workflow.

An alternative to the risk matrix is a SWOT (strength, weakness, opportunity, threats) analysis. This method separates risks in terms of internal weaknesses and external threats. It also identifies potential benefits in terms of internal strengths and external opportunities. Unlike the risk matrix, SWOT offers a more holistic picture of the risks and benefits inherent in doing work. SWOT is often part of the preliminary work for starting a project, but it can also help with BPM when it comes to revising or modifying work processes after they have been mapped.

Goals and Objectives

From the documents above, the mapping team should be able to extract a list of goals and objectives for the workflow under investigation.

The goals for a publishing process should be a list of what the publishing house hopes is accomplished in the workflow. This list could be the milestones created in the process or deliverables needed to trigger other processes. One example of a goal in the book design process might come from the development of a set of print-ready files and a preflight document of quality checks for fonts, images, color handling, and so on, in a print subprocess. The ebook subprocess might have a goal of a valid and accessible EPUB file. Add in an additional goal that addresses the needs of other digital formats, such as a PDF

Table 2.2 Example of SWOT analysis on expanding international rights department.

	Positive	Negative
Internal	**Strength** • Rights group can read and speak several languages. • Several members of rights group have worked for publishers in Europe and Asia. • New title management software has licensing component.	**Weakness** • Rights group down to three people covering translation, audio, serial, and media licensing. • Acquisition of new publisher in FY included few titles with World rights for all languages.
External	**Opportunity** • Literary scouts have expressed interest in representing publisher. • Interest in the translation of English-language titles strong in China and Europe.	**Threat** • Scandinavian and Japanese detective stories are flooding the market. Competition for licenses. • Pirated translations of content being released at the same time as English publication date.

or the Amazon ebook format, and the list of goals identifies what work is needed for the project. Ensuring that the team members have narrowed their focus to processes that create similar goals in this first step will help them identify what group of activities they need to map as a process.

While goals are often deliverables or results from a process, the objectives for a publishing process are targets for what the organization wants those doing the work to accomplish. These are either identified in the strategic plan or can be found in the key performance indicators (KPIs) and performance metrics that are part of a publisher's annual business plan. Objectives should be quantitative statements that identify what managers, departments, and other stakeholders desire to be accomplished for a specific period. Examples of objectives could be "the production department will create book designs for forty new titles and twenty reprints each season" or "the editorial board will meet every other week to review and discuss all proposals on the agenda."

As important as it is to include a list of objectives as part of the prep work on mapping work, the team needs to ensure that the objectives on the list do not end up being identified as the intended results in mapping a process. Goals are the actionable items or deliverables that are tied to a singular process, while objectives are defined on a company, not process, level. For example, a goal of a process could be "ONIX metadata is created for the book title" and an objective could state "Metadata formatted for block 1, 2, 3, 4, and 8 as defined in the ONIX 3.0 specification will be uploaded to all retail platforms two days after sales conference" which informs a KPI that states "All metadata for both new releases and reprints will be uploaded to major retailers in the ONIX format by the end of each week." Ensuring that the team keeps goals and objectives separate before starting to map a process helps the team from confusing process with function.

MAPPING THE WORK

After the framing documents have been collected, the process team can begin the work of interviewing those doing the work in order to create the map of a process.

Before the group starts to interview people to understand how work moves through an organization, there should be some understanding of what level of detail is expected from the mapping procedure. In the swim lane diagrams discussed below it can be easy for those doing the mapping to get caught up in the details of the work being done and attempt to record every activity in the diagrams. This attention to detail, which is important in publishing work, is often not needed in the mapping process. One way to ensure that the modeling team produces usable documents quickly is to define what kind of maps they will deliver on as-is processes at the end of the mapping process.

A two-level mapping process is often all that is needed for the assessment of the work being done. The modeling team can create a high-level map that shows the work being done and what actors are involved in the work. This type of diagram is meant to show the process without the details: manuscript acquired, manuscript edited, book designed, book printed, ebook made, book warehoused, book sold. This map should be supplemented with a second-level diagram that focuses on the contributions, that is, the deliverables or milestones each actor supplies in a specific process. An example of a second-level map might take the book printing process and break it down into the work that takes place in terms of the designed files for a book and the work done at the printers to print, bind, check, and deliver finished print books to the warehouse. The team should focus a second-level map around the milestones within the process: files delivered to printer, lithographic plates printed from files, cover files delivered to printer, covers printed, book blocks printed, book bound and covered, quality check of finished books, books packed into cartons. The goal here isn't to identify and record every single step in the process but to focus on an activity that triggers others in the chain of work.

The Interview Process

Before putting pen to paper, the modeling group should conduct interviews with those who are doing the actual work. Interviews are crucial in publishing houses where work being done may be carried out at different offices or by a variety of freelancers and publishing service providers. These interviews should be focused on how those who do the work spend their time and what resources they use to move work along. Interviews are preferable to only using a person's job description as job descriptions may not reflect the person's current day-to-day activities. For most of the 2010s, social media was often part of someone's job in a publishing house, but who that person was depended on the size of the press. Smaller presses had interns manage their accounts while corporate publishers initially put the responsibility on publicists or press officers. Few houses had a dedicated Social Media Marketing Manager and the work was often incorporated into another position without a change to the job description. A similar decision was made with ebooks when publishers hired a service provider to create the ebooks but never formalized the management of those conversions to production managers. Even in those publishing companies that update job descriptions at the time of annual reviews instead of when the company needs to hire someone, the descriptions rarely reflect the full extent of an employee's work. It's only through real discussions with the people doing the work that the extent of that work can be discovered.

Interview questions should focus on how the employee understands the scope of their work, what resources (databases, programs, systems, and so on) they use, how they manage the files they create, and where those files are stored or sent. The answers will provide a narrative of the process that will be broken down into individual activities and eventually turned into the process tracked across workers.

36 *Workflow and Project Management Theory*

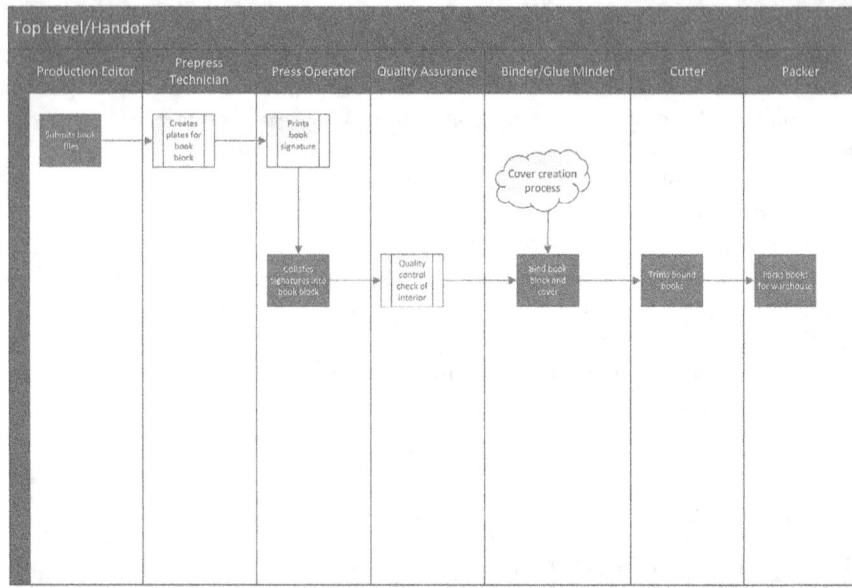

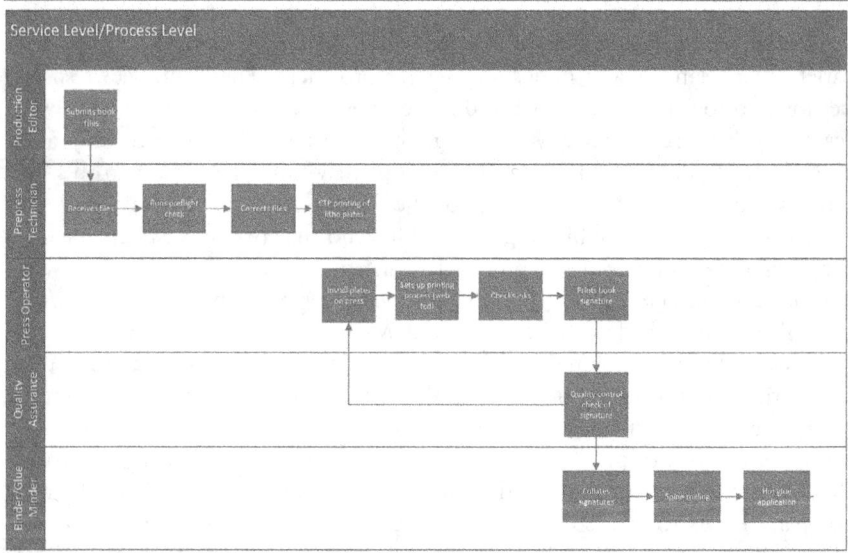

Figure 2.1 The level of detail between a top level, or handoff, diagram and a process level, or service diagram, provides two ways of looking at a process. In this example of printing a book, the handoff diagram shows when work moves between roles at a printing plant while the service diagram outlines the steps each role needs to complete to move the work to the next role. Please note, this image has been included for the visual overview; a higher resolution version can be downloaded at https://www.routledge.com/9781032516721.

Box 2.2 Interview Questions for Process/Activity Discovery

- What do you call this activity?
- What triggers this activity? Are there other triggers that can start it?
- What is the first process step to start the process?
- Walk me through the steps that are performed in this activity.
- How often is this step performed: every day/week/month?
- How long does the activity usually take?
- Who performs this step?
- How many people are needed to complete this activity?
- What databases, programs, and equipment do you need to do your work?
- Is there a specification you use as guidance for the activity?
- Any special terminology or jargon specific to this activity?
- What output is created in this process?
- Who needs to know when this activity is completed? To whom do you send your output?
- How do you communicate with others about the status of the work?
- How, when, and how often are team meetings on a project?
- How is this process step measured? What are the KPIs or metrics used?
- What frustrations do you have with the current process?
- What tools or support do you wish you had to improve the process?

Interviews should identify and define the terminology that different areas of publishing use in their work. The specialized nature of publishing is now such that employees within different departments will have their own acronyms and jargon that will often not be understood outside the functions of that department. For example, a publisher may have a current goal of increasing accessibility for their ebooks. Ebook production editors might talk about their work as it relates to A11Y (the shortened form of accessibility that comes from the A11Y project on digital accessibility), the web content accessibility guidelines (WCAG), and the European Accessibility Act (EAA). They may identify accessibility in terms of compliance levels and how they understand the publisher's focus in relation to these levels. When employees are asked to define their acronyms and jargon, they often do so in terms of work being done. In the ebook development example above, a developer may speak of level A, AA, or AAA compliance for EPUB files. The first level requires publishers to supply alternatives to audio and video used within a book, while level AA requires synchronized captions and audio descriptions for video, and level AAA requires sign language interpretation. The different levels require different activities that the employee may only talk about when asked to define their jargon.

The other reason that interviews are important is that the amount of work being done outside the house has increased over the last decade and departments are often dealing with the results of outsourced work without any control over how the work is performed. In areas such as proofing of manuscripts or the production of ebooks where the work is often handled by third parties, it is rare to be able to interview those doing the work. Instead, the team will need to rely on workflow documents provided by the outsourcing company. If those documents are not available the work may be noted as a process outside the scope of the map either by defining it as an outsourced process or by using the cloud icon to indicate that the work leads to a completely separate area not addressed on the map.

Creating Process Maps

The mapping of business processes is a way to visually represent what work is being done and the resources (people, systems, technologies) needed for that work. When this mapping is done correctly, the models will show who is involved in the current path that work takes and what resources that work consumes as opposed to what resources departments and managers assume are consumed.

While there are several different ways to record the work being done—and those who have worked with consultants on information systems, project management, or business process management may have seen a wide array of shapes and arrows that carry a variety of meanings as to how work takes place—this book will limit its discussion of the mapping of work processes to simple swim lane diagrams. A swim lane provides a visual of relationships between the actions performed by different actors over time. The work done during the course of a book project is generally linear in nature and there are defined processes associated with specific roles. Therefore, mapping book publishing processes can be adequately represented with boxes to define the process and arrows to indicate the relationships between processes. The representation of a process such as copy editing a book might move across the four lanes representing the production editor, the acquiring editor, the author, and the copy editor. A box in the production editor's lane might be "hiring copy editor for work on book project" with a line to a box in the copy editor's lane stating, "define hourly rate and availability." From there the sequence of processes of negotiating a freelance contract, distribution of the manuscript to and from the copy editor, copy editing the manuscript, and invoicing can all be indicated by linked boxes moving to the right of the diagram.

The purpose of the swim lanes is to visually capture:

- The actors who do the work and the role of the person/group in the process,
- The steps taken or what is done, and
- The flow of work that identifies the routes the work takes between actors.

Swim lanes are ideal for publishers as they take business process theory and boil it down to mapping a single input-output or trigger-result event, a mindset that aligns well with the way publishing houses traditionally think about work; most of the work that different departments do in a book project is triggered by the receipt of the manuscript. The output of that work may trigger other activities, but each trigger/result event needs to move the project closer to the initial completion of the project, often the

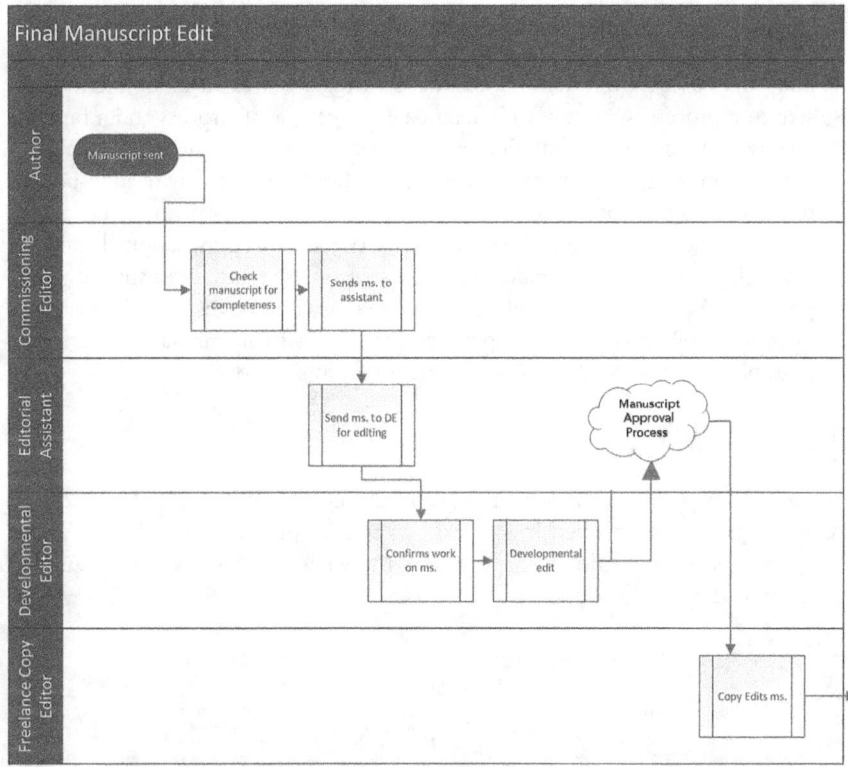

Figure 2.2 Example of swim lane diagrams for high-level editing processes. This swim lane follows a final manuscript from the author through different editors from receipt to copy edit.

publication of the title. This kind of focus makes the work done on a book project by a publisher very much a trigger-result-based series of work processes.

When trying to visualize the work done in the process of making a book, it can be tempting to record every action done by an individual or department, but it is not necessary to record how a copy editor uses reference titles for their work or how a marketer searches Amazon for comparison, or comp titles, that is, those titles they see as similar to the title in question. To ensure the mapping does not get mired in recording every activity and task, the BPM model provides a hierarchy of business areas, business processes, subprocesses, and activity/task as a way to think about work.

- The business area is the group of related processes. An example would be "editing a manuscript."
- Business processes define the work that needs to be carried out within the business area. They are defined by a trigger to start the process and result. Examples could be "executing a signed author contract" where the trigger is a deal memo from the acquiring editor and the signed contract is the result of

the process (which then triggers other processes including the licensing of the book for translation and the payment of any advances on signing).
- Subprocesses are work that may still have a trigger but result in an intermediate step in a process. One way to differentiate between a subprocess and a business process is to evaluate if the deliverables created are complete or essential. For example, in the process mentioned above, the draft contract may need to be sent to a literary agent for a round of negotiation before being executed. The negotiations could be a subprocess to the larger process of executing a signed contract.
- An activity or task is a single step or a series of steps that constitute a subprocess. "Writing a grant of rights for worldwide English publication" or "revising boilerplate splits as per negotiations with literary agent" are two examples of an activity in a contract negotiation subprocess.

MAPPING WITH STICKY NOTES

To start the mapping of a process the group should identify on a sticky note each activity or process mentioned in the process/activity discovery interviews. At this point the group should not try to organize the work into the hierarchy outlined above, only identify the work.

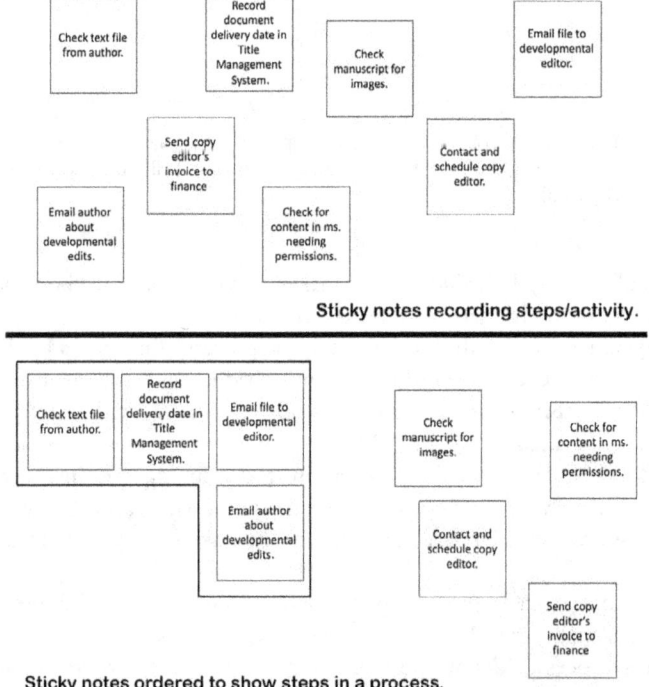

Figure 2.3 A comparison of randomized sticky notes recording tasks and organized sticky notes that show what tasks are part of a process or subprocess.

From this collection of sticky notes the group can organize the work into processes, subprocess, and activities which can be used to create a swim lane diagram. It is often up to the modeling team to identify the right level of detail in a swim lane diagram. It's rarely necessary to map out work on the activity level, but it is often beneficial to record those activities in a narrative, list, or table that supplements the diagram.

The swim lane will add the context of who does the work and who passes what to whom. A swim lane diagram should identify four aspects of a process:

- The trigger that starts the process,
- The subprocesses that are activated by the trigger,
- The actors who do those subprocesses, and
- The result that needs to be accomplished.

The trigger will often be a result from a previous process or some kind of signal that is sent outside the process to start it. Common triggers in publishing could be an author's acceptance of an offer for their manuscript, the payment for the sale of a title, a book fair, a sales conference, the compilation of weekly sales figures, and so on. The actors are those who are doing the work. Such actors may be an employee, or they may be a group, or even a process that is a necessary part of the work. The subprocesses are the work that gets done in response to the trigger.

A business process must also deliver a specific result. That result should be identifiable, countable, and essential to the operation of the publisher. The licensing of a foreign translation on a title is an example of a result. Here the result is identifiable: each license is a unique agreement with a different publisher in a different language. These licenses are also countable, a house can tally how many are done in a specific time, and they are also essential to the operation of that company as they generate revenue. Compare that to the sale of a book. Is selling one copy of a title distinguishable from another?

Once all the processes that were recorded on sticky notes have been either diagrammed or reserved as part of a list of associated tasks for the mapped process and those diagrams revised based on feedback from those interviewed, the team should now have a set of diagrams that trace the as-is processes of the publishing house and that team can start the work of assessment and revision.

Issues in Mapping a Workflow: Variation and Systems as Actors

Before moving to the analysis of a workflow, it is important to address two issues that often appear in the diagramming process that may not fit perfectly in the swim lane diagram for book publishers.

Variations of a process occur where some processes have the same triggers and results, but the work that takes place between the two processes changes depending on the goal of the process. The standard business example of this is when one compares the hiring of a temporary worker with the hiring of a permanent worker. The trigger of an empty position and the result of filling that position are the same, but the number of interviews and the focus of those interviews from the departmental team will be different from the process and focus of a Human Resources department. A more unique example of variation in book publishing can be seen in the process of creating a paperback that was licensed versus creating a paperback from a hardcover original. Both will start with the same trigger and result in files for the creation of a paperback book, but the number of actors involved and the editing processes will be different. One may require a complete redesign, copy edit (if the acquisition was of a book in American English by a British publisher), and a completely new marketing plan, while the in-house conversion title may only need a change in trim size and a new cover. It is worthwhile to map each major variation in order to record as realistic a picture of the work as possible. The more variances that can be mapped the better an organization can understand the constraints and scope of the work when updating the processes.

As mentioned above not every activity needs to be mapped. In most cases, individual activities can be described in a narrative or list, but in the case of data entry in management systems, those systems should be identified as actors in the process. Part of the modern publishing process often includes the addition of content management systems or title information systems that were bought to increase the efficiency of work or the flow of information across functions and departments. These systems are often databases that include metadata, schedules, and sample content for different titles or they may be repositories on a shared computer server where finished typescripts and sales material are stored. Regardless of what they do, they often are actors in the publishing process as they hold the work being done or act as delivery systems. In pre-digital times, realistic workflows were required to identify how paper forms moved through an organization. This often meant a swim lane for a mailroom as they transported work from one department to another. Identifying that work was key as it showed how insular departments were from one another; they understood their work, but they didn't understand the hand-offs that needed to take place to move work along. A manuscript may go from a copy editor to a production editor, or it may need to travel a more circuitous route from copy editor to a courier to an editorial assistant to the mail room to an author back to the assistant, and then to a production assistant before ending up on the desk of a production editor. Couriers and mailrooms have been replaced by email and warehouses have been replaced by content repositories but even these need to be identified in the process to ensure that the publisher captures the whole of the work done.

Assessment and Redesign of Publishing Processes

The final step in the workflow modeling process is to assess the work being done and identify what needs to be redesigned to align with the mission of the publishing house and any current goals or objectives. The assessment of a workflow can also identify the major problems—bottlenecks, too many handoffs, people who only coordinate but aren't involved in the work, problem actors, and so on—within that

Publishing Workflows 43

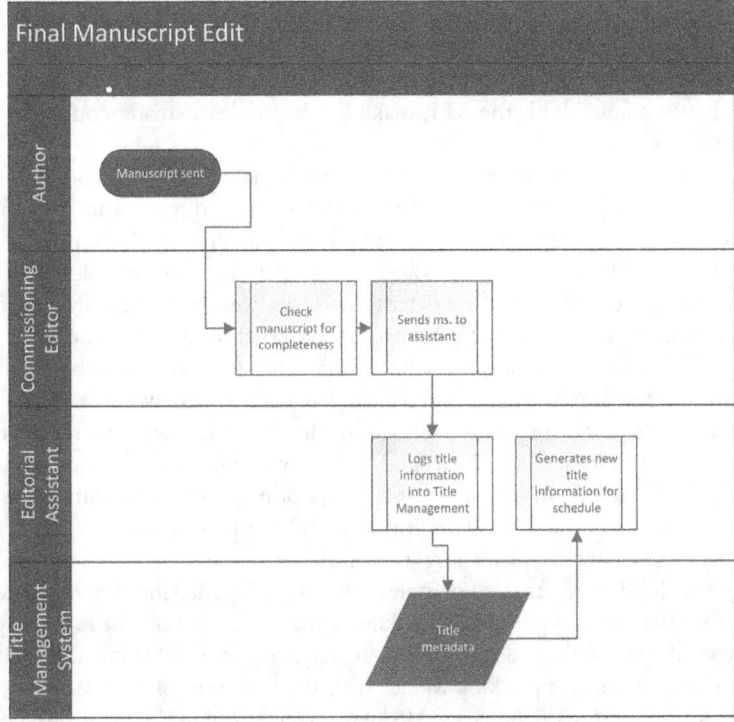

Figure 2.4 When systems are necessary for a process, they should be treated as actors and have a swim lane for their part of a process.

workflow. It is important to have some means of recording the lists as it will provide direction on the work of redesigning work. The duration of this assessment will depend on the nature of the house. A small publishing house with few employees that outsources most of the production and sales work will be limited in what they can redesign. The assessment may be better used to show where work can be done in parallel instead of in sequence as a way to increase efficiency. A large multinational publisher, on the contrary, may need to constantly assess and redesign their workflows as they acquire new companies or introduce new systems.

Assessment

The first part of an assessment should be to compare the results of the process with the desired outcomes for a process. These desired outcomes can be KPIs or other measurable objectives and provide a business context to the work. Assessing how the work that was mapped reflects the desired outcomes will show how well the work aligns with the company's goals. The results of the mapping process to create a signed author contract may reveal that the publisher's current workflow involves a contract manager, contract assistant, legal counsel, editor, editorial assistant, publisher, CFO, CEO, administrator to the CEO, subsidiary rights manager, royalty manager, the literary agent, and author. If a KPI is to shrink the time between draft and signed contract by several days, it should be clear that the process is not aligned with the KPI, making this process a strong contender for a redesign.

The next area for assessment is a review of internal and external problems and their effect on this process. Here the weaknesses and threats from the SWOT analysis from the framing documents may provide examples and solutions to problems that are identified in the evaluation of that process. In addition, there should be a consideration of other departments that were not originally considered in the evaluation of the process but could create disruptions if the process in question is changed or abandoned. One of the issues for some publishers with the "start with a markup language" trend from a decade ago was the reliance on having either authors or someone within the editorial department format a manuscript and all its associated metadata into a typescript based around a markup language. In an article on simplifying book and print publishing, Liam Borgstrom notes a presentation on XML workflows by Phil Madans of the Hachette Books Group where Madans "explains how the Hachette Book Group had difficulties in making the XML tagging less complex for editors" (Madans 2009, quoted in Borgstrom 2013, 9). While XML workflows became important in increasing the efficiency of production departments, it required buy-in from the editorial department that ended up taking longer with their delivery of a typescript as they had to tag the manuscript into a CMS that ended up requiring a quality control check (and corrections) on the production side. In some instances, it had the unintended consequence of delaying the delivery of content to those in the subsidiary rights department who needed a manuscript to send to foreign publishers to start the translation process in time to release alongside the initial publication of the English language edition. Here, the editorial assistants responsible for coding the typescripts and the subsidiary rights department were both unacknowledged shareholders who were negatively affected by the change.

The assessment of a publishing process can be completed by answering the following questions:

- Is the work being spread across too many actors and/or taking too much time to complete?
- Does the work move back and forth between two actors too many times? Can the work be rearranged for fewer handoffs?
- Are there any non-value-added subprocesses? This can be work like rekeying information into a system because that system isn't tied to the others.
- Are there other noncritical steps that slow down the process? Common noncritical steps such as submitting and processing paper forms have survived from a time when physical signatures were needed.
- What are the bottlenecks? Manager approvals and batch processes are places that often create a delay as the work is held until several requests can be done at once.

- Are there places where sequential work can be converted into parallel work?
- What are the exceptions to the standard process that have been created? Bad personalities and other difficult situations within a workplace can be a source of unique subprocesses. If the workflow was originally designed to work around a problem, it is often a good candidate for revision.
- What are the problems that are constantly being ignored? Has the organization created a workflow specifically to address work others should be doing? Not registering the copyrights because the person/intern who did this work left the company has become too common an example of this in the world of book publishing.
- Are there undocumented tasks or tasks that help to create a milestone? This often happens when the team finds a disconnect between activities or a step that doesn't have the same trigger as similar steps. A great example of this is the way imprints within large corporate publishers may end up bidding for the same book because editorial groups share information with sales and marketing teams but not with other imprints.

Once an assessment has been done on each process the modeling team should make a recommendation to the publisher on the next step for the specific workflow. The recommendations can include:

- **Leave the process as is**. For those processes that have been mapped and are aligned with the objectives and goals of the company, nothing more needs to be done.
- **Abandon the process entirely**. This is for those processes that may no longer align with the rest of the company or were created only to deal with the problems within a house. Great care should be taken when suggesting the dropping of a process. Making sure that the results of this process do not become unique triggers for other processes is required otherwise the abandonment of one process may cause another to cease to function as well.
- **Outsource the process**. This has become a common decision as there are more publishing service providers from India and China who can offer the same level of work as internal departments at a much lower cost.
- **Redesign the process**. After assessing a workflow and finding that it is not working as intended but is still essential and needs to be done in-house, a publisher may need to go through a redesign process.

Redesign Process

The assessment of publishing processes should help to clarify what recommendation the modeling team will suggest to management. In the case of leaving the process as is, nothing more needs to be done but for the other three recommendations, book publishers will need to redesign the process in a way that causes minimal disruption to other processes. This is particularly important when recommending outsourcing or abandoning a process. Almost every process within the creation of a book project is tied to other processes. Eliminating or outsourcing activities will often create a cascade of new tasks to other processes that are connected to the one being eliminated. Outsourcing a marketing campaign requires someone in marketing to manage the marketing company working on the book which may include answering questions, paying invoices, providing needed resources, and other operations.

When a book publisher needs to revise a process, the best practice is to move through the following steps:

- Write a course of action statement,
- Identify the means of measurement,
- Explain the consequence of inaction, and
- Develop and share process maps.

Course of Action Statement

The course of action statement should be a reiteration of the original stakeholder problems that the revision addresses, and should include information about how the current process isn't solving the problem. The statement should note where the as-is publishing process falls short and propose a solution to that problem. It should also include examples of how this proposed solution will address the problem and may also align with changes to the organization or the larger industry. Ultimately this should be a statement on why the publishing process isn't working and the proposed solution to that problem.

Identify the Means of Measurement

A course of action statement should propose a change, but that change will often require new resources; therefore, it is pertinent that after the course of action statement, the modeling group creates a list of the needed measurements, resources (including people hours), and changes to policies or rules. When suggesting what resources will be needed for a redesign, the modeling team may need to clarify what means of measurement are relevant for the new process. For example, a publisher may make the decision to shorten the editing process and, in the course of the revision process, they decide to take the sixty hours they identified as the average time it takes one person to copy edit a manuscript for the company and divide it across multiple editors. This division of work ends up totaling close to eighty hours due to the additional tasks of compiling and comparing changes from different editors, but multiple editors can work on the project at the same time. This means the work that would take one person two business weeks could be done by three people in one business week. The work is done faster but it takes more time and resources. The modeling team must be clear that the measurement of the time it takes to complete the work takes precedence over the costs of hiring additional editors.

Explain the Consequence of Inaction

When discussing the revision of a publishing process stakeholders, particularly those who are involved with the work in question, might push back and claim the process should be left as is. They may argue that the current process is working for them and is allowing them to hit their objectives. A redesign rarely has an easy implementation and the assessment that was previously done should provide some reason why the revision is needed. The modeling team should also prepare a statement on what might happen if the process stays the same and what that could mean for the organization. Inaction may not lead to catastrophe. It may only mean that a department will need to work harder to reach its objectives. This statement on the negative consequences of inaction needs to be clear.

Develop and Share New Process Maps

Once a team has identified those processes that might need to be reworked and gone through the process of creating an action statement and of understanding how a redesign will affect other processes as well as the benefit or deficit that such a change may cause, the next step is to start work on revised swim lane diagrams that show the desired workflow instead of the as-is workflow that was created in the previous step. This modeling should follow the same process outlined above, but with some minor changes. The redesign will respond to the mission statement and objectives, but it also needs to address the assumptions and risks outlined at the beginning of the process.

The team that has worked on the previous mapping work should take the process as it currently stands, identify the trigger, result, and any milestones, and then focus on the path of work across the swim lanes. The trigger, result, and milestones will give a sense of the essential steps in the workflow. The processes should develop around those aspects. As the team remaps the work, it must pay attention to the dependencies to ensure that any changes aren't deleting potential triggers for other processes.

One of the easiest redesigns is often to see what can be done in parallel and what might need to be done in sequence. Making these minor changes will often tighten up the process and make it more efficient. Playing with parallel operations that were previously locked into a sequence can shorten the time it takes to complete the work and better use resources that may be sitting idle. Just remember to ensure that the removal of a resource will not start a domino effect across the publishing house.

As the team works through the redesign it should double-check that nothing is missing from the as-is process. It can be easy to drop activities that initially appear outside the scope of the process in question, only to find in a redesign that those activities are key to the process. An example of this can be seen in the redesign of how cover mechanicals were being handled at a small publisher. The original process had an art director send a cover mechanical to the editorial assistant on the book who would send it to the author, managing editor, publicist, and acquiring editor for review. When the publisher was redesigning their workflow they identified a bottleneck at the editorial assistant who was delaying the turnaround on the jackets and covers. A decision was made that the art department would be the only stakeholders to check the jackets as it was assumed that the editorial assistants were only involved in an administrative role. What the team who was redesigning didn't realize is that the editorial assistants were the only ones in the process who were checking for typos and that the price on the book was correct on the cover and in the bar code. Price changes were occasionally made last minute and not always conveyed to the art department. The problem with the redesign didn't become apparent until books began to be released with printed prices that were different from what appeared on a retailer's point-of-sales system.

When a modeling team completes its work and shares it out to others in the publishing house for feedback, it can be a cause for celebration. A deep dive into process and how work moves through an organization will become necessary information for any publishers hoping to improve their efficiency. It will also help publishing houses embark on the next step of organizing work: addressing projects through project management theory.

References

BISG Workflow Committee. 2019. *Fixing the Flux: Challenges and Opportunities in Publishing Workflows.* New York: The Book Industry Study Group.

Borgstrom, Liam. 2013. "Simplifying E-book and Print Production." *Learned Publishing*, 26, 115–122. https://doi.org/10.1087/20130207.

Börsenverein des Deutschen Buchhandels. 2023."Der Buchmarkt in Deutschland 2022/23: Buchbranche engagiert und selbstbewusst angesichts herausfordernder Welt- und Wirtschaftslage." *boersenverein.de.* https://www.boersenverein.de/boersenverein/aktuelles/detailseite/der-buchmarkt-in-deutschland-2022-23-buchbranche-engagiert-und-selbstbewusst-angesichts-herausfordernder-welt-und-wirtschaftslage. Accessed 10 September 2023.

Federation of European Publishers. 2022. "European Book Publishing Statistics 2020." https://fep-fee.eu/European-Book-Publishing-1400. Accessed 3 August 2023.

Harmon, Paul. 2019. *Business Process Change.* 4th ed. Burlington, MA: Morgan Kaufmann. https://doi.org/10.1016/C2017-0-02868-9.

Jeston, John. 2022. *Business Process Management: Practical Guidelines to Successful Implementations.* 5th ed.London: Routledge. https://doi.org/10.4324/9781003170075.

Madans, Paul. 2009. "The Evolving Role of Authors and Editors." www.slideshare.net/toc/the-evolving-role-of-authors-and-editors-presentation-920817. Accessed 12 September 2023.

Masson, Sophie Veronique. 2017. "Going over to the Other Side: The New Breed of Author–Publisher." In *Publishing Means Business: Australian Perspectives.* Edited by Aaron Mannion, Millicent Weber, and Katherine Day. 69–86. Clayton, Victoria, Australia: Monash University Publishing.

Moore, Art. 2014. "What is Scope?" *BPMInstitute.org.* www.bpminstitute.org/resources/articles/what-scope. Accessed 5 April 2023.

Object Management Group. 2023. "Business Process Model and Notation." *www.bpmn.org/*. Accessed 5 April 2023.

Pickup, Oliver. 2020. "Is data the key to the future of publishing?" *Raconteur.net*. https://www.raconteur.net/digital-transformation/data-strategy-publishing. Accessed 5 September 2023.

Sharp, Alec and Patrick McDermott. 2008. *Workflow Modeling: Tools for Process Improvement and Application Development*. 2nd ed. Norwood, MA: Artech House.

Taleb, Nicholas. 2007. *The Black Swan: The Impact of the Highly Improbable*. New York: Random House.

Web Accessibility Initiative. 2023 "WCAG Overview." www.w3.org/WAI/standards-guidelines/wcag. Accessed 5 April 2023.

3 Project Management

When a publisher identifies a viable project, be it a new book title or the creation of an automated system, the company needs to manage it separately from ongoing daily work. A publisher needs to identify a project as work that will: (1) exist for a limited time, (2) require a team of employees aligned to the needs of that project, and (3) bring a different set of costs and benefits outside normal work. Making a book has a different set of needs than managing royalties or sharing reviews with authors. All acquisitions are projects as they focus on a core aspect for all projects, that of "objectives and outcomes" (Phillips, Bothell, and Snead 2012, 12). Having a project management office (PMO) or a group of project managers can help publishers manage their projects more effectively, but an understanding of the core principles of project management can help publishers evaluate different paths to publication and find the one that works best for the stakeholders within a publisher, whomever they may be.[1]

The Project Management Institute (PMI), an organization that offers certification and education of project managers, defines a project as "temporary efforts to create value through unique products, services, and processes" (PMI 2023). The project must bring about business value creation or create a change in the organization. This business value creation can be a new product or a new process, provided it adds value to a company. Project management is built around the notion that the nature of the work involved will take place within a specific time period and then end when that time period elapses. There is a novelty in projects that make them separate from the regular flow of work: they are, by their definition, nonrecurring. This means the issues that arise will not have the same solutions as the previous project, nor will the solutions discovered for this project apply to future projects (Thomsett 2022, 16). Compare this to a day-to-day operation like the allocation of royalties, a standardized process that processes a variety of financial information on book sakes in the same way as the information is transmitted. Managing finances is ongoing, the design of a print book takes place within the span of a few weeks.

This chapter will provide an introduction to project management theory and how projects are started and completed within an organization. The following chapters will expand upon the theory by looking at the two types of life cycles a project can have: linear and iterative. The linear project life cycle, covered by the

DOI: 10.4324/9781003403395-6

next chapter, is a project where there's a clear sense of deliverables at the start of a project and where each step in a project is dependent on the one before it. The traditional book from a publisher is the most pertinent example. The iterative life cycle, covered by Chapter five, is a project that evolves several times over its life cycle. The project starts with an idea of what the main deliverables are, but loops through a project management process several times to gain feedback from the marketplace. A mobile phone app or online platform is the most common example of the iterative project life cycle for book publishers.

Publishers that are reorganizing to become more project focused will need to determine how project management fits within their organization. It could mean creating a PMO and hiring a certified project manager, as is common at several of the largest global publishers, or it may mean identifying roles within the organization that can take on the needed work. I will not focus on the training and certification of project manager in these next three chapters as that is an industry that extends far outside the scope of this book. Organizations like the Association of Project Management (APM) in the United Kingdom, the Project Management Institute in the United States and the Australian Institute of Project Management can provide those readers interested in certification with more information about the certification process. It is not uncommon to see midlist and small publishers make a production manager or editor a *de facto* project manager. This is often a result of a publisher's functional-based focus where the needs of ongoing operations and projects are seen in terms of job functions and not needs. An alternative to giving editors the title of project manager is to support those employees in training to become certified project managers and promote those roles to create an equilibrium within departments between operational and project work.

For those employees who move into a role centered around project management, the core resource will be the collected knowledge provided by the Project Management Institute on their website (pmi.org) and in their *Guide to the Project Management Body of Knowledge* (PMBOK). These resources are the foundation for most of the certification courses and the countless study guides available for becoming a project management professional (PMP). The information provided by PMI can be overwhelming and often requires those studying for certification to set aside several months or more to work through and translate the theory into their role within the publishing industry. Other resources that may help those in the industry get a grasp on project management include Jack Ferraro's *Project Management for Non-Project Managers* (2012), which is written for the functional manager who wants to understand project management, Dave Barrett's *Understanding Project Management, a Practical Guide* (2022), and Michael Thomsett's *Little Black Book of Project Management* (2022). These books outline project management that focuses on teams and people over theory.

Project Management and Book Publishers

Book publishing's relationship with project management is unique within the media industry. It has a similarity with other media companies in that the project work within a house can be characterized as centered around the creation, production, and distribution of a product. This mirrors the work done in the film, audio, and gaming industries, but book publishing diverges from these other media industries in their focus on releasing and maintaining multiple formats beyond the project's close. Film companies are not releasing new films into theaters, on physical medium, and streaming on the same date and maintaining those formats for an extended period of time. Music and video game companies can be seen as similar to book publishing in their support of multiple formats upon release, but there is often an exclusivity with some content to certain platforms and formats. There isn't an expectation that a new video game release will be available for all current and previous consoles the way there is an expectation that books will be available from all bookstores and ebooks will be readable on all e-reading devices including older or discontinued models. And the audio industry doesn't feel the pressure to work with sheet music publishers to publish tablatures and scores on an album's release day the way book publishers are expected to have audiobooks available when their print and digital books release.

Traditional project management focuses on the life cycle of a project and defines the release of a deliverable as the end of the major work on a project. In book publishing that period is often the time it takes from manuscript delivery to the first edition's publication. Post publication, the people and resources who worked on the project are reassigned.

Functional Managers Versus Project Managers

Because of their temporal nature and specialized focus, projects need a dedicated project manager to shepherd the project through its life cycle and protect the team members from the addition of new responsibilities by other departments within the organization, often called job creep. In order for a project team to be successful, its project manager often needs to have autonomy outside the functional organization of a house. That means the project manager needs to be able to guide cross-functional teams, where team members come from different departments within the company, without having to consult with each team member's department heads. For industries like book publishing that are structured around functions, this often means the organization needs to rethink its organizational structures. One way of achieving this is to create a PMO within the house that supports project managers the way departments support functional managers. The PMO allows project managers the same autonomy as departmental managers. Even without a PMO, including project managers as part of the organizational structure means that those project managers will need to be as involved as a functional manger in employee issues such as salary, review, and advancement. Projects cannot be seen as work outside the employee's job description that are not considered in annual reviews. This will hide the work that is being done within an organization, giving a false sense of the costs for work being done. It will also lead to employee burnout that can create a hiring cascade.[2] In an attempt at recognizing both the organizational and project work that takes place within a company, most of the largest global book publishers have moved towards a matrix model that uses a divisional structure instead of, or alongside, a directional one. In a divisional structure, employees are grouped around projects instead of being grouped by their specialization of work. In other words, editors are part of teams with production, marketing, and sales instead of only working with others in the editorial department and leaving the cross-departmental communication to a manager. These organizations will tend to have a project manager on the same level as functional managers, such as a managing editor or a production manager. A reorganization towards this divisional structure or a matrix structure, which creates a hybrid of the functional and divisional structure, needs to be a key concern for executives and directors as revealed in research done by Frania Hall on organizational structures within publishing. Those publishers who are already reorganized around projects find the matrix structure one that "is more likely to fit the new creative economies that are emerging; [that] will cope better with the more fast moving fragmented markets" (Hall 2019, 300).

To give an example of how a matrix structure should be used within a publishing house I offer a high-level example of work that would be needed for the launch of a new online interface to provide Open Access (OA) digital copies of print titles at an academic or STM publisher. The OA project needs to accomplish the following:

- Determine which frontlist and backlist titles need to be available as OA,
- Identify the parent organization for its participating authors and setup a relationship,
- Determine the type of OA (diamond, gold, green, platinum, bronze, or hybrid) the publisher needs to provide for different clients or authors,
- Develop a process for identifying which new titles need to be published as OA,
- Develop the section of a publisher's website where these OA titles will be found,
- Manage a database of the complete work,
- Manage the metadata for these titles so that they are discoverable on the company's website as well as in search engines,
- Test the user's experience in finding and reading the material on the publisher's website to make sure the titles are accessible, and
- Create a publication schedule for OA titles to ensure that backlist titles are being added to the OA library.

In a functional organization, team members will have these projects assigned by a departmental manager and the work they need to do for the OA project could be in competition with core job responsibilities including the acquisition of new titles. If left to a departmental manager, the work of an OA can be assigned to an employee who has the time to engage with the project instead of those employees who are best suited to work on the project. This often leads to the failure of a project before it starts. It is the dreaded "I don't know why I am here, but my manager assigned me to this team" situation where a department sends the employee who is least needed for departmental work, but not the employees directly affected by the project. If the team members are lucky enough to work in a publishing house that has moved from a functional to a divisional or matrix structure, the correct editors will be available for involvement in the OA project and that work will be folded in with their workload and list of responsibilities. The work is not supplemental to their existing job but incorporated into their job requirements.

The Project

Like the adage about training a novice carpenter to use a hammer and suddenly everything looks like a nail to them, once managers and executives begin to apply project management principles to their work they tend to apply PM to all aspects of their work and personal lives. They will start talking about how to be more efficient in meal prep or create spreadsheets to manage their children's day. But there is a big difference in managing operations and managing projects. As mentioned above, projects have three very specific aspects:

1. A project must have a defined start and end date and be temporary in nature.
2. It must produce a unique output. That can be a product, service, or other kind of result.
3. The work must end when the defined goals or objectives of that project are complete or if that project is completed.

If the work in question is ongoing without an end date or isn't creating something unique for the company, then it's not a project. Most financial and inventory work cannot be seen as projects, but the work needed to convert a manuscript into a product to be sold has a defined start and end date. That book product will be unique in terms of not only content but constraints than other books and the work done on that book by different departmental employees will cease once the book has been published or moved to the backlist.

The Project Team and Project Life Cycle

The step after ensuring that the work in question qualifies as a project is to create a project team that has the skills that align with the needs of that project throughout the project's life cycle (PLC). A PLC will be split into phases that focus on specific processes. In project management literature, the number of phases in a project life cycle will depend on the project's needs and the nature of the organization. In *Understanding Project Management*, Dave C. Barrett identifies four generic phases that capture the basic life cycle for any project:

- Initiating,
- Planning,
- Executing, and
- Closing (2022, 8).

Other authors have built upon this core group of four by either expanding one of the phases into multiple phases or adding a monitoring phase between Barrett's "executing" and "closing" ones. Wayne Turk offers an alliterative alternative that adds team building as a phase of project management: proposal, planning, people, processes, product (2008, 52). The next chapter will look at a six-phase life cycle for book publishing that turns Barrett's executing phase into three distinct phases for development, quality control, and release. These additional phases could all be considered part of an execution phase, but the work involved is so specialized that they require their own phase within the project, especially as they are also three areas in book publishing that will continue to change with technology and the marketplace.

Each of the phases in the life cycle of a book project will have specific project deliverables that inform subsequent phases. These deliverables will be tangible and verifiable products created by the team members and the larger organization that indicate the progress of a project. For example, an acquiring editor will distribute a business case for acquiring a book proposal that will often provide the information other departments need for their work, including publicity announcements, marketing plans, and pitches to foreign publishers for translation licenses. That document may also help to inform the planning of the book project in the next phase.

Project teams should, therefore, create deliverables with a list of acceptance criteria attached. The acceptance criteria will identify the expectations of that deliverable in terms of cost, need, and quality. In the editorial department criteria are often defined in terms of a word count, number of illustrations and author responsibilities. In publicity it can be the number of galleys sent out. A more complicated example can be seen in how a production department defines acceptance criteria for an ebook file. When submitting an ebook to an online distributor, the files must pass a validity tests. This is the most basic level for an acceptable ebook file, but the validity at a retailer does not mean the ebook also supports the accessibility needs as defined in legislation such as the European Accessibility Act (EAA). Therefore, the production department may need to create stricter acceptance criteria than what is required by retailers to ensure their ebooks conform to the needed level of accessibility. If the criteria are not adequately defined for a book project, work such as making ebooks accessible as well as valid becomes work that sits outside what was considered in defining the project constraints and can often lead to team members working on accessibility in ebooks outside their normal working hours leading to burnout and turnover.

Project Constraints

One of the main ways of thinking about a project is how the organization will deal with the constraints put upon the project. In traditional project management, the quality of the results for a project is limited by the following three constraints:

- Cost,
- Time, and
- Scope.

Figure 3.1 The three constraints of project management in their iron triangle format.

These three constraints are often referred to as the triple constraint (Project Management Institute 2023) or as the Iron Triangle (Caccamese and Bragantini 2012). In every project there will be two constraints that will be fixed, forcing a project manager into the position of having to decide if a project will be "fast, cheap, or good–pick two." If the scope and time to produce a book are set at the project's start, the only constraint that can be changed is the cost and a publishing house can hire more people to meet a deadline. Project managers need to ensure some flexibility in one or more of these constraints in order to respond to change, lest the organization come up against the deadly triangle where all three constraints are fixed, and the team is unable to alter the scope, schedule, or cost of a book which often results in a decline in the product's quality.

Project Initiation

Processes that are involved in the initialization of a project primarily consist of creating documents that define the work being done and the goals of that work. This work should include identifying the project (book proposal), stakeholders (author, retailers, publisher's parent organization, employees working on the book, etc.), and the project's value (net income from P&L, or other means of determining ROI (return-on-investment)) as well as defining a preliminary budget (P&L) that outlines what resources the publisher may need to commit to the project based on the information in the other initiating documents. This work goes towards defining the project's viability. Viability will depend on the goals and deliverables and what business areas will be affected by the project.

The ROI for a project is determined by comparing the project's monetary benefit to the project's costs. A project should have a positive ROI, that is the benefits should be greater than the costs. For example, if the team evaluating the value in developing an in-house audiobook studio, for a list of twenty titles published annually, estimates the costs of material and labor for building the actual studio to be around US$20,000 and the cost of hiring a narrator and audio editor to be around US$5,000, the studio would need to see around US$6,000 net profit for each title to have a positive ROI within a single fiscal year. While this is an overly simplistic example of how to figure out the ROI of a project, it does capture how a project team needs to define the financial support from its organization compared to an estimated value created by a project in its earliest planning. This process often takes place within publishing at an editorial board meeting or through some other workflow in evaluating book proposals.

Project Planning

The planning phase of a project outlines what work needs to be done and is often accomplished through the creation of a project management plan and/or a work breakdown structure (WBS). Planning can also include risk assessments, revised budgets, and updated schedules that include major milestones. This information is not always outlined in specific documents by a house and may be part of a deal memo, status report, or P&L statement. This stage requires frequent iterations of a publishing plan to account for changes in scope, cost, and time. One such iteration can be seen in the revision of a P&L based on feedback from sales and marketing and the concerns raised about the book and the author in an editorial meeting or peer review. The planning and organizing is where most of the preliminary work for a book project is defined and often requires the most attention from managing editors who will need to determine if the project can be done in-house or needs to be assigned to freelance and third-party services.

A work breakdown structure is a hierarchical representation of the project's deliverables, tasks, and subtasks and is often accompanied by a network chart that shows the critical path of the work. The two documents offer a visualization of the project as manageable work components and provide an organized view of the work required to accomplish project objectives. The WBS is similar to the mapping of a workflow, but it is focused on the work specific to this project. The work should be deconstructed into tasks and subtask so that each activity can be easily understood, estimated, and assigned. The results should have a similar level of detail as the service level diagrams from a workflow mapping activity.

The WBS typically follows a hierarchical structure, with the project deliverable or major milestone at the top level. Below that, it breaks down into several levels of

58 *Workflow and Project Management Theory*

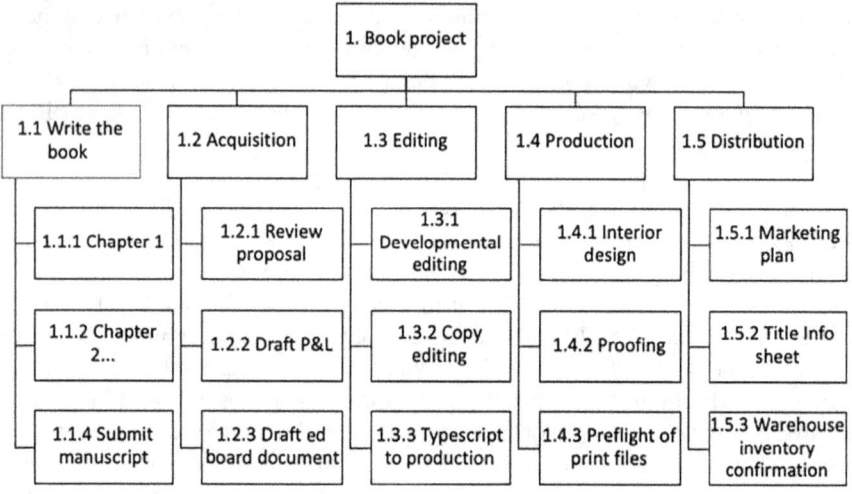

Figure 3.2 The high-level work breakdown structure for a book project shows the divisions of labor needed to move from idea to book.

sub-deliverables and work packages, each representing a distinct component of the project. This diagramming of deliverables can be supplemented with a network diagram that places the deliverables in relation to one another to give an indication of their relationship to one another. Combined with the WBS breakdown chart, a network diagram can give a project manager a better sense of the sequence of work to better estimate the schedule and allocation of resources throughout the project.

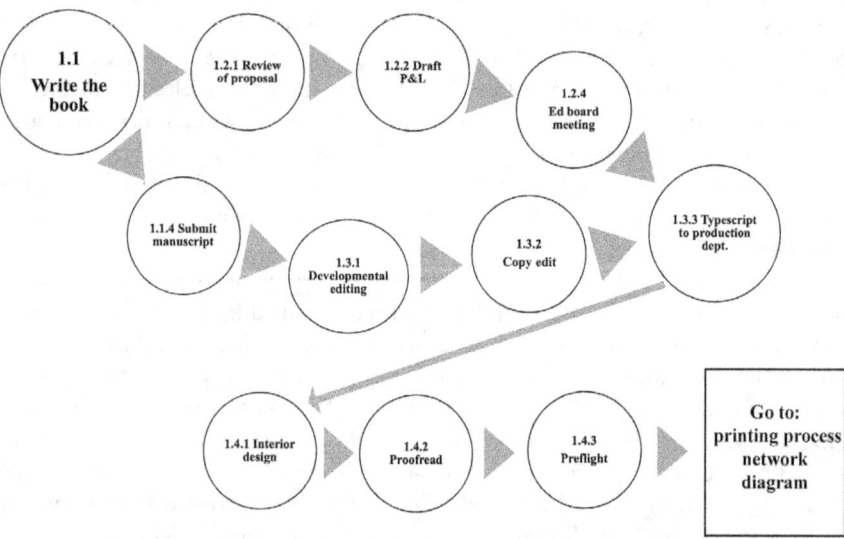

Figure 3.3 The network diagram identifies the critical path of work in the tasks outlined in the work breakdown.

Creating a WBS, like other deliverables in the planning phase, should be seen as an iterative process. The WBS needs to be flexible so that it can change to feedback from the shareholders and change as the project progresses. The WBS should not be seen as a document that is created in and then confined to the planning stages of the project.

In addition to a WBS diagram, the publisher should also develop a network chart, or flow diagram, that identifies the critical paths within the WBS diagram. For example, in Figures 3.2 and 3.3 the drafting of the P&L is a task in the acquisition process, but it is not a trigger to start the editing processes, whereas line editing requires that the developmental edit task is finished before it can start. The WPS process can be considered a visualization or portrait of the project while the network chart provides the narrative of that image (Ferraro 2012, 192). In most cases the WBS will come before determining what roles are involved, so a simple diagram that shows the relationship between tasks is sufficient.

Project Execution

Executing the project is where the planning gets put into action. This phase will have a heavy focus on schedules, cost, quality, and procurement. The phase will include the development, testing, and deployment of the product that was defined in the goals and objectives. In terms of publishing, it is the work that is carried out in the production, marketing, publicity, and sales departments as well as any work involved in the distribution of a book's physical and digital editions. Throughout the development, testing, and release phases the team will need to rely on a communications plan so as to coordinate with other team members and outside groups. Along with the actual development of product, this phase also requires the monitoring and control of the quality of the work done. The final part of this phase is the release of the main deliverable to the intended audience.

Project Closing

The last process group allows for the project team to document the work done and evaluate the quality of that work, which can lead to better management of future projects, but it is also a phase that publishers shortened, if not skip altogether.

The closeout of a project often can take one of many paths depending on how successful the team was with the project.

One type of closeout is the handoff where the project team delivers its completed work to another team that will handle the next iteration or the next evolution of the product. In terms of book publishing, this handoff is most common after the publication of a hardcover edition of a book. Post-publication, the production team that was handling the hardcover may hand over production files, a schedule, and any production and editorial notes to a paperback production team that will work on the paperback edition when it gets released in a future catalog season.

A second type of closeout is one where the project is complete, and the project team can be released from working on the project. This type of closeout will often include a post-project review or a postmortem on the project where the team evaluates the process of doing the project. A postmortem for a publishing project should be carried out within the first month of release and include those involved in the project. The meeting should be a closed meeting of just the book project team for an honest assessment of the project. It should focus on high or low points in the process for editorial, production, and distribution instead of being a data-driven review of the orders and sales, although this data will be key to talk about the project's goals and objectives. The team members should also have a space where they can talk about what they were most proud of doing on the project and what they are taking away from the project. The point is to review what went well and what could be improved upon internally.

The last type of closing that is worth mentioning is when the project is not completed and the organization decides to close the project, deeming it as unsuccessful. In the case where a project keeps getting extended to the point where it continues to consume resources without producing a deliverable, the publisher may need to cancel it and move on. Common book projects that fit this description are large reference works where work-for-hire authors fail to deliver, or a celebrity or business memoir where the personality attached to the book moves on to work on other projects.

This simple outline of a project life cycle is meant to give a general idea on how a project is structured for work to be completed. The next two chapters will focus on two common approaches to a project that an organization can use depending on what it hopes to achieve. The next chapter will focus on the predictive or linear PLC, which is also commonly referred to as the waterfall method. That will be followed by a chapter on the iterative development cycle, which includes the popular Agile method.

We will address these two development cycles and delve into the benefits and deficits of each for book publishing. For most companies the predictive/linear cycle should feel familiar. It's designed so that the deliverable is defined at the start of the project cycle. Each process is completed before moving to the next one. For publishing it often means the writing of a book is complete before it is edited, or the design is complete before it is made available.

Notes

1 While book culture glosses over the publishing process to focus on the "art of the book," the goals of publishers are not always book focused. Small presses may be focused on raising awareness of poetry in general and not just one title. Corporate publishers, especially those now owned by investment firms, often fixate on financial growth. The needs of the stakeholders can be just as important as the final book in terms of publishing success.
2 It is common in book publishing that when an employee leaves their work is distributed to others in the department while the company hires a new employee. These same people who are now handling more work are also the people responsible for scheduling and conducting interviews as well as training new hires. The added work exacerbates burnout in the department and it is not uncommon to see a high turnover in a department as it struggles to return to "normal" workloads.

References

Barrett, David. 2022. *Understanding Project Management*. 2nd ed. Toronto: Canadian Scholars.

Caccamese, Andrea and Damiano Bragantini. 2012. *Beyond the Iron Triangle: Year Zero*. Paper presented at PMI® Global Congress 2012—EMEA, Marseilles, France. Newtown Square, PA: Project Management Institute. https://www.pmi.org/learning/library/beyond-iron-triangle-year-zero-6381. Accessed 5 June 2023.

Ferraro, Jack. 2012. *Project Management for Non-Project Managers*. New York: AMACOM.

Hall, Frania. 2019. "Organizational Structures in Publishing." In *The Oxford Handbook of Publishing*, edited by Angus Phillips and Michael Bhaskar. 291–309. Oxford: Oxford University Press.

Phillips, Jack J., Timothy Bothell, and G. Lynne Snead. 2012. *The Project Management Scorecard*. London and New York: Routledge.

Project Management Institute. 2023. "What Is Project Management?" https://www.pmi.org/about/learn-about-pmi/what-is-project-management. Accessed 5 June 2023.

Project Management Institute. 2004. *A Guide to the Project Management Body of Knowledge (PMBOK®)*. 3rd ed. Newtown Square, PA: Project Management Institute.

Thomsett, Michael. 2010. *The Little Black Book of Project Management*, Third Edition. New York: HarperCollins Leadership.

Turk, Wayne. 2008. *Common Sense Project Management*. Milwaukee, WI: ASQ Quality Press.

4 The Linear Project Life Cycle

Most publishers have been creating books using some type of linear project life cycle (PLC) model—even if they would never call it that—for the past several decades, if not the past two hundred years (Wright 2009). The linear PLC model follows a progression where the work completed in one phase builds upon what was done previously and provides the inputs for the next one. After a proposal is reviewed, the acquiring editor goes through an acquisition process that results in an author contract. That contract will provide information for editing and production schedules. When the author's manuscript is accepted, it will go through one or more editing processes before being sent as a typescript to the production department for an interior design. The files produced from that process are used by the printer to print the book and by the ebook developer to create the code. As the book is being designed, the marketing and promotion campaigns are started to raise awareness of the title before copies are sent to retailers. After the release, the publishing house can evaluate the different work within the book project and determine what worked well and what needs to be reconsidered in future projects. This sequence for the traditional book project is a near perfect example of a linear project life cycle.

While I will refer to this model as the linear PLC throughout the book, other names for it include the predictive development life cycle, the plan-driven life cycle or waterfall model (Wysocki 2011, 23). The waterfall model is particularly illustrative as it has an automatic visual representation of how work moves from one process to the next as water flows down a hill. Another way to visualize this model is as a staircase where each step leads to the next. The model's name isn't as important as a clear understanding of how a sequence with identifiable milestones (manuscript, typescript, marketing plan, finished book) generates a clearly defined goal (complete printed and digital book). The linear PLC should not be conflated with the iterative model addressed in the next chapter, even as managers push to include the iterative, or Agile, model into work done at a publishing house as it has become a leading model at tech companies. Unlike the linear PLC where a product is created and released, an iterative PLC develops a product over several iterations of producing a product, sending it to market, and then refining it based on feedback from the marketplace. This is not a model that works for the creation of books, unless the company is looking to release new editions of a book every few months with new content that reflects a reader's desire. The iterative PLC does work for other areas

DOI: 10.4324/9781003403395-7

of publishing such as journal publishing where articles exist in pre-print, print, and post-print formats individually and as part of a specific issue. It is also essential for publishers looking to develop online platforms or apps for handheld devices like T.S. Eliot's *The Waste Land* app developed by Faber and Touch Press or *The John Murray Learning Library* from Hachette UK and Trellisys.net where the publishers create new content and interactivity over time.

The publishing industry has used a linear PLC, even if they didn't call it that, as its main method for creating a book for several hundred years. It outlines how content creation, production, and distribution sectors work together to develop content and release it to a waiting audience. Even with the variations on how a book is created in the different segments of the industry, almost any linear PLC for a book project can be seen as having six distinct phases:

- Initiation the project,
- Planning the project,
- Development of the project,
- Quality control,
- Release, and
- Closing and maintenance.

This sequence expands upon David Barrett's generic four-phase process mentioned in the last chapter to reflect the most common methods of developing a manuscript into a saleable book. The vague executing phase has been broken out into three distinct steps: development of the project, quality control, and release. All three phases describe the work that needs to be done to make the deliverable for the project, that is, the execution of the project, but for a publisher the work to edit, design, and create a book in print and digital formats is very different from the work needed to release the different formats for a book. These phases are also often handled by different departments within the publishing house: the development and quality control being part of the content creation and content production groups and the release being handled by those involved in content distribution.

The variations seen between academic, trade, and educational publishing can all fit within this sequence. Most book projects start with a proposal or commission which will go through a vetting process within the house that leads to an acquisition that initiates a book project. This is followed by a series of planning events that includes the creation of a contract, identification of the means for evaluation, the drafting of a schedule, and the creation of a preliminary budget. Once the manuscript is received, different departments begin to develop parts of the book project (Advance Information (AI) sheet, typescript, sales plan, etc.) in an order that moves the project towards a successful release into the marketplace. Because of the current digital nature of book publishing that generates multiple formats for different markets, the different formats need to be examined for quality before the formats are released into the marketplace. Once available to readers, the publisher can move this from frontlist to backlist and prepare for future printings that may include corrections of typos or other maintenance on the book.

64 *Workflow and Project Management Theory*

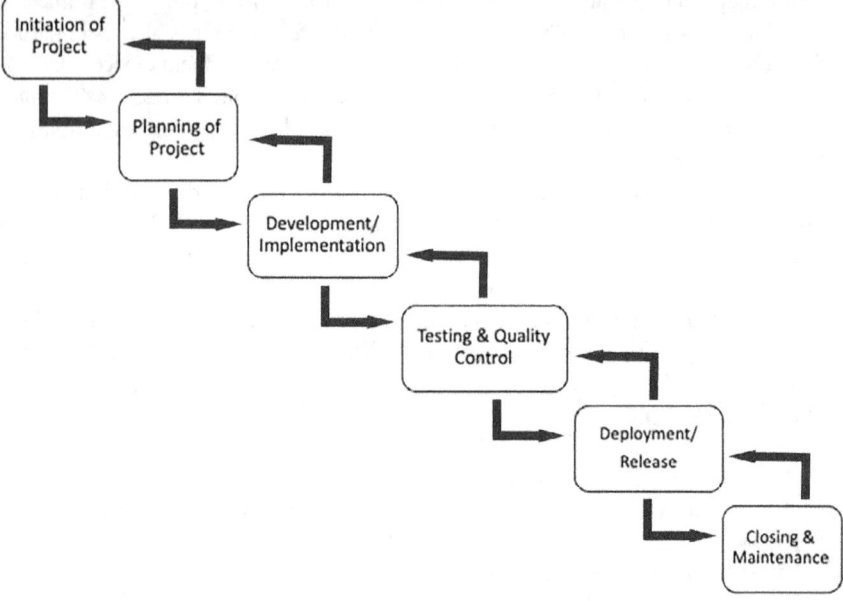

Figure 4.1 A linear project life cycle with six stages represents the major work needed for a standard book project.

The Book as Linear Project

To simplify the hundreds of tasks that are carried out in a house to convert a manuscript into a book and the variations of those tasks across different publishing areas and different publishers, I will use the concept of the book project. The book project represents all the work done by a publishing house and those hired by the house to create a finished textual product that can be distributed in a variety of formats to bookstores, retailers, organizations, and individual readers. Each publisher managing their book projects will need to experiment and modify their work until the processes align with their resources and needs. What works for one publishing house might not work for another, but the overwhelming body of work that is carried out in the different publishing industries still aligns with the six-phase model described herein.

When thinking as a project manager, one needs to differentiate between a book and a book project. The finished book is a deliverable or goal of the book project that will continue to exist after the book project is over. The planning, development, quality control check, and release of the book from a manuscript is the book project itself.

The management of these book projects can be handled several different ways within a publishing house. The toolset needed will depend on the size of the publishing house and the complexity of the project. For small publishing houses that outsource most of the work, Google Drive or Microsoft 365 (with Visio added if any workflow diagramming is needed) may be all that is needed. Mid-sized publishing companies have moved to using one of the dozens of software platforms designed around project management. General project management software like Basecamp, Asana, Monday.com, or the suite of products from Atlassian (Confluence, Trello, Jira, etc.) are popular within the book publishing industry as a way to oversee all of the book projects currently in process. These services help publishers who are managing dozens to hundreds of book projects over a season. More targeted project management software for the book industry is also available. Two such platforms are Title Management from Firebrand Technologies and TEP from Klopotek. Both are software platforms designed around the book publishing workflow and support the needs of the project for editorial, production, marketing, and sales departments. The marketing, publicity, and sales departments may also need to supplement the general platforms with ones specific to customer relationship management (CRM) like Hubspot or Salesforce. Before considering which of these software platforms—or any of the dozens of others not mentioned—to use, a publishing house needs to first understand the costs of the platform in terms of annual fees and training within the organization and what departments or project teams will benefit from having access to the platform.

It should be clear to anyone who has worked in publishing that every book is unique enough that it needs to be considered its own project. Each book project will go through the life cycle process outlined in the rest of this chapter. Even within a series, each book will have a different word count with text that needs to be edited and laid out for both a print and digital page. Each book will have a unique cover,[1] price, ISBN, and other metadata. Individual printings will also have different print quantities that can originate at different printers or from different printing methods. How a publisher handles this process will help them decide what software will best help them manage their projects.

Whatever the book project may be, part of the initiation process is to identify the work needed in the next phases. A publisher might not need the project charter discussed below, but they will need to have at least a preliminary budget, risk analysis, and schedule before they move forward with the acquisition of a proposal. The publisher will also need a plan to manage the workflows within each of the phases. Copy editing cannot start until after the manuscript has been developmentally edited, peer reviewed, revised, and accepted. The specific order of operations in a publishing house requires the group to have a robust means to convey the necessary information from phase to phase, what project management defines as a communications plan. A book designer I know often submits queries to the proofreader about grammar with their interior designs. These notes provided a context to the proofreader and also indicated to the proofreader where they may need to focus on content as well as design. It should be no surprise that the designer also added detailed notes on unique aspects of the interior and cover for the production editor and typesetter. This communication by the designer to those working in later phases helps with the efficiency of the project and shows that there are multiple ways for teams to communicate. I've had project teams use similar commenting features in production environments as well as messaging apps such as Discord, Slack, and WhatsApp over the long email chains and comments coded in hierarchical shades of editorial marking that are still favored in some houses. Publishers need to remember that it's not a house's history with a procedure or a manager's preferred platform that is important, but that the team working on a project has an effect way to communicate and can also provide an archive of the decisions made.

Initiation of the Book Project

Every book project within a publishing house starts with project identification and selection. An acquiring editor at a company has communicated the genres they are looking for to literary agents and through calls for manuscripts, an editorial version of a request for proposal (RFP). After the book proposals have been received they are vetted and the most promising of the proposals is selected for discussion at an editorial meeting where the group evaluates the proposal and decides on how to move forward on the project. As part of the evaluation a commissioning or acquiring editor will draft a financial analysis of the project in the form of a profit and loss statement (P&L)^2 as well as identify when a manuscript will be turned in by the author, creating a major milestone in the book project's schedule.

This first phase of a book project really focuses on requirement gathering: identifying what is needed to get the project done and then selecting the process that makes the most sense. The selection process often comes down to thinking about the project in terms of the three constraints of time, cost, and scope. The following types of documents will help a publisher or publishing team to define the scope and goal of the project, evaluate the work that needs to be performed, and identify the potential benefits of the project:

- Business case,
- Project charter, and
- List of stakeholders.

Business Case

The business case is a document that explains the project and identifies the demand or opportunities for the organization. For most book projects this is simply the editorial cover letter that accompanies a proposal to an editorial board meeting. For larger projects such as multi-year reference works and anthologies, the editor may need to create a more detailed outline of the benefits, risks, and costs for engaging in the project. The business case/editorial letter should state how the project matches the publisher's mission and provides some sense of the value the project would bring to the publishing house. This value could be prestige in terms of publishing an award-winning author or it could be a guarantee of a bulk sale to the author's organization. In some cases, the value may come from the creation of a new subgenre, as happened with Travis Baldree's *Legends and Lattes* and the cozy fantasy genre. The goal of this document is to have a commissioning editor explain why the company should exert effort and expense to bring the product to market. Speaking of expenses, the business case/editorial cover letter should also include a financial analysis on the investment in the project such as the return-on-investment, the rate of that return—how quickly the book can theoretically earn back the development costs including author advance—and the project's net value, all of which are often found in the standard P&L.

The letter may also need to include a feasibility statement that identifies the timeframe for the author to write a manuscript and the author's track record with previous titles. In addition to explaining project feasibility, an editor might also want to outline how to move forward with the project in terms of products. For some book projects this could be a recommendation to acquire the proposal with an option for an initial publication of hardcover and digital edition followed by audio a few months later and softback with a revised ebook a year after initial publication. Other options could include hardcover followed by soft and ebook, a softback original with an ebook or even ebook followed by either hard or softback. Additional recommendations may suggest a reworking of the proposal so that it aligns more with the books the publisher offers or to pass on a proposal if the feedback from the editorial meeting and peer reviews was negative.

Project Charter

The project charter will go into more detail than the business case on what work will be done and provide the specific costs and resource needs. It is also often ignored in the acquisitions of books or, at best, addressed in a deal memo from the editor. The work to define the following elements will ultimately help the publishing house in understanding the book project and what resources it needs. A book project charter should include:

- **Goals**. What will be achieved and how those achievements align with the organization. An example can be: "to publish a book as a hardcover and ebook in the Spring 2025 season."
- **Objectives**. The specific and measurable outcomes of the project. Often these take the form of KPIs that identify a baseline for the team to work towards: "to produce a valid and accessible ebook that will release at the same time as the hardcover edition."
- **High-level list of requirements**. Feasible, attainable, achievable, and unambiguous needs for the project. An example of one requirement could be that an author needs a specific advance to cover living and research expenses.
- **Budget**. The project's costs compared to its benefits.
- **Team roles**. Employees who need to be involved with the project.
- **Milestones**. Scheduled deliverables that indicate progress.
- **Risks and how to manage them**.

It can be argued that a charter is rarely needed for a single book project. The information it addresses is often covered elsewhere or is dealt with in the planning stages, but being aware of the information needed for a charter will provide for greater efficiency in the book-making process. It will also be invaluable for projects that might extend beyond a single title such as a proposed series or a multi-authored reference work that may take years of development. In these cases, a charter can provide the publisher with a more defined outline of the cost and work that will be required over an extended period of time and different titles. In the case of a non-book project, such as the development of a digital asset management system, the information in the project charter can be used to evaluate the offers that come in from service providers.

List of Stakeholders

The last document in the initialization phase should be the identification of stakeholders or those who are either actively involved in the project or who will derive value or be otherwise affected by the project. In publishing this can be a list that includes employees, authors, vendors, investors, and customers (Phillips 2019, 149). The identification of stakeholders in the initiating phase will help define what work and communication is needed throughout the project and may influence an understanding of the project's value and viability. For example, in the early 2000s there was a race among different labs to clone the woolly mammoth. As a result, science editors were often reviewing proposals from scientists and their labs purporting to have the next breakthrough. In one case, a trade science editor had acquired a proposal by a group of scientists who were very close to extracting viable DNA from a frozen woolly mammoth and was pitching the book at their sales conference. The project had a solid narrative and came from a known research lab in this field. It had the promise of being a lead title for the publisher, but in the middle of the editor's presentation, an executive in the audience noted that the authors were in competition with a research lab also working on cloning a woolly mammoth; but this research lab was a subsidiary of the publishing house's corporate parent. The editor had stumbled into a new concern for publishers in this age of private equity ownership: a conflict of interest for the publisher's parent company. As more and more publishers are purchased by similar companies and become part of a portfolio of companies for investors, editors may need to be more aware of their parent company's other financial interests when evaluating a proposal. For those interested in learning more about the relationships of stakeholders and corporate responsibility, I would point to Angus Phillips's chapter on "Publishing and Corporate Social Responsibility" in the *Oxford Handbook of Publishing*, which also outlines the effect of stakeholders on both the project at hand and the reception of the publisher's product by the larger community (Phillips and Bhaskar 2019, 147–161).

Stakeholders are both internal and external parties that will be affected by the project. A partial list of stakeholders involved in a book project may include:

- The author who created the manuscript,
- The literary agent who is managing the relationship between author and publisher,

- The commissioning editor who will have the book as part of their acquisition portfolio,
- The various editors who schedule and work on the book,
- The designers who are creating the print and digital layouts,
- The printers who need to schedule and print the book,
- The warehouse managers who need to store the finished books,
- The retailers who are selling the different formats,
- The financial department which manages the money owed to vendors and authors,
- The marketer who is scheduling, budgeting, and managing the book's marketing campaign,
- The publicist who is arranging author interviews and book reviews for the book,
- The salespeople (domestic, international, special sales, translation, and other subsidiary rights) who will have the book as a product that needs to be considered in their budgets, and
- The investors in the publishing house or the house's parent organization.

In terms of publishing, the initiating phase for several projects make up the editorial board meeting. Every commissioning or acquiring editor who brings a potential book to the meeting will have to identify what the book project would be and what value it would bring to the publishing company. The goal could be to acquire a title for a future publication list in an established series or it could be to republish a backlist title to commemorate a publication anniversary or new work from the author. The deliverable can be a book, or a book with supplemental digital material, or a large anthology in a new subject area. The proposal for these projects also will need to explain how they tie the project to the publisher's mission and how they will add value to the publisher. This is commonly an estimate on the number of copies that a publisher can expect to sell of a title. The editor's reasons for acquiring the book often covers the business justification, rationale, and creation of value.

Planning the Book Project

After a book project has been identified and evaluated, the project will move to a planning phase. This phase provides a chance to clarify the project's scope and objectives as well as define a schedule and define needed resources if that was not done in a project charter. In the case of a book acquisition, the editor may need to redo the budget and schedule based on the results of the proposal going to auction.

The work needed in most straightforward book projects will also focus on creating a set of documents called the project management plan that should identify the following:

- The project's scope,
- The activities to be performed/work breakdown schedule,
- A complete project schedule,
- A list of team members,

- A communications plan,
- Expectations in terms of quality,
- Risk management matrix with accountability, and
- A revised budget from the project charter now tied to the actual work being performed.

The scope should be a clear outline of what will be produced in the project. There's an inclination to write this scope in a more descriptive form that explains the product instead of the project. For instance, a sentence like "This series of language learning titles will teach primary school children the basics of different languages through the use of Chet, a puppy and mascot for the brand" is a good pitch for an editorial meeting, but a scope needs to be focused on the project and specific about deliverables and timing: "The Chet series of language-learning series will release the first dual-language (Spanish/English) title, *Chet at the Vet*, in print, ebook, and audio early in the spring season."

The activities/work breakdown schedule and project schedule should provide more detail on what work needs to be performed and when it is due. Project scheduling can be done with milestones and a Gantt chart. Milestones identify key deliverables and when they should be completed within the project. A Gantt chart shows the interdependencies and timing of different tasks in a project.

The means of communication will depend on the team members. The team members should define who is in what role and the responsibilities for those roles. This list is primarily to help the team members know who they can contact with questions. Independent publishers may not need this as there is only one acquiring editor and one production editor, but large publishers may end up with team members in different offices throughout the world. That situation leads to the need for a defined means of communication. Will the team have meetings on video chat? And if there are team members in London, New York, and Singapore, what time works best for those team members? If video doesn't work, can the team use a messaging service such as Slack or Discord. Is the team allowed to use public messaging services to discuss projects? Teams will also need to consider how their decisions are being recorded and communicated out. In most publishing houses a managing editor and

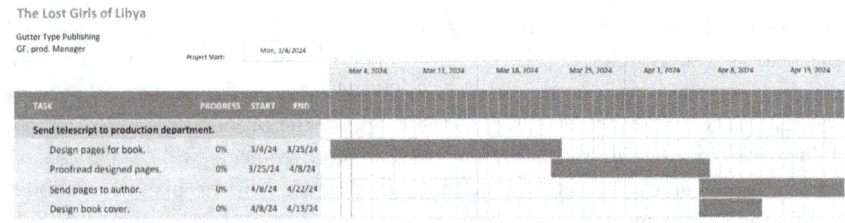

Figure 4.2 A Gantt chart showing the length of time for content production. The chart shows the time a process will take in a sequence or if it can be completed simultaneously with another process. Please note, this image has been included for the visual overview; a higher resolution version can be downloaded at https://www.routledge.com/9781032516721.

production department will meet regularly to discuss titles in production. Delays may pushback a title's release date, prompting the production department to update the schedules and send a status report out to the whole company. This is often a large document that can cover multiple seasons. In some houses the report may only go to department and project managers or only the editorial and production staff, who, in turn, are responsible for communicating changes for their specific projects to the marketing, sales, and promotion people on the project team. Both methods will work, but depending on the volume of titles produced, one method may be more effective than the other.

The expectations of quality define what is expected at launch. In terms of print books this could be defined as the trim size, page count and inserts up to the specification needed for a four-color printed book. In terms of ebooks this could be an indication of what level of accessibility is needed for the book.

The risk matrix with accountability should be a document that lists any potential risks that the team has identified and the potential impact of those risks on the project. This is similar to the risk matrix explained in Chapter two. Any major risks that are identified as probable should have a contingency plan in place. In addition, the matrix should also have a column that defines accountability. It's one thing to identify and plan for risk, it's another to assign people to monitor and respond to them. In terms of book publishing, the range of risks can go from the common—manuscript delivery is delayed by author, similar products release to market before the release date—to the improbable—massive paper shortages (Parente 2018) and vehicles transporting finished books hijacked and never found (Sellers 2010).

The budget in the planning phase should be more detailed than that of the project charter. The project charter may include a cost estimate based on a company's previous projects. This revised budget can provide better estimates for the project. For example, the company should have an idea of the cost to copy edit a manuscript based on the company's history, but if the book in question is several thousand words longer than the average, the costs for copy editing could be greater than the costs identified in the charter. And if the book also includes images that require a full-color insert for print, those costs may not have been part of the estimate for printing. With an internal digital project this becomes more pronounced as most publishers outside the corporate multinationals are not doing multiple projects to the point where they have a sense of what a budget for a management system might be at in the initiation phase. It may be the most informed guess, but it still needs to be reviewed and revised in the planning phase and periodically checked when the project is underway.

Development of the Book Project

After the planning, those involved in the project can turn their attention to the actual creation of major deliverables. This is the stage where a book is created or where the software or app is developed.

In terms of a book project, the development will include all of the work in editing, designing, and printing the book as well as any work in developing the ebook or digital files for online databases. The main deliverables at the book creation phase are the book files that will go through quality checks in the next phase. In addition to the major deliverables for the project, this phase may also include an update to the project plan based on change reports that can include:

- **Status report**. This document will compare the actual work to the schedule and budget and note where the two may vary. In terms of book publishing, this is often a weekly report and meeting with a focus on the major seasonal titles or the titles that are soon to be released.
- **Issues log**. A record of issues that arise in the actual development process. This could be notes about how a publisher's in-house template for print is causing issues in the ebook conversion process, the quality of work from freelancers, or even about how the publisher's website cannot support aspects of a redesign.
- **Schedule change**. An up-to-date schedule is needed in every project, and any changes made to a schedule need to be communicated to those who are doing work in the next two phases.

Quality Control of the Book Project

For most products that go through a linear process, the team will need to be able to ensure the quality of the products being developed. Often this means that after the development of the key deliverables for the project there needs to be a stage of testing or quality control to make sure the deliverable works as outlined in the project charter. The management of quality may need to begin in the earliest stages and managed throughout, a process called quality assurance. It is important to understand the difference between quality control and quality assurance. Quality control (QC) "inspects products at the end of the line" and identifies issues that will lead to delays in release while quality assurance (QA) means

> having frequent checks at multiple stages, [to] find issues and identify and incorporate resolutions in the next stage of the process. That way nothing makes it to the end to be sent back, and if it does make it that far, only a few components are affected.
>
> (Kreischer 2019, 59)

During the creation of the project charter or a project management plan the book project team should decide how and when quality will be checked. For most books it will often be a QC check before the release of the book, but anthologies and digital products may need QA checks and revised scheduling throughout the development phase.

Book publishers should understand how quality management ensures that print and digital products are complete and accessible before being released into the market. For print this might mean that someone at the press will send photos of concerns to their contact in the production department or the designer for feedback on the results. For those cover designers who often push the limits of cover design—embossing the title of a book and adding glow-in-the dark ink and spot gloss on top of that embossed title, for example—they should understand the need for more spot checks on quality as the more times a cover has to go through a press, the more likely that mistakes will occur leading to larger print runs increasing the waste and potentially the costs for a book project.

Ebooks and other digital editions have made the need for quality assurance essential in a book project. Several of the most common problems in ebooks will be discovered through a visual inspection at the time of delivery for different milestones. Problems may include issues with the display of text, the failure of chapters to start on new pages, or the misplacement of images. In addition to the visual inspection through the development process, ebook developers will need to perform another level of QA after the design is complete that confirms the files are valid and accessible. This process is often done through software that checks the file against ebook specifications and accessibility requirements.[3] Without this second level of QA, the ebook could read fine on the screen but not include necessary information in the code that could result in it being rejected by an online distributor.

Box 4.1 Sample Ebook QA Guidelines

A set of quality management guidelines is essential for publishers creating an ebook format. While print books have a fixed page design for a fixed page size, ebooks can display on dozens of screens of different sizes and are rendered by different programs on e-reading devices. Therefore, ebooks require more testing than print. Publishers will need to create guidelines through trial and error and constantly update as the landscape changes, but here are some basic guidelines that the publisher should follow to ensure a quality ebook.

Visual Guidelines

- Does the text display on the page as intended?
- Is the text legible in the smaller font sizes?
- Are paragraphs, block quotes, and lists consistently indented?
- Are all hyperlinks, both internal and external, correct?
- Are all declared fonts displaying correctly? Are the right terms italicized?
- Is there any print-centric language present that may confuse the reader (e.g., "See reverse of this page.")?
- Are images resized to fit on a single page on the e-reader?
- Are there tables and charts? Are they readable?
- How do the books read across different devices?

> **Coding Guidelines**
>
> - Is the file valid?
> - What are the file naming conventions for: the final EPUB? The HTML and CSS files? Assets within the EPUB (images, video, scripts)?
> - Are the stylesheets in conflict?
> - Is the necessary metadata present? Is it correct?
> - Are images converted to RGB from CMYK and tagged appropriately with semantic elements with alt text?
> - Does the EPUB load quickly on devices?

Developing solid quality management strategies is difficult and takes not only time but serious investment. It is also complicated by the different needs of print and digital where one format can be managed through quality control before release while the other needs quality assurance throughout the development process.

This schism between formats also raises the need for continuous improvement for projects that might not fit the standard print/digital structure. In the next chapter I will show how iterative project management is built around releasing multiple versions based on user feedback. This PLC is standard for mobile apps where new content and features are added in response to user reviews. For publishers, continuous improvement plays a small role in a book project, focusing mostly on typos and printing issues. As companies move beyond the book, continuous improvement will play a bigger role when the content becomes part of a digital product such as a learning system, app, or digital library. Book designers should be familiar with Adobe's continual improvement efforts that include multiple updates throughout the year.

Release of the Book Project

Release is a straightforward process. After the book files and printed copies are created and checked for quality, the formats are released to the marketplace or deployed by the organization. The details of the work done by the marketing, publicity, and sales departments in this phase are covered in the last chapter of this book. For publishers who are launching a new platform, the release stage would be when the platform goes live, and the publisher can begin to track how users engage with it.

Closing of the Book Project

The last step within this linear sequence is often defined as a mix of closing the project and performing maintenance. Once a project had been released, or, if the organization has determined that the project is no longer worth pursuing, the project team will need to document the work done for future reference before moving on to the next project. In the language of project management theory, a project can have one of four ending types:

- **Addition**. If a project evolves into an ongoing operation that requires a staff and budget, it is added to the organization's business. The creation of a content distribution system is one example of the addition ending.
- **Starvation**. When the organization cuts all resources to the project, regardless of whether the project is completed or not is considered starvation. In some cases, the author may be months or years late with their manuscript pushing the book project out of the current publishing pipeline or it might be that the sales of titles in a series have dropped to a level that no longer makes it financially feasible to continue with the series.
- **Integration**. Here resources are moved elsewhere in the company and the project ceases to have support. One example of this kind of project close is when a publisher who had created a dedicated ebook team to develop processes for creating in-house ebooks moves those team members back to a general book production team and incorporates the creation of ebooks as part of the production process. Depending on where the team was when they were integrated into another group, it may be that the project was never completed as the team was never able to complete a model for creating and testing ebooks for all their titles.
- **Extinction**. This is the most common ending for book projects. Extinction means that the project's goals were achieved. When a book is released, the project should go extinct.

A book project should be considered closed once it has moved to the backlist. At that point licensing new editions or correcting typos and grammatical errors within the book become operational concerns rather than maintenance problems. Some publishing professionals, primarily those in production who are responsible for the backlist, might feel that a book project is never complete, but a key aspect of a project's definition is that it needs to end. The book may require some kind of work over its life, but the life cycle of a book project ends when the team responsible for the book project moves on to other projects. One person managing some aspect of a book does not a project make.

Concerns

While the linear PLC for a book project reflects the way the publishing industry has thought about project development and management for decades, if not shortly after the adoption of Gutenberg's press, the model does have some limitations in how it deals with change throughout the course of a project. The linear PLC can be inflexible once it begins. The completion of one phase of a project can discourage team members from requesting changes or corrections discovered in the next phase as it can disrupt the entire project plan. The idea within the model is that the discovery of problems initiated in previous phases should require the team to revert a project back to a previous phase. This makes sense in the testing phase when a book or internal project might have functional issues that require a rework of the product in the development phase, but if there are minor issues in the process and scheduling of a project, the team should not need to step back from the development phase to the planning phase and delay a book's release and impact the project sales for that week or quarter.

Another challenge in the linear PLC is that it assumes that the requirements for the book will not change over the course of the book project. If a book is proposed as a 256-page hardcover with a manuscript due in twenty-four months, those assigned to that book from their respective departments can start planning the work needed based on their understanding of the book from that proposal. But the author may require extra time or deliver a manuscript that runs well over the expected page count. The reality is that book projects are often subject to changes in scope, deadlines, and other factors that will affect all stages after the project plan. Active communications can manage keeping others informed of the changes, but it usually means employees are inundated with updates and may lead to divergent schedules where departments aren't using integrated planning programs.

A capacity for managing change should be built into any model for project development. As noted above, at any point in the linear process the team can step back to revise the project based on new information. The team may also decide to sunset a product and replace it with a new one that has gone through a parallel process as the original product but reflects the users' needs that emerge after a release cycle. An example of this is the way Microsoft handled the release of new versions of its new Windows operating system (OS). New Windows OS releases would replace older versions, which would require the users to install the newer version over their current OS. This often required the user to be active in the purchasing and implementation of the new OS every few years. The parallel in textbook publishing is where instructors, students, and bookstores switch to a new edition every few years as a publishing house releases new editions. The next chapter will explore the iterative PLC's solution to this churn: to never close a project. Instead of a finished product released to the marketplace, companies release perpetual beta versions that are constantly being updated. This means the user no longer needs to purchase a new version of an operating system or textbook every few years but have access to a product that is in a constant cycle of updates.

Notes

1 Even books released in series with a uniform cover from Gallimard's La Pléiade line and the Piccola Biblioteca Adelphi series from Adelphi need some changes made to information on both the front and back cover.
2 That is, if the publishing house believes in their P&L statements as something more than a means to justify an advance. As Mike Shatzkin notes in *The Book Business*, "the practice of constructing P&Ls on a book-by-book basis is itself a logical fallacy. The idea of an individual book making a profit or loss makes sense only if there is no publishing house…you [can't] actually just 'add up' all the expenses for each book to subtract from the revenues to produce a profit calculation." (Shatzkin and Riger 2019,. 74–75)
3 To understand how problematic non-accessible ebooks can be for readers who have low-vision or are blind, Ka Li, an accessibility and usability consultant from the Canadian National Network for Equitable Library Service, offered a demonstration on how screen readers perform different ebooks with coding issues at the 2019 Ebookcraft conference in Toronto. His presentation walked through ebooks that failed with screen reading software.

References

Barrett, Dave. 2022. *Understanding Project Management*. 2nd ed. Toronto: Canadian Scholars.

Kreischer, Noah. 2019, July. "Working Smarter to Improve the Workflow: Use Lean and Agile Principles to Produce More Training Content Faster and at Higher Quality." *TD Magazine*, 56–61.

Li, Ka. 2019. "The User's Perspective: Accessibility Features in Action." *Ebookcraft 2019*. https://www.youtube.com/watch?v=FoXkwG6rn3k&list=PLRthkZj3fAc0lLDpJ8o39BzGVLwE-usi1&index=7. Accessed 13 September 2023.

Parente, Susan. 2018."The Scarcity of Paper—Pulp (Non)Fiction." *Sheridan*. https://www.sheridan.com/insights/the-scarcity-of-paper-pulp-nonfiction/. Accessed 13 September 2023.

Phillips, Angus. 2019. "Publishing and Corporate Social Responsibility." In *The Oxford Handbook of Publishing*, edited by Angus Phillips and Michael Bhaskar. 147–161. Oxford University Press.

Project Management Institute. 2004. *A Guide to the Project Management Body of Knowledge (PMBOK®)*. 3rd ed. Newtown Square, PA: Project Management Institute.

Sellers, John A. 2010. "'Flanimals Pop-Up' Shipment Missing—No Joke." *Publishers Weekly*. https://www.publishersweekly.com/pw/by-topic/childrens/childrens-book-news/article/41889-flanimals-pop-up-shipment-missing-no-joke.html. Accessed 13 September 2023.

Shatzkin, Mike and Robert P. Riger. 2019. *The Book Business*. Oxford University Press.

Wright, Alex. 2009, Autumn. "The Battle of the Books." *The Wilson Quarterly*. http://archive.wilsonquarterly.com/essays/battle-books. Accessed 13 September 2023.

Wysocki, Robert K. 2011. *Executive's Guide to Project Management: Organizational Processes and Practices for Supporting Complex Projects*. Medford, MA: Wiley.

5 The Iterative Project Life Cycle

A publisher's work in the creation of print and digital books is best reflected in the linear PLC model discussed in the last chapter. Most book projects have a set of defined final products (monograph, EPUB ebook, audiobook, PDF) and each manuscript goes through a specific sequence to create those products. In some instances, such as academic and professional publishing, there may be projects including ongoing series or the publication of conference proceedings where the creation of individual volumes follows a linear PLC, but the series as a whole requires the publisher to evolve the series over time in response to market and user needs. De Gruyter's series on German literature, *Studien zur deutschen Literatur*, began in 1968 and currently offers over 150 titles in the series. In dealing with the series, De Gruyter has had to adapt their production processes for the volumes several times as this series spans major changes in printing technology including phototypesetting, digital typesetting, and POD. The series has also expanded to include offering EPUB, PDF and Open Access versions of the titles in the series. With each release, the publisher needs to address changes in the industry for new titles while maintaining the availability of previous titles, though not necessarily adapting previous titles to modern needs. For example, no titles prior to 2019 are available as EPUB publications but all titles have been converted to PDF for institutional access and the tables of contents of each volume are available through De Gruyter's website (https://www.degruyter.com/serial/stdl-b/html#volumes). All of the work to modernize the series and make it available online did not take place in one iteration. The same process can be seen in the development of other apps and services that publishers are creating for use on tablets and phones. This requirement that they should respond to user needs and modify products cannot rely on a linear PLC so instead must turn to an alternative means of conceiving of the project's needs. The iterative PLC model, commonly referred to as the Agile model, is an umbrella term for the different methodologies that had arisen from the need to develop a product over several iterations. Some of those methodologies include lean development, extreme programming (XP), crystal, Agile Unified Process (AUP), Dynamic Systems Development Method (DSDM), Scrum, and Kanban. In most cases the methodologies mentioned above are primarily used for large software development projects and are rarely part of the world of book publishing.[1] The two exceptions are the Scrum and Kanban methodologies which have been adopted by publishers for the management of series—De Gruyter currently lists over 520 active series that need to address the same developmental concerns as *Studien zur deutschen Literatur*—and other customer-facing projects like phone apps as well as internal projects including implementation of new management systems in book publishing.

Unlike the linear PLC model that delivers a final product after a lengthy planning and development phase, Agile focuses on the project as a series of iterations where much smaller but fully functional deliverables called the minimum viable product (MVP) are released every few weeks. One way of understanding this in terms of manuscript development is that the book project starts as a short story that is released for sale and then developed into a novella that is released that then becomes a novel which is released in hardcover, digital, audio, and paperback a year later before it becomes a series. In each version the original short story is still the core part of each product.

The goal in the iterative life cycle model isn't to address a long list of goals and objectives the first time through the process, but to identify the smallest but most essential part of the product, quickly develop it, and release it in order to get feedback that will influence the next iteration. We can see this feedback loop in narrative development in the writing projects found on online community publishing apps such as those offered by Wattpad Webtoons Studio and Tapas Entertainment where authors develop serial narratives by drafting parts based on the feedback on earlier sections by readers.

One reason for the appearance of the Agile method as a method for project management in book publishing is its success in other industries. The Project Management Institute (PMI) contends that "more than 70% of organizations have instituted some type of Agile approach, while more than 25% of manufacturing firms employ Agile exclusively. PMI research suggests that Agile-based projects are nearly 30% more successful than traditional [linear] project management" (Davidson 2019, 33). For publishing executives those statistics, along with the overall sense that Agile leads to more success with a leaner process, makes it a tempting tool. But books are not and cannot be iteratively based. Agile is for projects that have a high uncertainty on what will be delivered or new products that does not have a clear indication of the time and cost needed for development. Agile's place within the book industry is with new digital ventures in the industry. Apps like the Barefoot World Atlas from Barefoot Books or Curious World featuring Curious George are examples where an Agile model is more beneficial than a linear one. In both cases the publishers developed apps based around a book or series, but throughout the process the content and interactivity began to grow. In the case of the Barefoot World Atlas the publisher began with the text and hand-painted illustrations from the print book that explored different countries and regions of the world through their animals, architecture, and culture as the foundation for the app and then expanded the product to include multimedia content that provided audio and images. The app also took the physical maps from illustrator David Dean and turned them into a virtual globe that users could spin and zoom. Barefoot Books then experimented with live data for each country's entry so readers could see the real-time temperature, CO^2 emissions and exchange rates.

After the app was released in 2012 the publisher continued to develop the app releasing several expansion packs that offered more multimedia entries on subjects such as world art and international football. More expansion packs and versions were released in 2014 including full translations into French, Japanese, German, Spanish, and Catalan. As Apple's IOS evolved, Barefoot also needed to address the bugs and errors created between their app and the new operating systems. The app remains an ongoing project for Barefoot Books that has now had four major versions released. Unlike a print book where an updated edition is a new product that needs to be repurchased, the parent who bought the Barefoot World Atlas app in 2012 has access to all subsequent versions including the current on their tablet.

The Agile Model

Rapid releases by software companies can make an Agile project appear as if each iteration is a minor update to fix buggy software, but the speed of their releases often hides the amount of work that needs to be completed in a short amount of time. For a publishing house to start to begin to understand how to utilize an Agile model for a project, they need to start with an understanding of the guiding principles for this model. Agile was created by seventeen experts of different iterative methodologies during a conference at the Snowbird resort in the American state of Utah in 2001. The goal of this meeting was to define the parameters on how to create quality products quickly so that developers could move between the methodologies and not get attached to using the slower linear model. The group came up with twelve guiding principles on how to use these methodologies as well as the decision to group them all under the title of Agile.

Box 5.1 Twelve Core Principles for Agile Project Development

1. Customer satisfaction by early and continuous delivery of valuable software.
2. Welcome changing requirements, even in late development.
3. Working software is delivered frequently (weeks rather than months).
4. Close, daily cooperation.
5. Projects are built around motivated individuals who should be trusted.
6. Face-to-face conversation is the best form of communication (co-location).
7. Working software is the principal measure of progress.
8. Sustainable development, able to maintain a constant pace.
9. Continuous attention to technical excellence and good design.
10. Simplicity—the art of maximizing the amount of work not done—is essential.
11. Best architectures, requirements, and designs emerge from self-organizing teams.
12. Regularly, the team reflects on how to become more effective, and adjusts accordingly.

The guidelines, like the methodologies themselves, focus on customer response, change within a project, and require a lot of interaction between team members who need to self-organize. The Agile methods prefer to give team members autonomy and free them from the hierarchical and functional structures dictating how the individuals work. For companies who aren't engaging with customers for continuous improvement of a product, aren't willing to give the project team the freedom to dictate their course of work, or release every few weeks, Agile will not be an improvement on the linear cycle.

For those publishing projects that do require iterative development, an understanding of how a product develops over several iterations is essential for its success. In an industry that manages hundreds of thousands of linear PLCs a year, having a case study on iterative development over several years can help reframe how a team will approach the work. One such case can be found in the development of an ebook library by online information provider ProQuest. The company acquired Ebrary, an online library of 170,000 scholarly titles, in 2011 and Ebook Library (EBL), an online collection of more than 300,000 ebooks, in 2013. Ebrary and EBL were offered as separate services to US and UK libraries until the company launched the Ebook Central platform in 2016. Ebook Central not only integrated the title catalogs of Ebrary and EBL, but it also added functions for libraries such as an access-to-own option and patron driven acquisitions, a feature where libraries acquired books based on actual patron use, and note-taking, highlighting, and citation building[2] for users (ProQuest 2016b). In 2016 ProQuest also added Chinese-Language titles to the Ebook Central platform with user interfaces in both traditional and simplified Chinese characters (ProQuest 2016a). In 2017, the company added expanded digital tables of contents that allowed users to go directly to subsections of chapters, an updated naming convention to help users keep track of their downloaded titles, as well as making the platform conform to level AA for the W3C Web Content Accessibility Guidelines, meaning it offered keyboard navigation, browser magnification, and ability to work with screen readers (ProQuest 2017a, ProQuest 2017b). In 2018 Ebook Central offered DRM-free titles and added features such as reader reviews and tags from the LibraryThing platform as well as author photographs and bibliographies (ProQuest 2018). In 2021, ProQuest launched the SimplyE mobile app that allows patrons to browse, borrow, and read ebooks on their handheld devices without having to go through the several layers of logins common to academic libraries (ProQuest 2021). In additions to the iterations of Ebook Central, the company has also been integrating services from their other partnerships and platforms to improve metadata and discoverability in the larger ProQuest databases. The Ebook Central currently used at universities around the world is very different than the one that launched in 2016, but the libraries that purchased access have not had to repurchase it as they do with printer reference works.

The Agile Project Life Cycle

The life cycle phases for an Agile project can be defined in a similar way to a linear model, but the nature of the work in the Agile model is such that instead of a

82 *Workflow and Project Management Theory*

progression where early phases only influence later ones, the iterative nature means the release phase can now inform the planning phase of the next iteration. Project teams can learn and adapt their work based on past experiences in working with the product. The process continues to start with a list of requirements that provide definition for the project, followed by the planning, design, and development of the deliverable before release, but upon release, the team returns to the requirements phase and recalibrates its work based on what was learned in the last iteration and the process begins again.

While the phases may move in a circle instead of a series of steps, it should be obvious that this model follows the general project life cycle of initiation, here called requirements, followed by planning and execution. It's not too far from Barrett's four generic project life cycle phases of initiating, planning, executing, and closing (Barrett 2022, 8). The major change is that the closing of a project folds back into the next iteration's initiation phase. In this model, execution takes place in both the development and release phases. Testing and quality assurance are also addressed across these two phases.

When comparing the two models in terms of process there may be some questions on how to deal with the constraints of time, scope, and money. Because of the iterative nature of Agile, the whole sequence from requirements to release are

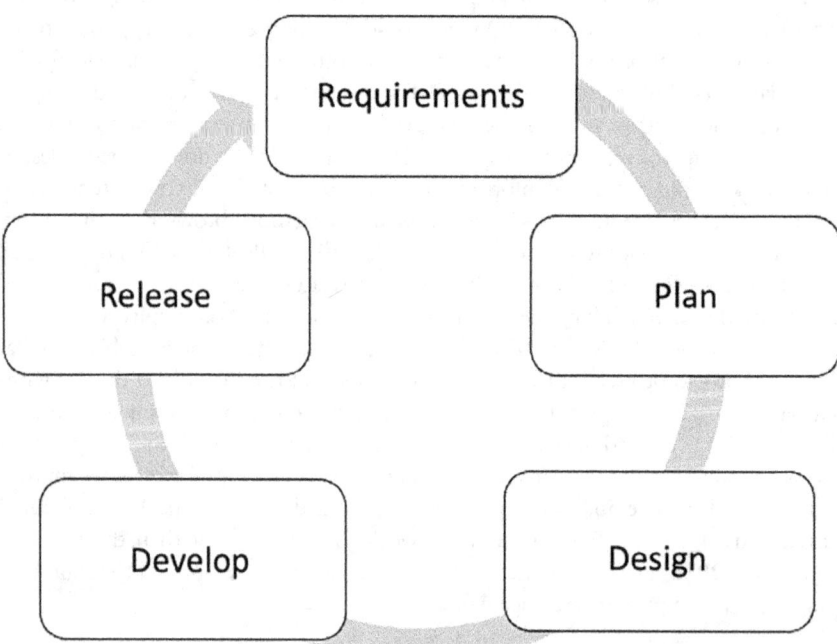

Figure 5.1 Unlike the linear model where processes are visualized as steps from initiation to release, the Agile model is better visualized as a cycle where once one development cycle ends, the next one begins.

often limited to a short period called a sprint. Sprints are commonly only two weeks to a month long, although they can be as long as needed. They are meant to be short so that the scope of the requirements within each iteration are much smaller than what is expected in the linear model. This means a sprint's constraints will be smaller, but the needed resources (people and equipment) will continue to be needed over several product releases instead of becoming free to work on other projects.

Because of a sprint's narrow focus, the iterative model should be used for book projects geared towards new technologies where there's little understanding of what customer needs will be. This can be the development of an app for a book series that might not start with a clear goal, an interactive website for a book that will provide interviews, or video content of author presentations and interactive features that have yet to be created. The model can also be used when customer feedback is required for product development. The development of educational product that integrates with online learning systems provides a use case on how academic and textbook publishers can use this model for their book projects. It doesn't make sense to develop an entire digital library of textual and multimedia resources for a specific subject the way publishers created print textbooks. Online learning systems can provide specific curricular needs that inform the development of a product specifically for a class. It can also take the feedback from a professor or student and update the content to align with their needs. The online learning systems are already responding to user needs throughout the semester; why shouldn't the content providers as well? For book publishers this also means that students are now both stakeholder and QA tester instead of a passive consumer. The user plays a much bigger role in the development of a product developed with the Agile method requiring organizations to make space to listen to the user.

Agile projects will eventually reach a final closing phase, but the close often means that the company is completely done with the project and will no longer work on it. In our example of ProQuest's Ebook Central, the EBL and Ebrary platforms are no longer available. Unlike a linear book project where the print product exists well after the project closes, once an app or service ceases to be viable, the project goes through an extinction where team members are released from the project and the company will either shut the service down or no longer provide support or updates, meaning it will eventually become incompatible with operating systems.

The Requirements Phase

Similar to the initiation phase in the linear model, the requirements phase in an iterative model will produce documentation that identifies the project's goals similar to what gets identified in a business plan and project charter. In the iterative model the business plan outlines the goals, parameters, risks, and a budget for the current iteration. Unlike the linear business case that provides extensive information for the project, this plan should be straightforward and clear on what will be delivered in a single sprint and how much it is expected to cost. The project charter should include a project vision (what the team wants to get done), a project mission (why the team wants to do this), and what the success criteria will be for a successful project. The requirements on the first phase may also include a plan for how often the team will release. The milestones and objectives identified in the charter will inform what user stories and epics, groups of related user stories, are essential. The user stories themselves will dictate the nature of each iteration and are developed in the kickoff session, a meeting run by the project manager or Scrum Master, if using the Scrum methodology, where the project team and project owner discuss what they feel is needed in the upcoming iteration.

User Stories

User stories are an integral part of several different iterative methodologies. They capture and communicate the requirements of a project from the perspective of the end user or consumer. Instead of developing a list of goals and objectives only from the perspective of the team working on the project,[3] user stories capture work that needs to be done and what value that work brings to the project for team members and users alike.

The first step in creating user stories is to create user roles. This can be done through surveys, interviews, or other means of information gathering, or through the development of user roles that will provide some characteristics and context for this user. In a project focused on creating apps for learning management systems, the users might be students, teachers, school administrators, and IT personnel who will interact or manage the app in an academic environment. In each case these roles will have different needs from the app and those needs will become user stories.

After defining the user roles, the team members should start to record what they think those users will need as user stories. The stories need to provide a concise description of a specific feature or functionality in a way that is measurable. One common method for developing effective user stories is to use the INVEST principle. This principle defines a good user story as one that addresses the following criteria: the story should be Independent of all others; it should be Negotiable in terms of priority and resources; it needs to be Valuable to a user; it needs to be Estimable; it needs to be as Small as possible and still conform to the other criteria; and it needs to be Testable within the iteration. With a principle such as INVEST in mind, the project owner and project team should create their user stories with the following process:

1 Define the stories in the following format: "As a [type of user], I want [goal] so that [reason/benefit]." This is the format of a user story. The point of the user story is not only to identify the goal, but also understand why the user wants that goal. For example, an editor using a title management system might have a user story that reads: "As a commissioning editor, I want to be able to upload chapters of a manuscript so that marketing and publicity can pull them from the system instead of requesting them from the department

assistants." A publicist's story for this same need could be: "As a publicist, I want to be able to download manuscripts on a chapter level as PDFs so I can send them to media outlets as part of a pitch for an interview." There will be dozens if not hundreds of user stories gathered, and some will focus on the same need from different perspectives.
2. The project should review broad stories ("I want access to the management software so I can see future titles") and break them down into user stories that focus on a single action that can be completed within a single iteration, or sprint ("I want a weekly report on future titles so I can plan the marketing budget").
3. The team also needs to define how it will consider stories to be completed.
4. The project team will need to prioritize the user stories in a rank of importance with the most essential ones at the top as they need to be completed in early iterations. Teams may want to establish a technique for prioritization such as the MoSCoW (Must, Should, Could, Won't) method where teams assign an M,S,C, or W to the user story and then sort on those letters.
5. Teams should assign a duration or amount of effort it will take to complete the user story. Some teams may use a point system here to identify a user story's complexity and the resources needed. The points will help the team to identify what can be accomplished in a sprint. If a sprint can only have a maximum of eighty points, the stories chosen for the MVP cannot add up to more than eighty points.
6. Once the user stories are ranked based on some means of identifying the value of the task, similar stories should be grouped into epics. Epics are collections of related user stories that have a similar value and can be achieved in a sprint. Together the epics and single user stories define the MVP.
7. The user stories not picked for the current iteration become the product backlog where the team will create the next iteration's MVP after a reprioritization, or backlog grooming.

If it isn't already apparent, this type of initiation phase can be labor intensive. The iterative model does not subvert or break the project management constraints that were identified earlier. It only shortens the duration of development and refines the scope around that duration. Multiple iterations with their different MVPs will naturally expand the scope, but it does so while it is in creating value in the marketplace. The *Barefoot World Atlas* app that is currently available in the Apple store added functionality and content over an eight-year period, but users always had access to its original content as the app grew.

The Planning Phase

Once the user stories have been selected as the MVP, the team should be able to address how to schedule the work across team members so that the stories are resolved within the current sprint. Most of the identification work that is part of a linear PLC takes place as part of the requirements phase when team members develop and rank user stories in a kickoff meeting. An Agile planning phase will deal with a set number of user stories that have an assigned point value indicating the amount of work the task needs. The team can translate that point into a duration based on the number of people working on it and use that duration to identify a deadline. This is often called a timebox. If team members mark that it will take two hours to develop a data entry screen based on a user story, then the people working on that screen have only two hours to complete that task. Timeboxing also applies to meetings including a daily standup meeting. If the meeting is scheduled for fifteen minutes, the project manager needs to keep the meeting to fifteen minutes. For people comfortable in the linear model, this fixation on time can be extremely stressful. Agile assigns fungible time to every small task in a way that can feel as if it is the next generation of Taylorism complete with a timer and a to-do list, but an iterative PLC relies on removable sticky notes over check boxes as the main means of tracking the progress of a task.

Kanban Board

The planning of work across an iteration gets complicated quickly. There may be several dozen user stories that are being worked on by different team members concurrently. When the project is being designed, the team will need to provide a sense of where all these user stories are in terms of completion. Teams will need to use a tracking tool to know who is working on what and when it might be done. There are several programs such as Atlassian's Trello that allows teams to create digital lists for tracking of work, but Kanban, a low-tech method developed by Taiichi Ohno that has been in use for decades as part of Toyota's lean manufacturing process, has an elegance to it. Kanban is a visual model where tasks are written down on cards or sticky notes and grouped on a signboard, or Kanban. The Kanban is divided into different columns that indicate the status of the work. The most common columns are:

- "To Do,"
- "In Process,"
- "Due," and
- "Complete."

As the team works on different activities the cards move between statuses. This provides a visual map on what tasks are in process and what tasks are needed. It also gives individual team members some autonomy, for instance, to move a card into the "Complete" column, claim the task they want to do from the "To Do" column, and move it to "in process." The decision on what task to complete is aided by the card which defines not only the user story but can also include notes on acceptance criteria, an indication of the priority (MoSCoW) and the effort (points) or duration (timebox) for that task. Beyond listing basic information on the cards, teams can also color-code the cards to define the type of work needed (editing, coding, documenting, content creation) and create rows on the board to act as swim lanes. The way a team decides to structure a board needs to provide that team with a way to quickly see the work in progress and what work needs to be done.

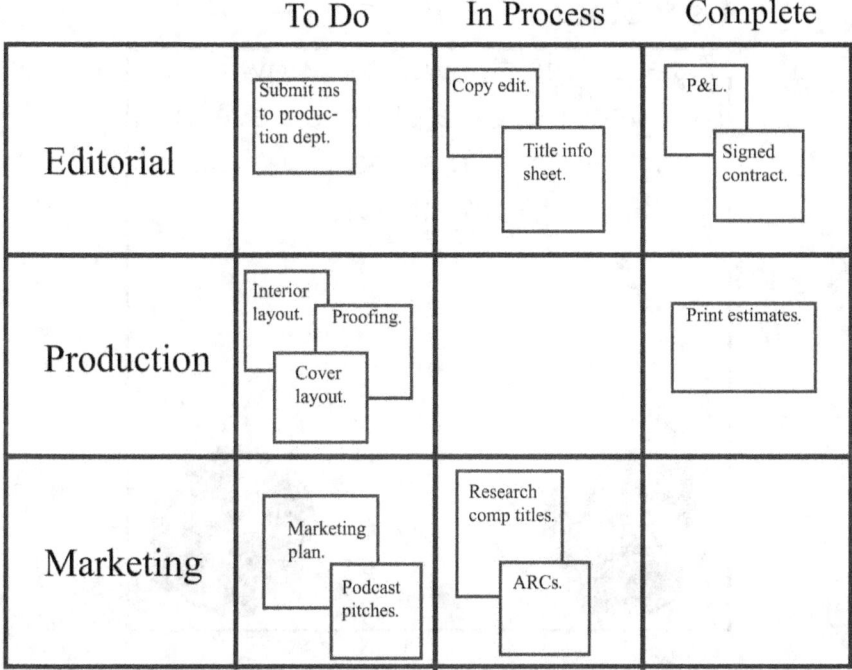

Figure 5.2 A Kanban board can provide a quick visualization of what work is completed and what work needs to be done. The board can use rows in a way similar to swim lanes to identify different team members, while the columns indicate if the work is yet to be worked on, is in process, or is completed.

The Design Phase

Unlike the linear PLC where the design is folded into the planning phase, Agile keeps the design separate as both planning and design are intensive. Every iteration focuses on a new MVP, so every design phase will create new deliverables that need to integrate with the work from previous iterations. This kind of iteration can be seen in the apps released by textbook publishers who have had to revise their apps to work with different operating systems and course management software as well as improve upon or add new content. Complete Anatomy, a three-dimensional anatomy platform designed for the medical field developed by 3D4Medical, is an app that has gone through multiple iterations over its nine-year history. The app started as a different product called Essential Anatomy, which was more focused on presenting straight anatomical illustrations, but evolved into one that allows users to isolate different anatomical systems and zoom in on specific areas. Since its release in 2015, the app has released over seventy updates across three different versions (3D4Medical 2023). The updates included bug fixes as well as new interactive features, new languages, and the addition of new content. In 2021, the company introduced a new female model that reflected new research into female anatomy (3D4Medical 2021). What would have traditionally been seen as a

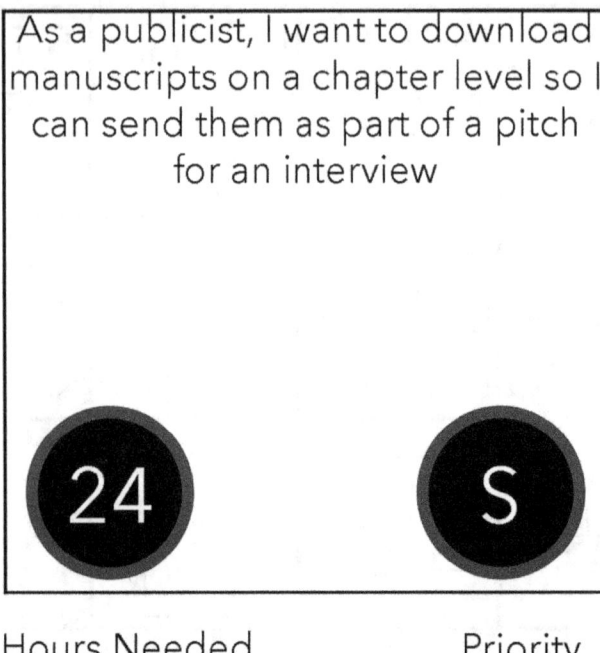

Figure 5.3 The cards or sticky notes that are placed on a Kanban board will have the user story or task at the top of the card. The cards may also include an indication of the time needed to complete the task (hours or points) and the priority of the task (MoSCoW). This card indicates the user story will take twenty-four hours and has the priority of "should" complete in the MoSCoW terminology.

revised edition or the development of a series of titles is now a digital product that incorporates revised material into the app first purchased by the user.

In order to manage the development of new content, team members working in the design phase will often develop the outline of the needed content and interactive features as a series of wireframes and prototypes. Wireframes are straightforward outlines of how the content looks on the page using only boxes and arrows with descriptive titles. Prototypes will provide design elements and color as well as a sense of interactivity to suggest the look and feel of the final product. These wireframes and prototypes will then be passed along to those working in the development phase as directions on what work needs to be done.

The Development Phase

The development phase in a cycle of an iterative PLC is similar to the development phase in a linear PLC. It's where the main deliverables for the project are created. But unlike the linear mode, these development phases focus on the current MVP, "that version of a new product which allows a team to collect the maximum amount of validated learning about customers with the least effort" (Ries 2009). Whereas the linear PLC develops a product that gets released once, here the product being developed is completed with the expectation of gathering feedback and going through more cycles of development. As shown in the Complete Anatomy example, the versions that are released often include updates to the content or introduce new aspects of the products that will inform future cycles. In the example of the introduction of a new female model in the Complete Anatomy app, the company developed new anatomy and dissection courses around that new model that became available over several updates to the app. Because the focus in a single iteration is only on a core set of features, the time to complete the work can shrink down to a matter of days. This short cycle will need a new means of managing it. That is where the Scrum methodology comes into play.

Scrum

Scrum is an Agile methodology that prioritizes the current iteration's work over almost anything else. It is designed to give team members autonomy in breaking down the priorities into specific goals that can be completed within a short part of a cycle that is only one of several iterations of a project.

The Scrum methodology is rich with specialized vocabulary. The name itself comes from rugby and is meant to indicate a team that does not have a typical hierarchical relationship. Each team member can decide on what work they will do in each sprint. The work is timeboxed and if an action is not complete within its timebox, that user story may be abandoned for a future sprint, or the team member will dedicate time outside the project to complete the story by the end of the sprint.

Scrum Roles

The Scrum team is often a small group of highly specialized workers who are self-organized around responding to the needs outlined by a product owner. They rely on a Scrum Master to protect them from distractions or other departments within the organization. A Scrum team is expected to breakdown the user stories presented by the project owner into small tasks that can all be defined in points and timeboxed to indicate the effort needed to complete the story.

The product owner represents the stakeholders and is responsible for identifying the expected outcomes in the current sprint through the identification and prioritizing of user stories. There are hundreds of user stories for each project and the project owner will need to prioritize these as well as identify the acceptable criteria for the team.

The last person involved in a Scrum is the Scrum Master. The Scrum Master's role is understood in terms of servant leadership. The Scrum Master does not define what team members do but is responsible for removing the obstacles that team members identify as stopping their work. The Scrum Master also has the job of protecting the team members from non-essential work and non-essential meetings that take place outside the sprint.

Scrum Meetings

While it sounds as if Scrum's self-organization means that team members are working on their own, there are established meetings for a sprint. The main types of meeting within a sprint are:

- **Kickoff**. This planning meeting is where the user stories are defined and the time for the tasks is set. This can also include budget information and the product specs for the version that will be released at the end of the sprint.
- **Standup**. These are daily meetings between the Scrum Master and the team members. These should be short meetings, often 15 minutes. In the meetings, team members should identify what they completed the previous day, what they are working on today, and any obstacles or diversions being added by others in the company.
- **Sprint review**. Upon completion the team should have a review that evaluates the work done or not done and any issues that arose in terms of the project or morale or interactions with the rest of the company so that they can be resolved in the next sprint.

Scrum Tracking

As sprints tend to be short and intense periods of work, the tracking of the work is essential. There are certain methods that Scrum teams will use to track the project and sprint. This chapter has already discussed how to use a Kanban board which can work in a sprint, but Scrum teams also need to manage their backlog.

The two major backlog documents are the product backlog and sprint backlog. The product backlog is a list of all the user stories that have been created in the project and will define the stories for future sprints. The sprint backlog are only those stories that were identified for the current sprint that are not complete.

An alternative to backlog spreadsheets and sticky note Kanban boards is an executive dashboard. The dashboard is a visualization that tracks the backlog and status of user stories, but it can also include information on where the sprint is in terms of the cost, time, and scope. In addition to keeping track of constraints, executive dashboards have become popular because they often provide information on how quickly the team is completing their tasks in the form of either a burndown chart or a velocity chart. The velocity chart tracks how quickly the team is completing tasks across the different sprints (the velocity) compared to their initial estimates. The team's velocity can be used in a future sprint to adjust the number of hours or points that can be realistically completed. A burndown chart focuses more on the work done over the time, indicated as a sloping line recording the decrease of open tasks as the sprint progresses. The burndown chart provides visibility into the project's progress, highlights any deviations from the plan, and helps the team make informed decisions and adjustments to achieve their objectives.

While the tools used in Scrum look as if they provide a clear map on the work that is completed and the work that needs to be done, Scrum, like most Agile

The Iterative Project Life Cycle 91

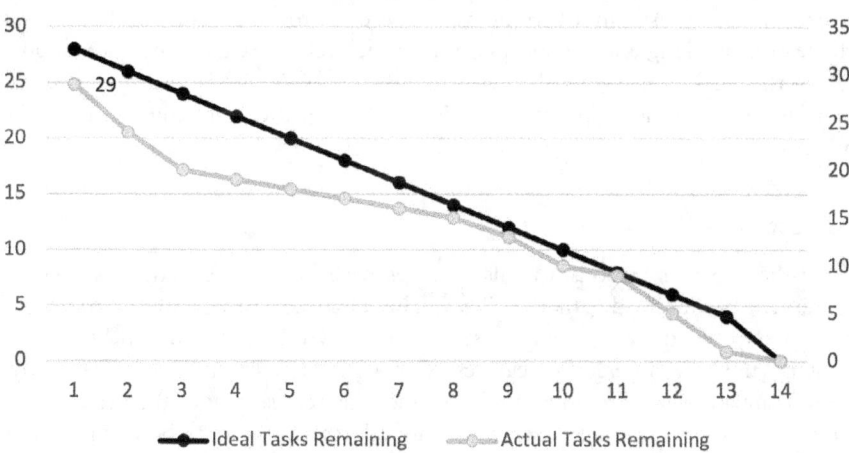

Figure 5.4 This example of a burndown chart shows the actual work that is completed as compared to the expected completion rate over time. The y-axis shows number of tasks and the x-axis the number of project weeks.

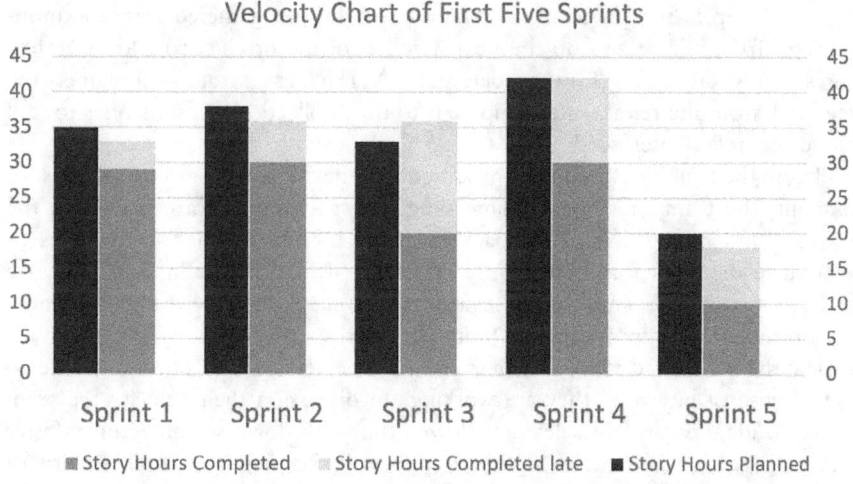

Figure 5.5 A velocity chart will measure the work completed against the work scheduled across multiple sprints. This will give the team a sense of how quickly they are completing tasks compared to their initial estimate. In this example, the team is having to complete work beyond the timebox allotted.

methods, is fundamentally focused on managing uncertainty. The tools mentioned above should be used in a Scrum-based project to revise goals around how well the team is working and the reception from each release. Unlike the linear model where the market gets what the organization creates, Scrum is meant to evaluate what needs to be done in every iteration and revise the requirements and plans accordingly.

Release

After the project's responses to user stories have been developed, it is time to release the product and gather feedback. The release can be either a minor update to address bugs or new operating systems or a new iteration that includes new content and new interactive features. Generally, releases are made frequently. Most companies aim for either weekly or monthly releases but as the project goes on and the most important user stories are addressed, the time between releases may become longer as the team deals with the more complicated user stories (the stories marked as "could" in the MoSCoW method) or on new content that can be as intensive as content that was part of the initial release. Both the Barefoot World Atlas app and the Complete Anatomy app have released significant additions of content in major updates.

Repeat

The final step in this process is to take the information gathered from the monitoring of the release and do the next iteration of the product to add more features. How are those features determined? The Agile team will gather the feedback from the release and compare it to their collection of user stories to find those that reflect user needs.

Before the team goes back into picking up the next epic or list of user stories for a sprint, the team should take some time after gathering information from the tracking and monitoring of feedback from the users and other stakeholders to reevaluate the work that needs to be done. This is often done in a retrospective meeting where the entire team evaluates the feedback received and identify opportunities for improvement. During the retrospective meeting the team will review the completed work and may evaluate the velocity and burndown rate to get a sense of how well they are working. In discussion their velocity the team needs to identify any obstacles that slowed the work down so the Scrum Master can manage those obstacles in future sprints. In keeping with Agile's spirit of continuous improvement, the team should focus on the experience and note what could be improved for the next sprint. The last step before starting another sprint should be a project backlog refinement. Here the team should add any user stories that came from the retrospective meeting and review the backlog of user stories. This review will include a clarification of user stories based on the previous work done as well as a ranking or prioritization of user stories to identify what stories may form the epic or group of user stories that will be addressed in the next sprint.

The identification of user stories to be addressed in the next sprint moves the team from the end of the current iteration into the identification of the requirements for the next iteration. From here they can begin the next round of work.

Iterative Publishing Projects

Book projects continue to align with the linear model as the industry continues to fixate on the complete final product as the only goal of their work. But that's not to say the iterative model hasn't been used in experiments around the development of manuscripts. Examples include projects such as A Million Penguins from Penguin UK and book projects from authors McKenzie Wark and David Weinberger who both released beta versions of their manuscript online as a way to collaborate with readers (Wark 2006, Weinberger 2001). Similar to the projects from Wark and Weinberger, A Million Penguins was a "wiki-novel" that was open for contributions over a five-week period and was managed by Penguin Books and the Institute of Creative Technologies at De Montfort University (Mason and Thomas 2008). All three of these projects would move through several iterations where author, editor, reader, and commentor would work on the development and release of a chapter. They may not have been as structured as a standard Agile project, but the collaborative iterations followed Agile's spirit. While Penguin's wiki-novel ended up being archived upon completion, both Wark and Weinberger would see their project get acquired and turned into traditional linear PLCs that resulted in the books *Gamer Theory* (2007) and *Small Pieces Loosely Joined* (2002), respectively.

Another example of iterative publishing can be seen in the Swoon Reads venture that is part of Macmillan Children's publishing group. The imprint allowed readers to submit their manuscripts directly. Other readers are able to read, comment, and rate the submission before they are acquired for print publication. The work with the highest rating from readers and the editorial team is acquired and published in a print and e-edition from the press (Lodge 2012). The model mixes crowdsourcing with an Agile framework to create a different model for book acquisitions. This community-based acquisition model uses the iterative processes of Agile to not only identify publishable books but to begin developing a marketing buzz for a book during its development.

Educational, academic, and professional publishers are also using Agile as they move away from a reliance on selling print material to content that can be integrated into online learning systems. The Complete Anatomy app mentioned above is just one of many projects coming from textbooks and academic publishers as they evolve print products to content that exists as a book or series of books in several formats as well as content that has been deconstructed into chapters or articles available on a school's interactive learning platform or as an app for handheld devices. The move towards these online systems for classroom management allows professors to provide digital access to relevant parts of a text instead of requiring the purchase of a whole collection. This disruption in the market has forced publishers such as the one publishing this book to rethink the value of a "book" in terms of academic use and rethink ways to provide the needed content in a way that works for publisher, student, professor, and administration.

Agile is also suited for projects focused on helping book publishers with the management of work. Lonely Planet, the travel guide publisher, uses Scrum to develop their publications. The house found that prior to Scrum, "the development of a book was very sequential and required many handoffs" that created a lengthy development phase. They began to use the Scrum framework where the different departments, authors and photographers were involved as a team to "incrementally develop the book chapter by chapter following the Scrum framework" (Sliger 2011).

Concerns

For all the advantages this model provides book publishers when dealing with cutting edge digital resources, the nature of an iterative PLC has issues that need to be understood by publishing organizations before starting to implement it with their employees.

For a publishing house that centers the release of its key books around important dates and focuses most of its work around seasonal lists, the multiple delivery dates that come with iteration often mean timelines that will not fit with its established production calendar. That, combined with the reality that a release may be nothing like what was originally described, means that the workflows a publisher has will need to be completely revised. Iterative projects will have multiple releases across multiple seasons. They are book projects that require multiple cycles of not only content creation and production but also multiple cycles of marketing and promotion. Unlike a book, where most marketing and publicity ceases a few weeks after publication, iterative book projects may need a promotional push every few weeks as new versions are released.

Iterative development also requires a high time commitment to projects from highly skilled team members, creating an added human resource cost. The skills and job requirements for Agile team members can be problematic for an industry that continues to claim it does not need employees with specialized skills. The idea that a publishing house can teach new employees what they need to know through mentorship and on-the-job training will not work in an iterative environment. Publishers engaged in this kind of project will need to hire people who have project management training or a skillset that aligns with the needed project management work. Unfortunately, the candidates with the necessary project management training also tend to be in demand at other media companies as well as other industries developing platforms and apps for their industry including fintech (financial technology), medtech (medical technology), and edtech (educational technology). For an industry that is notorious for low salaries, the competition for good employees means publishers will need to change their culture and begin to either offer competitive salaries with those other industries or begin to provide a means to allow for current employees to get the necessary training in project management.

The last concern in incorporating iterative PLC into a book publisher is that iterative project management theory requires a focus on documentation as part of each cycle. In the Agile methodologies, teams need to track KPIs for the latest product release as well as update the backlog of user stories that will be used to create future MVPs. User feedback is also essential in the requirements phases of a cycle and will need to be collected through interviews, surveys, and other means of user outreach with each release. All this documentation will need to be tied to their specific version of the project requiring version control management, which becomes one of the first activities dropped by overworked employees on a tight deadline. Without the time to document the work done, an iterative process can quickly become unmanageable for new team members should those working on the project leave the company.

Notes

1 The major types of projects where other Agile methods outside of Scrum and Kanban are used are massive digital projects like EBSCO's Ebook Manager or large multi-year developmental projects that may focus on Open Access initiatives where the deliverables available expand over each iteration as the project goes through each sprint.
2 ProQuest also owns RefWorks, a web-based citation manager.
3 The needs of the team are included but those needs are addressed as user stories as well. User stories can include any needs from team members, stakeholders, or users.

References

3D4Medical. 2021. "The Story Behind Our New Female Model." https://3d4medical.com/blog/background-to-the-female-model. Last accessed 5 June 2023.
3D4Medical. 2023. "Product Updates." https://3d4medical.com/updates. Last accessed 5 June 2023.
Barrett, Dave. 2022. *Understanding Project Management*. 2nd ed. Toronto: Canadian Scholars.
Barefoot Books. 2020. *Barefoot World Atlas*. https://www.barefootbooks.com/digital-apps. Last accessed 5 June 2023.
Davidson, Jeff. 2019. *Everyday Project Management*. Oakland, CA: Berrett-Koehler Publishers Incorporated.
EBSCO. 2023. "EBSCO Ebook Manager – One Year Later." www.ebsco.com/blogs/ebscopost/2334265/ebsco-ebook-manager-one-year-later. Last accessed 5 June 2023.
Lodge, Sally. 2012. "Swoon Reads Introduces Crowdsourced Publishing Model." *Publishers Weekly*. https://www.publishersweekly.com/pw/by-topic/childrens/childrens-industry-news/article/55210-swoon-reads-introduces-crowdsourced-publishing-model.html. Last accessed 15 September 2023.
Mason, Bruce and Sue Thomas. 2008. *A Million Penguins Research Report*. Leicester, UK: Institute of Creative Technologies.
ProQuest. 2016a. "Key Chinese-Language Titles Now Available on the ProQuest Platform." *Proquest.com*. https://about.proquest.com/en/news/2016/Key-Chinese-Language-Titles-on-the-ProQuest-Platform. Last accessed 15 September 2023.
ProQuest. 2016b. "ProQuest Launches Ebook Central." *Proquest.com*. https://about.proquest.com/en/news/2016/ProQuest-Launches-Ebook-Central. Last accessed 15 September 2023.

ProQuest. 2017a. "Ebook Central Enhances Accessibility for Researchers." *Proquest.com*. https://about.proquest.com/en/news/2017/Ebook-Central-Enhances-Accessibility-for-Researchers. Last accessed 15 September 2023.

ProQuest. 2017b. "ProQuest Enriches Ebook Central® Platform User Experience." *Proquest.com*. https://about.proquest.com/en/news/2017/ProQuest-Enriches-Ebook-Central-Platform-User-Experience/. Last accessed 15 September 2023.

ProQuest. 2018. "Ebook Central Platform Enhances Discovery via the Syndetics Unbound Service." *Proquest.com*. https://about.proquest.com/en/news/2018/Ebook-Central-Platform-Enhances-Discovery-via-the-Syndetics-Unbound. Last accessed 15 September 2023.

ProQuest. 2021. "ProQuest, NYU Pilot Program Offers Students and Faculty Instant Access to 150,000 Ebooks Via App." *Proquest.com*. https://about.proquest.com/en/news/2021/proquest-nyu-pilot-program-offers-students-and-faculty-instant-access-to-150000-ebooks-via-app. Last accessed 15 September 2023.

Ries, Eric. 2009. "Minimum Viable Product: A Guide." *Startup Lessons Learned*. http://www.startuplessonslearned.com/2009/08/minimum-viable-product-guide.html. Last accessed 5 June 2023.

Sliger, Michele. 2011. *Agile Project Management with Scrum*. Paper presented at PMI® Global Congress 2011—North America, Dallas, TX. Newtown Square, PA: Project Management Institute. https://www.pmi.org/learning/library/agile-project-management-scrum-6269. Last accessed 5 June 2023.

Wark, McKenzie. 2006. *GAM3R 7H3oRY, version 1.1*. New York: Institute for the Future of the Book. https://www.futureofthebook.org/gamertheory/index.html. Last accessed 5 June 2023.

Wark, McKenzie. 2007. *Gamer Theory*. Harvard University Press.

Weinberger, David. 2001. "The Making of the 'Small Pieces Loosely Joined' Draft Site." *Smallpieces.com*. https://www.smallpieces.com/history.html. Last accessed 5 June 2023.

Weinberger, David. 2002. *Small Pieces Loosely*. Cambridge: Perseus.

Part II
Project Management in the Three Areas of Publishing

6 Content Creation Project Management[1]

The job of the editor is project management.

In a short interview with *The Bookseller* in 2018, Rachel Faulkner-Wilcocks, a senior commissioning editor for Avon at HarperCollins UK describes her role as one that involves "a lot of reading, but the role is largely project management, and I spend a lot of time working with designers and marketers, as well as editing and strategically planning" (Pace 2018b, 41). Faulkner-Wilcocks's comment is echoed by other editorial professionals in similar interviews with the magazine (Alexander-Jinks 2019, Pace 2018a, Williams 2019) and reflect the now common appearance of "project management" as a job responsibility for editorial employment at British and American publishing houses.

Publishing culture has had a history of describing the editorial department in a way that disguises their obsession for schedules and to-do lists. Editors are often portrayed as a type of midwife (Frankel 2008, Hem 2012, Nabhan 2021) or alchemist (Aronson 1993) and most of the literature about book editing focused on the developmental work they perform (Ginna 2017, Germano 2016, Gross 1993, Rabiner 2003) over the day-to-day managerial aspects that composes a modern editor's job description.[2] This fixation on the author and their writing process dominates the industry's view of editorial work so much so that the bulk of the work done in most editorial departments is often identified with a focus on manuscript reading, as seen in the quote from Ms. Faulkner-Wilcocks. This chapter will forego any discussion on the work involved in the development of a manuscript with the author as it has already been addressed by the authors mentioned above. Instead, the focus will be on the work that leads up to an acquisition and the work that comes after the manuscript delivery that initiates a book project. I will follow the idea from Roger Stoddard that "authors do not write books. Books are not written at all. They are manufactured by...artisans, by mechanics and other engineers, by printing presses and other machines" (Chartier 1992, 53) and view the editors involved with a book project as the artisans and engineers who transform the author's manuscript into a designed book targeted to an audience.

When the author delivers a manuscript, it is only the start of several publishing activities within the linear PLC that include:

- Developmental edits,
- Legal reads,

DOI: 10.4324/9781003403395-10

- Rounds of page design from the designer/compositor,
- Copy edits and proofs,
- Cover designs for a designer based on feedback from the editor and sales reps,
- A marketing strategy for social and traditional media,
- Advanced reading copy mailings to media outlets and reviewers,
- Licensing of new titles to foreign presses, reprinters, and multimedia companies,
- Sales meetings and conferences, and
- The distribution networks for print and digital books.

Each of these activities will, in turn, have multiple steps and can involve several employees. The work for licensing books includes the subsidiary rights agent who licenses the translations, the contracts department who creates the contract, the finance department who assigns the advance and royalty to the main author contract, and a rights assistant who may deal with the correspondence and invoicing of the licensee.

In all areas of the industry including trade, academic, textbook, STM, and educational, editors are the ones responsible for evaluating potential projects for the company, rejecting those that are not viable, and crafting a project plan for those that could bring value to a publisher. They manage authors, agents, and other publishing professionals to ensure that the book project they brought to the company reflects the company vision. Their work is the work of managing schedules for the dozens of book projects that make up a seasonal list that is presented to sales teams who will use that information to pitch the titles into the marketplace.

The Editorial Workflow

A clear outline of the editorial department's workflow is essential in a book project if the project team is to outline the specific deliverables editors are responsible for delivering in each of the six phases of a book's linear PLCs. The editorial workflow should show the department's work in sequence and in relation to the other publishing departments who develop books and sales material from the documents they create.

As there is no one way for a manuscript to move through an editorial department, each publishing house will have its own unique set of processes for evaluation, acquisition, and management of a book project. For independent trade houses who are working on manuscripts they initiated or are themselves writing in an effort to build the press, the workflow may be split between two people: a publisher who manages the entire acquisition and editing process, and a production editor who is responsible for the financial management and production work for the book. Larger independent publishers may have an editorial board of three or four people that include the publisher, acquiring editors, and a marketing/promotions manager. The number of actors doing that work will change depending on the company's size. For a mid-sized publisher, the editorial board may consist of several editors, publicists, and sales and marketing people evaluating the proposal; independent and small boutique presses may have one person in several roles.

In almost all cases the content creation workflow within the house follows this pattern:

- A proposal for a project is submitted,
- The proposal is evaluated for value and viability,
- An offer for the manuscript is made,
- Contractual issues are negotiated and agreed upon,
- A preliminary schedule is created based on a contractual delivery date,
- The draft manuscript is delivered,
- The draft manuscript is evaluated in terms of its quality and scope compared to what was proposed,
- The draft manuscript goes through either a developmental edit or a peer review,
- Manuscript is accepted by the publishing house,
- Accepted manuscript is distributed to other departments,
- A tagged typescript is sent to the production department, and
- The typescript is copy edited.

Different houses will combine or modify some of these steps depending on their needs. For example, a publisher that is acquiring content from a book packager may only need to evaluate the proposal and negotiate the contract for the book. The work of editing and designing is handled by a book packager. On the other end of the spectrum is the acquisition of a licensed property from another media company that may require the publishing house to develop the story idea itself and find someone to write the manuscript based on that idea. If the press is lucky, the media client may provide an outline of ideas they would like to see developed but are also open to new ideas from the publisher. The *Nikki Heat* series based on the television show *Castle* is one example of this, children's books for *Bluey*, *Peppa Pig*, and *Paw Patrol* are others. The author who writes the book for these licensed properties is often hired under a work-for-hire contract where the manuscript, like the cover and marketing plans must receive approval from the media entity. This requires a very different workflow from a small literary fiction house. Between the two are companies like Running Press, an acquisition by the Hachette Book Group that developed a successful business selling mini editions through spinner displays at the registers of bookstores. Their displays are filled with small books and kits designed to be purchased by impulse, examples of which include books such as *The Love Sonnets of William Shakespeare* (2014) shrunk into a book with the dimensions of 6.99 x 2.22 x 8.57 cm or the *Harry Potter Golden Snitch Kit*, (2023) complete with a plastic Golden Snitch. Academic titles such as this one will need several rounds of peer review by subject experts as part of the evaluative process both before acquisition and acceptance. Textbooks and anthologies may have a series editor as well as a volume editor who manages the contributors that write content for the collection.

Whatever type of book project is being acquired by a publisher it is often similar to other publishing projects previously managed by the publisher. Established publishers tend to stay focused on subject areas where they have experience in producing and selling books. Conglomerates are able to manage a large number of new releases in a wide range of categories from celebrity memoir to children's picture books because they have workflows in place that can evaluate and produce books quickly. Here's where the publishing house's culture becomes relevant in the workflow. Large publishers are able to produce books efficiently, but the attention and focus that helps them complete work has also made these companies risk adverse to experimental titles. The mix of workflow and culture is such that it emphasizes proven subjects over others. It is often up to small literary presses such as Jacaranda Books and Sort of Books to take a risk with authors who are taking risks with their narratives. Small presses have a different set of goals and objects from multinational publishers. Instead of focusing only on growing the bottom line, small publishers can justify acquiring a project around an experimental manuscript because it expands readers' understanding of narrative or presents narratives in new ways. Even though selling out of several editions is not the main goal of the book project, these publishers have recently found themselves in the position of having their publications nominated for and winning several major literary prizes. Sort Of Books published the 2022 Booker winner Shehan Karunatilaka while Wave Books, a small poetry press, saw their publication of Tyehimba Jess's *Olio* win the 2017 Pulitzer Prize in Poetry. Of course, this winning of awards is often more of a risk than a reward in terms of the publishing process. Awards can mean more attention for the press and the book, but it also means a redesign of a cover to include a starburst, more work for a publicist to manage requests for the author, and most importantly it often means an upheaval of scheduling of books with printers. For a publishing house that only offset prints its first edition and then moves to POD, an award-winning title can increase the demand for the title from bookstores several-fold requiring the production department to schedule a reprint over the publication of new titles. The reprint process, common at the multinational trade houses who rule the bestseller charts, can be disruptive, if not devastating, to small presses who can see the sales on a title spike up to 350 percent in the weeks after an award announcement (Lagios and Méon 2021). It also means the potential for a return of 30–60 percent from those same bookstores (Thompson 2012, 284). The mix of goals, workflows, and a publishing house's culture dictate not only what projects the house will pursue but what its expectations for that title are and how it responds when reality is vastly different from that expectation.

Editorial Project Management

The editorial tasks of proposal evaluation, list building, manuscript preparation, and the development of publication schedules align with the core activities of the initiation, planning, and development phases of a book project's life cycle. It's this work from the editor in the early phases of a book project's life cycle that sets up a book project for success and is as important as the work of editing the book, even if it is never mentioned in reviews or talked about as part of the work that goes into creating a book. The editor's work of initiating and planning a book project will guide the others working in the latter phases of a book project.

Initiation of the Project

The initiating work for projects requires someone—the project team in linear projects and the project owner in Agile—to create the planning documents that describe the project's goals and provide an indication of its value for the organization. This is often outlined in a business case, a project charter, or, in the case of a publishing house, a publishing proposal form. The form should provide context on the proposal and how it aligns with a company's mission and goals. The editor should provide a description of what the book hopes to achieve either as a restatement from the author's pitch letter or as their own summary: "The author's latest project is the first book to address the history of bubble gum from ancient times to its height of popularity in 1960s America." After an editor defines what the project is and what value it brings to the publisher, an outline of when the author is proposing completion and a publication season will provide information for a preliminary schedule. The proposal form should close with a sense of the book's financial impact for the company. What kind of advance is the author/agent looking for and what is the right advance for this book based on the production needs (full-color, glossy pages, complex cover treatment, etc.) and a list of sales figures of similar titles to give some sense of the costs for doing this book and the benefit of publishing this book. The form should also mention what rights to the work the author is granting the publishing house to identify any opportunities for licensing and selling the work outside bookstores.

That form is then provided to the editorial board along with the original proposal. Unlike other initiating projects, the recommendation on how to pursue will come not from the proposal writer but from the board reviewing their project.

Box 6.1 List Development

The initiation of book projects is an essential part of an acquiring or commissioning editor's job and helps with another essential part of an editor's role: list development. Most proposals will never go beyond the initial review, but from a project management viewpoint, that evaluation and rejection is still work done in the initiation phase of a project. While this work by the editor may not be collected and analyzed as the number of ARCs sent out or the number of pages edited in a day, it is an essential part of the operation of a publishing house that has real costs and benefits attached.

In order to get a realistic understanding of the work that is being done by editors early in the process, a publisher should encourage some kind of tracking of manuscripts that have been rejected and why. Some editorial departments may create a shared document, a forum on a chat program, or use Trello to create a place to record evaluated proposals or brainstorm ideas for future titles. Depending on the nature of the editorial department the implementation of a shared means for list development could be problematic. A competitive culture often means editors don't share ideas or proposals they have evaluated with one another. In large corporate publishers or those publishers that rely on editors working in different offices, imprints or editors might start bidding against one another in book auctions. Rethinking how editors communicate about the evaluative work they do provides greater transparency among editors and can lead to a more efficient and more cohesive work culture.

The system in place for tracking projects should be simple. A spreadsheet that tracks each proposal reviewed by the editors will provide the department with a sense of projects that never made it beyond the first phase. At this point the tracking of the projects would only need to identify the project, the tasks performed as part of the evaluation, and an indication of the date completed.

When a project gets the green light from an editorial board the next step in the initiation phase is for the editor to contact the author and agent about contract terms. These terms, once negotiated and approved by both parties, will provide the information for the project charter. In some houses this may be called a deal memo or an acquisition memo. It will outline the book in terms of topic, size, and delivery date and define a communications/delivery plan for the manuscript that indicates how the author will deliver the manuscript and how the editors will evaluate it. A publishing project charter will also need to include a profit and loss (P&L) statement or some other financial evaluation to give a sense of the costs for

Table 6.1 A template for evaluation of and task recording for potential titles.

Project title	Ed.	Task	Date completed	Notes
The Politics of Owls	GR	Received proposal	20 February	
The Politics of Owls	GR	Evaluation of manuscript	24 February	Subject not a match. Pass.
Lost Girls of Libya	GR	Received proposal	1 March	Award-winning journalist. Focus on human rights in Africa.
Lost Girls of Libya	GR	Evaluation of manuscript	15 March	Has potential. Will pursue.
Lost Girls of Libya	GR	Readers' reports received	14 April	2 positives, 1 negative. Will share feedback with author after ed meeting.
Lost Girls of Libya	GR	Comp titles researched	28 March	Two from our backlist with sales figures.
Lost Girls of Libya	GR	Profit and loss statement	14 April	Advance based on discussion with agent. Sales numbers based on comp titles.
Lost Girls of Libya	GR	Decision to move project forward	18 April	Yes.

turning the manuscript into a book with a special focus on those requirements that are outside the ordinary (a copy editor who can edit in both English and French, a sensitivity reader who will also evaluate illustrations for a children's book).

Stakeholders and risks are rarely identified by the editor in their memos, but it is necessary work that can help better define the book project for later phases. A new author may require some extra time in the editing and proofing processes. A complex book design might mean more time required for printing. These risks may become notes in a schedule or title management platform and are essential information that will also provide a benefit when included with planning documents like the acquisition memo.

The project initiation phase will also often include the drafting of an author contract. This contract relies on the acquisition memo to fill in the required information in the company's boilerplate on royalties and the author's information. The author contract will identify the author and the expectations of that author in terms of work for the book project. The author's contract will define the project constraints for the author in terms of when the author needs to submit the book (time), the book's focus (scope), and an advance against royalties (resources). In addition to the advance the contract should also identify the expected word count for the project and if the author is expected to handle the permissions and indexing for the book. The contract needs to identify what rights the author is granting the publisher and how the proceeds of those sales will be split between author and publisher. While the contract is primarily an agreement between author and publisher on what is being granted by the author to the publisher, it also serves as a record on what work will be done by the two parties. For publishers with a sales force that includes personnel focused on non-traditional outlets (corporate sales, museum sales) and the subsidiary rights department, the expansion of sales beyond domestic bookstores can change how the publisher views the book and what grant of rights will be needed from the author in a contract negotiation. A same-day release of multiple translations on a new book or a co-edition with foreign publishers on a heavily illustrated title are two examples where a publisher can benefit from thinking about the needs in the production and release phases in the initiation phase.

Project Planning

The project's scope and schedule as well as any activities that comes out of the initiation phase documentation will become the foundation for a book project's planning phase. The identification of the activities and the expectations on those working on the tasks identify the constraints for the project. For those working on non-fiction titles, the editors should be familiar with the needs of editing non-fiction—checking sources, rewriting jargon, ensuring that chapter, paragraph, and sentence length align with audience expectations—and any specialized copy editing or unique design elements that will be handled by a production department. It will be up to the project manager in consultation with the managing editor to create the project plan for the book project. This will include any needed meetings, a schedule of milestones and delivery dates, and any modes of communication between all parties who are working on the project.

The way the team communicates will depend on who is doing the work. At a house where the work is done in-house, the communication plan could use messaging services, email, or even in-person meetings.[3] For those publishers who use offshore publishing service providers, meetings may only involve the title liaison who represents the work of several others within the provider. These communications of changes or response to completed work may need more time to filter down to the person doing the actual work on the book, and this delay may affect the book's schedule.

In a standard book project the planning phase can start when an offer is made or after the signed contract is received. A managing editor or team leader will take the milestone dates from contracts and the publishing proposal form and use them as the foundation for a preliminary production schedule. The schedule will also need to account for the book project's complexity. The schedule for turning a manuscript into a paperback original YA fantasy novel of about 70,000 words with no images will be different than a historical biography with three sixteen-page glossy inserts, copious footnotes, and an index. But the editorial and production intricacies aren't always clearly outlined in the notes found in a management system and that level of detail is rarely highlighted in deal memos or acquisitions forms, therefore developing some system of tracking assets alongside edits is often necessary.

The other important task within the planning phase for a book project is the development of an itemized budget for the book. The P&L that was generated during the initiation phase will be more focused on the benefits that come from the expected sales against the cost that comes from the book advance. Overhead and production costs are often in the P&L, but for many publishers these costs are often hidden within the automated calculations in the P&L creation activity. An editor isn't weighing the costs for different weights of paper for the book or calculating the costs of a freelance copy editor in their P&L, but once the proposal has been accepted, these editorial and production costs need to be provided in detail. A good book budget will outline:

- Paper,
- Copy editing,
- Proofreading and quality control,
- Cover design (labor and permissions),
- Permissions (text and illustration),
- Creation of illustrations (if needed),
- Typesetting/book design,
- Printing and binding,
- Ebook production, and
- General overhead.

Most of these costs are incurred by the editorial and production departments with production responsible for the paper, book design, printing, binding, and ebook creation. The editorial department will also be responsible for estimating the costs for the editing work that not only is carried out during the editorial process but often during the proof reading and indexing that will take place after the page designs are complete (Bullock 2012, 43).

Although it's rare for publishers to do so, this planning phase is also the spot when the publishing team may need to create a Work Breakdown Schedule (WBS) for the project. Most single-author books will not need their own WBS, but book projects with multiple authors and multiple editors that will take years not months to publish may need clarity on where they are in the process and who is managing what. A general WBS for the work done on a book project can provide a visual outline on the press's process. This WBS will also provide the managing editor or editorial project manager with a list of activities that needs to be scheduled.

Development of the Project

The publishing professionals involved with content creation will do most of their work in the initiation and planning phases for a book project but spend most of their time on the project in the development phase. The main work in content creation in this phase is the developmental, line, and copy editing carried out once the manuscript is received.

In addition to the editing work, editors will also need to update any planning information for the book project and create an Advance Information (AI) or Title Information (TI) sheet. The updates may include an accurate word count and number of illustrations so that the house can have a more accurate sense of how many pages will be in the printed book. The AI or TI sheet will be a summary document that goes out to all marketing and salespeople to help them prepare the work they need to do for the book's release. The document will include key information about the book (title, author, ISBN, price, release date). It should also include two summaries of the book: a sales handle and a long description. The sales handle should operate as an elevator pitch and express the main idea of the book in a single sentence. The longer summary should be about four to six sentences that explains both the book's focus and its importance to the marketplace. It will often be directly copied from the summary of the editorial cover sheet or the publishing proposal form. In addition, the commissioning editor will include an author bio, also from the publishing proposal form, and any blurbs they might have received from other authors. The final part of the AI sheet should be focused on marketing. The sheet may include a list of comp titles that provide the sales and marketing departments with titles that indicate the book's style or subject matter. It can also include sales points and marketing ideas focused on how to market and sell the book to retailers (Squires 2017, 31). This can include information about awards the author has won or larger cultural trends that could make the book appealing to book buyers at bookstores.

Quality Control, Release, and Closing

Those involved in creating the content are involved with the quality control and release phases in a support role to the content production and content distribution team members who have key roles in the later phases of a book project. The quality control work includes checking that the cover has the correct title—important for those books that revise titles based on feedback during sales conferences—and for typos within the flap copy as well as confirming that the right price and ISBN are on the cover and in the bar code. Now, if that publisher were to release multiple formats at the same time, errors in format and identification metadata can be spread across formats. Quality management is also checking a copy of the finished format and ensuring that the text is complete and legible and that it displays correctly on digital devices.[4] The content creators' role in the testing and quality control phase is often to confirm that the files from the production department reflect the goals and objectives for the books as stated in the initial proposal.

Once a book is released into the marketplace, the project should be considered closed. Depending on the legal and editorial requirements outlined by the publisher, the editorial department may collect the manuscript drafts, correspondence, internal documents, and schedule into an archive that will be stored in a repository for future editions. In the case of a hardcover release the archive may provide the initiation and planning documents for the softback or special edition.

The most common maintenance work at the time of a book project's close will be the management of errors and typos. It is a rarity for a book to come to market without any errors. It is often only after the release date that the author, editor, or a reader will immediately find these errors and, in the case of the author, send frantic emails about the typos to their editors for immediate correction in the digital edition. The publishing house will need to plan on how it will handle these corrections. Some publishers will identify this work as the responsibility of the person managing the backlist. Others will have a process where the acquiring editor manages these changes and is part of a reprint meeting or works with the production department to make the changes on the next edition.

Publishers will also need to decide how they want to manage corrections in digital editions. In the pre-digital days when publishers and printers stored the designed pages on film, it would mean a physical cutting and changing of the film. In the digital age the revisions are easier to make. PDFs that are part of collections that go out to libraries might be generated during a reprint or new edition. Corrections for EPUB can be fixed directly in the files without the need to regenerate the ebook from the design files, but that will also mean that ebook files may diverge from the print files causing multiple versions to exist. It's up to the house to determine the most efficient way to manage the maintenance of its books.

Version Control and Asset Management

The idea of version control on both a macro and micro level has existed in book publishing for a long time. On a macro level, publishers manage editions, revisions, and updates to their books. On the micro level, a publicist may keep fifteen versions of a press release on their computer while editors are trained to store multiple versions of an author's manuscript with comments on edits in a digital folder in case there are legal or production questions that arise before the book is sent to the printers. For the publisher deciding how to ensure that the corrected version is available for distribution and managing an archive of completed work is often a project in itself. The digital manuscript on a publishing house's network is the modern equivalent of the hydra. Editors may remove four of the five different edits from the server after the book files have gone to the printers only to find nine more undated versions of the book scattered across the network ready to be accidentally used instead of the final files.

For an example of how complicated this process can get, Bill Martin and Xuemei Tian provide a case study in *Books, Bytes and Business* of a small academic press that not only publishes monographs but also is responsible for annual conference proceedings and journals both in digital and print formats. The publishing house in the case study generates far more versions of its publications than what the readers can access. The case study traces the issues the house has had in maintaining the correct version to use even with the help of a management system for editors and contributors (2016, 170–172).

Publishing houses need to set rules on how staff manage and retain their versions of the manuscript. To start the publishers will need a standard file naming convention (FNC) to be used across departments. There are worksheets and best practices online for creating an FNC, but a standard format for a publisher is the author-title-department-date-version convention (Rodzvilla-Publishing PM-Marketing-28 September 2023-Draft). A naming convention will help with both differentiation and discoverability. Therefore, the publisher needs to decide what information is most important. Is it the department or the date or the author title? The convention used above indicate the author is listed first which means that all versions will appear under the author's name in a search and will require the searcher to read to the end of the file name to clarify the version and ownership. Compare that to a department/author/title/date/version: Marketing_Rodzvilla_Publishing_PM28_September_2023_draft. This one identifies the ownership of the draft over the authorship.

The conventions needed will depend on the workflows within the publishers and the needs of those doing the work. One final suggestion is to not use ISBNs in the naming convention. Few people in a publishing house think of books in terms of their ISBNs.

The next step after defining the FNC policy is to create a retention policy for manuscripts and other documents produced during a book project. This policy will dictate how long documents for a book project should be available on the network before being digitally archived. With the introduction of digital editions, including the need for different versions of ebooks for different retailers, the file retention needs for a publishing house will often extend beyond just keeping a single version of a book. A house now needs to not only maintain PDFs for print and library lending services like ProQuest, but also create unique ebook files for different vendors including Amazon, Apple, and Barnes and Noble. Special editions and interactive versions of ebooks also require production departments to store and update those files accordingly. The abilities afforded by going digital may have reduced the house's physical footprint, but it has required companies to expand their digital storage needs and retention periods. A sample of what the publishing house may need to keep as a record of the book project in their digital repository includes:

- Cover design files,
- PDFs of the designed book,
- Final book files (XML, InDesign, QuarkXpress, etc.),
- High resolution files for images, illustrations, or other visual material,
- Email archives on the project,
- Meeting notes on the title,
- Folder for corrections and typos,
- Change memos,
- Marketing, publicity, and sales material (AI sheets, catalog copy drafts, etc.), and
- Postmortem notes.

The folder in the repository should be seen as a history of the title's process from manuscript to the printers. Small publishing houses may also include digital copies of reviews, contracts, licenses, and financial information, if needed.

For some publishing houses, particularly those who work with titles that include illustrations, version control can require a Digital Asset Management (DAM) platform as well as a repository. The platform should work with, or be part of, the content management systems a house uses in their digital workflow. While some companies may decide to build their asset management system in-house, what Simon & Schuster did with their Digital Asset Bank, most houses license a platform or cloud service that best matches their archiving needs.

A publishing house's DAM or MAM (media asset management) will primarily provide the publisher a way to store media files such as:

- JPEGs of book covers,
- PDFs of press releases,
- EPUB files for different e-readers,
- Interior photographs,
- Book trailers,
- Author interviews,
- Scanned review clips, and
- Digital galleys.

The difference between the DAM and the digital repository is that the digital repository should be a record of the work done on the book project and the DAM includes material relevant to the ongoing work for a title. The DAM is a resource for material for active book titles. It is where someone in the publishing company should go if they need content for licensing and sales.

There are several options for both repositories and DAM systems for all publishers. I have consulted with small presses that put together a DAM using Drupal and a few extensions. Midlist publishers will often use commercially available software such as Documentum, ResourceSpace, and CONTENTdm. Even a portable hard drive that has been organized by season and project and is maintained by a dedicated staff member can work as an adequate repository.

Content Creation and the Agile Method

For those publishers who are developing digital products including apps for smartphones or learning management systems, the work described above may be completely transitioned into an iterative project life cycle model. Whether the publisher is organized completely around projects or uses a matrix model, an iterative project will have a different set of activities for the sponsoring editor. In an Agile model the commissioning or sponsoring editor takes on the role of project owner and becomes responsible for the development of user stories and setting the requirements for the project. In an Agile model the content creators will often be involved in the initiation and completion of each iteration. Their focus will be in the project identification and selection workflow with most of the editor's work centering around the following activities:

- Project definition,
- Cost/benefit analysis,
- Risk assessment, and
- Change management.

Project Definition

It's up to the editor to figure out what content needs to be created and edited, who can work on it, how much it will cost, and how quickly the content can be created.

The determination of the scope is the first step. Allowing the project's topic to change or expand, what project managers call scope creep, can be deadly for an industry that follows tight margins like publishing. Scope creep can mean a book goes from straight text to one with a few illustrations to one that is four-color and heavily illustrated. The focus of the book may not change, but the scope has and that changes the budget for the book project.

User Stories and the MVP

The sponsoring or commissioning editor acts as the product owner in an Agile book project. This means they will need to generate the user stories that the project team will work on developing. Unlike the traditional book project, where an author outlines the book's scope and provides a roadmap of where the book will go, a digital project may need the editor to start from nothing and build up the list of requirements. The project will require user stories on more than just textual content. There will also be user experience stories, coding stories, multimedia stories, testing stories, distribution stories, and so on. The translation of a book project into an app requires editors to think well beyond the digital page. When Faber released The Waste Land app around the introduction of the iPad in 2011, it provided the published poem by T.S. Eliot as well as multiple audio and video performances. The app included the text of the poem, a facsimile of the original manuscript with Ezra Pound's notes, and copious footnotes on the poem. Included in the app were over thirty-five expert video perspectives on the poem. That is only the content for the app. How the commentary, performances, facsimiles, and notes would interact with the poem also needed to be determined as did the means for how a user would scroll through the poem, start multimedia performances, and whether the app would allow them to highlight or copy the text from the app. All these decisions were user stories that developed over several iterations spanning a decade. In 2013, these iterations would include the addition of readings by Jeremy Irons and Eileen Atkins, revised icons, and other optimizations for Apple's updated operating systems. It would not be until 2022, the centenary of the poem, and a decade after its release, that the app was finally available for the iPhone. Other products such as Jane Austen and David M. Shepard's interactive edition of the *Annotated Pride and Prejudice* or Mark Z. Danielewski's interactive edition of *Only Revolutions* provide similar examples of how publishers can develop Agile projects based on print books.

The complexity of these online products makes it pertinent for publishers to not only have experienced project managers to help develop these products but also to have staff who understand how to work in this model. The user stories for those interactive books and apps mentioned above were not the result of the product owner alone. They would need a focused kickoff meeting where the entire team would develop the hundreds of user stories needed and the narrowing down of those stories into an MVP and product backlog.

Analyze Cost Versus Benefit

At the advent of the current ebook revolution, there was much talk about how ebooks would reduce developmental costs, meaning that digital copies with the same list prices as a print book would make more money for the publisher. This argument was often heard from agents and authors when they were looking to increase their royalty rates during contract negotiations, but as Bharat Anand points out in *The Content Trap*, content industries need to consider the fixed costs that are outside formats as part of the cost (2016, 73–74). Ebooks may not require paper or warehousing, but they still go through the same development and design process as a print book. Agile projects that do not have a print counterpart, such as a mobile app, tend to have their own developmental costs that are not shared with other editions. The addition of multimedia content and interactivity are unique costs for this format and are often expensive as they require agreements with third-party developers, as was the case for the Eliot, Austen and Danielewski titles mentioned above. In addition, the time needed for the creation of the products and the iterative nature of the product will require the publisher to develop a new method for identifying and measuring the project cost against sales; a method that is more common in software development than in book publishing.

Risk Assessment

It's important to carry out a thorough risk assessment so that the working group is prepared not only for issues that may pop up in the project's development, but also for the larger issues within the press, such as the schedule of other books, marketing concerns near book fairs, availability of copy editors and proofreaders with the required specialization, and so on.

This risk assessment, no matter how it is done, should be completed around the same time as the cost/benefit analysis and project definition, and then incorporate the concerns raised during their creation. It should also include contingency plans for any of the problems that might be not only severe but also highly probable.

Emerging Technologies: Community Publishing, Analytics, and AI

As book publishers modify their editorial workflows and rethink the organization's models to respond to market needs and employee requests for a better work-life balance, they must also acknowledge that they are a decade or two behind how the Internet has changed content creation through social media sites, and the displacement of desktops and laptops by handheld devices. Community publishing sites including Wattpad Webtoons Studio have been engaged in a method of serialization that reflects the best and worst aspects of the Agile method that has been a part of fanfiction sites for over two decades. Publishers like Quirk Books have had some success with the remix culture of fanfiction and community publishing in titles such as *The Meowmorphosis* (2011), *Android Karenina* (2010), and the best-selling *Pride and Prejudice and Zombies* (2009), but they haven't looked past the content to see how the roles of reader, writer, editor are changing over the course of a narrative and how the sites are using analytics to promote content.

Community publishing sites such as the aforementioned Wattpad Webtoons Studio, Tapas Entertainment (which operates the Tapas webcomic platform, the Radish serialized fiction app and the Wuxiaworld fantasy fiction platform), and Royal Road (which focuses on serialized fantasy), are more than places where writers can create serialized remixes and fanfictions. The sites have active communities of hundreds of thousands of writers and readers who are developing and editing hundreds of thousands of stories a year and building fan bases for those story worlds. While these sites may appear as infinite slush piles to editors comfortable with the traditional agent and proposal processes, the users of those sites have created a rich system of metadata that rely on detailed tags and ratings to provide a key to what is worth reading (and publishing). One of the few publishers who has experimented with content creation models that reflect these online communities was Macmillan's Swoon Reads. Swoon Reads actively engaged with readers of young adult fiction to evaluate and vote on manuscripts to turn into finished books. In pointing to these writing communities, I would also include the online fanfiction communities that are the precedent for most of these platforms as examples of ways readers and writers are rethinking how narratives are created. Moving beyond the subject matter, we can start to see rudimentary acts of editing, production, and distribution that users engaged in that would help to create two global bestselling series: E.L. James's *Fifty Shades of Grey* (2012) and Anna Todd's *After* (2014).

Other content industries outside book publishing have adopted a variety of business analytics practices to identify microtrends in content creation and consumption. These different areas of analytics include content analytics and natural language processing. This type of analysis can be as innocent as tracking word frequencies across a specific time period, exemplified by Google's Ngram Viewer (https://books.google.com/ngrams), or it can help to create clickbait titles to lure in readers. Some experiments in Digital Humanities, such as Jodie Archer and Matthew Jockers, work on understanding commonalities between bestselling titles as outlined in their book, *The Bestseller Code* (2016), or Franco Moretti's research on publishing corpora, both of which are associated with the Stanford Literary Lab, provide examples of how analytics and algorithm can be used in book publishing.

The final emerging technology is the use of AI in services such as ChatGPT and Google's Gemini. These new assistive technologies can help writers cut down on the time it takes for them to write a novel. In some cases, genre writers have found ways to have the AI generate new locations and characters that they can plug into their romance or mystery format to quickly create a new cozy mystery or an Amish romance title. Services like ChatGPT can also provide more robust responses than a Google search for information on a topic. As of this writing these services have generated a bit of a panic within the publishing industry and writing communities with some organizations advocating for clauses in book contracts to restrict authors from using the services. Other organizations including the Authors Guild in the United States have begun to advocate for compensation to authors who have had their work used in the training of generative AI. While this emerging technology is still in its infancy it offers several different advances to content creators. It may help speed up the time it takes to create content, but it can also be used to generate summaries and abstracts of a book and rich metadata on the book. It could also promise the next generation of automated grammar and spellchecking within word processing programs which could facilitate faster copy editing.

Notes

1 Workflow diagrams for this chapter can be downloaded at https://www.routledge.com/9781032516721.
2 Work that until the end of the twentieth century was primarily seen as labor for the female assistants and administrative staff. The evaluation of manuscripts and author relations being the domain of the more senior male editors. This division of work provides the foundation for the nostalgia for "the golden age of editorial autonomy and art-based editorial practice" of mid-century publishers (Childress 2019, 90).

3 Provided employees are working in the office on the days of the meetings.
4 This in particular has been hard to accomplish across publishing. Hachette's original ebook for JK Rowling's *Casual Vacancy* had corrupted code that made only a few words display on some pages at different sizes (BBC 2012). The Kindle version for Neil Stephenson's *Reamde* included a repeating section of the book that was not caught until several months in the market (Driscoll 2011).

References

Alexander-Jinks, Stephanie. 2019. "My Job in 5." *The Bookseller*, no. 5836, 36.

Anand, Bharat. 2016. *The Content Trap: A Strategist's Guide to Digital Change*. New York: Random House.

Aronson, Marc. 1993. "The Evolution of the American Editor." In *Editors on Editing*, edited by Gerald Gross. 10–21. New York: Grove Press.

The Authors Guild. 2023. "Survey Reveals 90 Percent of Writers Believe Authors Should Be Compensated for the Use of Their Books in Training Generative AI." https://authorsguild.org/news/ai-survey-90-percent-of-writers-believe-authors-should-be-compensated-for-ai-training-use. Accessed 3 August 2023.

BBC. 2012. "JK Rowling's The Casual Vacancy Ebook Suffers Glitches." *BBC*. https://www.bbc.com/news/technology-19759117. Accessed 3 August 2023.

Bullock, Adrian. 2012. *Book Production*. London: Routledge.

Chartier, Roger. 1992. "Laborer and Voyagers: From the Text to the Reader." *Diacritics*, 22, 47–61.

Childress, Clayton. 2019. *Under the Cover: The Creation, Production, and Reception of a Novel*. Princeton, NJ: Princeton University Press.

Driscoll, Molly. 2011,September 30. "E-book errors in Neal Stephenson's 'Reamde' annoy Kindle users." *The Christian Science Monitor*. https://www.csmonitor.com/Books/chapter-and-verse/2011/0930/E-book-errors-in-Neal-Stephenson-s-Reamde-annoy-Kindle-users. Accessed 3 August 2023.

Frankel, Ellen. 2008. "On Midwifery and Gatekeeping: Memoirs of a Jewish Editor." *Nashim: A Journal of Jewish Women's Studies & Gender Issues*, 15, 165–174. https://doi.org/10.2979/nas.2008.-.15.165.

Germano, William. 2016. *Getting It Published: A Guide for Scholars and Anyone Else Serious About Serious Books*. 3rd ed. Chicago: University of Chicago Press.

Ginna, Peter. 2017. *What Editors Do: The Art Craft and Business of Book Editing*. Chicago: University of Chicago Press.

Gross, Gerald, ed. 1993. *Editors on Editing*. New York: Grove Press.

Hem, Erland. 2012. "Editors as Midwives." *Tidsskriftet den Norske Legeforening*. https://tidsskriftet.no/en/2012/12/editors-midwifes. Last accessed 3 August 2023.

Lagios, Nicholas and Pierre-Guillaume Méon. 2021. *Experts, Information, Reviews, and Coordination: Evidence on How Literary Prizes Affect Sales*. Working Papers CEB 21-011, ULB—Universite Libre de Bruxelles.

Martin, Bill and Xuemei Tian. 2016. *Books, Bytes, And Business: The Promise of Digital Publishing*. London: Routledge.

Nabhan, Gary. 2021. "Editors Direct Writers with Caution, Inspiration, and Guidance." *Garynabhan.com*. https://www.garynabhan.com/news/2021/08/editors-direct-writers-with-caution-inspiration-and-guidance. Accessed 3 August 2023.

Pace, Lara. 2018a,May 11. "My Job in 5." *The Bookseller*, no. 5799, 55.

Pace, Lara. 2018b,May 25. "My Job in 5." *The Bookseller*, no. 5801, 41.

Rabiner, Susan and Alfred Fortunato. 2003. *Thinking Like Your Editor: How to Write Great Serious Nonfiction—And Get It Published*. New York: W.W. Norton.

Squires, Claire. 2017. "Taste and/or Big Data?: Post-Digital Editorial Selection." *Critical Quarterly*, 59, 24–38. DOI: doi:10.1111/criq.12361.

Thompson, John. 2012. *Merchants of Culture*. Cambridge: Polity Press.

Williams, Debbie Jane. 2019, June 28. "My Job in 5." *The Bookseller*, no. 5848, 48.

7 Content Production Project Management[1]

The one department at a publishing house most likely to have detailed work breakdown schedule (WBS) and swim lane diagrams for its procedures would be the production department. The move to completely digital creation processes that involve multiple content platforms and outsourcing to one or more companies requires production editors to rely on diagrams to guide the work they need to do. For a production department at a small academic press, knowing that the submitted typescript is part of a book project that will be printed print-on-demand (POD) with digital files hosted on the publisher's site to meet the Open Access agreement with the author's institution means a different workflow than a book project with a traditional offset print run that needs to be warehoused and an ebook available through online sales channels. At conferences and book fairs including The London Book Fair, Ebookcraft, and the annual China Digital Publications Conference, production people from all types of publishing houses present their workflow documentation as part of their talks on managing digital-first publishing, digital rights management, and quality assurance.

The Production Workflow

If book publishing appears to the general public as a magical process managed by distant gatekeepers, the spells and incantations for that transformation are found within the production department. A basic set of activities for a production department to convert a typescript into a book ready for the marketplace includes:

- Schedule preparation,
- Copy editing of a typescript,
- Interior text design of front matter, main text, and back matter,
- Cover design including blurbs and cover copy,
- Proofing of text and cover for issues in the design,
- Proof reading of text and cover for typos or other textual errors,
- Corrections to files and secondary proofing,
- Specification and request for estimates with printers,
- Quotation submission to different printers for pricing and availability,
- Creation of PDF files for printer,

DOI: 10.4324/9781003403395-11

- Creation of PDF files for promotional reading copies,
- Creation of EPUB and ebook files for different e-reading services,
- Creation of HTML files for website,
- Delivery of files to printer,
- Quality control of printed output (F&G of printed and trimmed sheets or digital file),
- Quality control of different ebook editions on different readers,
- Quality control of cover samples (color, typos, ISBN, bar code, price),
- Confirmation of receipt of print books at warehouse, and
- Confirmation of ebook files at online retailers.

The list provided above assumes that the house has full-time production employees and relationships with different printers, but as is the case with all of project management, every publishing house will need to figure out the best way to handle the work mentioned above based on its staff. For small publishers moving between POD and offset printing, a production manager might need to research and establish relationships with new printers who offer different pricing for short-run printing. In addition to the printers, the production department will also be in contact with the freelance book designers and book packagers who will submit work that requires rounds of quality checks by someone in the production department to ensure that the work was done to the publisher's specifications.

For large conglomerate publishers the estimates and orders they place with printers can include the delivery of specific paper for both the book block and the endpapers as part of their print order, a specific color cloth for binding in the binding order, and paper for the slipcover on hardcovers as part of the cover order. There are different options for each and the choices often depend on both availability and the print budget of the book. The cost of printing 15,000 hardcover copies of a 256-page work of fiction from a best-selling author on 60-pound uncoated paper stock with a glossy jacket without any special treatments in a demy octavo size (216 x 138 mm) is going to be less than 7,500 copies of a 36-page, four-color children's book printed on glossy stock in a crown quarto (246 x 189 mm) with a cover that embosses the work's title and includes a spot gloss on the illustration. Those titles are targeting different audiences who have expectations on a book's look, size, and feel. The production department will also make estimates based on input from the marketing and sales departments on what features can help the book stand out in a bookstore.

This complicated network of relationships between editorial, sales, marketing, printers, warehouses, and outsourced companies is one of the main reasons why production departments were the first departments to record and revise several workflows for their book projects. A publisher's production department needs to maintain control over the chaos of creative work to ensure that each title meets the expectations of quality for the company. As Rachel Comerford, Senior Director of Accessibility Outreach and Communications for Macmillan notes, "if a book has a lifespan, the manuscript development phase is childhood and a project manager's involvement begins at one of the toughest phases: adolescence"

(Comerford 2018). Moving a book from manuscript to a designed product means a balance between what the book needs and what the market wants. Narrow margins and compact text blocks can make a design fit a book's extent as specified in the initiation documents, but it can also make the print reading experience difficult for readers. The alternative is adding a few signatures and bumping the price above that of comp titles. On the digital end the production department also needs to manage the creation of ebooks where bad coding can force images to split across pages vertically or create several pages of blank space between image and text making the ebook look incomplete or amateurish. Production is where the house needs to figure out how the manuscript can look comfortable in its own cover. Unlike the other departments where a lack of clear process is not necessarily visible in the deliverables, any undefined tasks within the project management work for the production department, specifically in the areas of planning, development, and quality control, will affect the products from the publisher that go out to customers.

Production Project Management

In a book project the production staff will support the editor during the initiation phase by providing timelines and costs for the creation of different formats based on the editor's ideas on how many images or charts a book needs, or how interactive the digital products need to be. The real work of the production staff begins after the project is acquired. Here production will take on a primary role in the planning, development, and testing phases. Each phase will have a branching list of requirements around the needed formats. The needs of the print format will be different from those of an ebook. And both will have a different set of needs in terms of creation and quality control than an audiobook.

Initiation of the Project

While those involved in content creation often do the lion's share of a book project's initiation, production needs to be involved if only to provide background information on what is possible in terms of timing and resources. If the book project in question is a heavily illustrated financial reference guide that is aimed at a general audience and needs to have a cover price that is comparable to non-illustrated books on the subject, the production department will need to source quotes from both local and offshore printers that include not only the time and cost to print the books, but also an estimate on the shipping costs and schedule if the book will need to be shipped over sea as well as land. Production people are essential in the initiation process to inform on what's possible in terms of a timeline and budget as they understand a book project's variable costs as they pertain to the actual design and development of the needed formats that dictate the rest of the book project.

Project Planning

As mentioned in the chapter on content creation, the profit and loss (P&L) calculation should be considered a cost-benefit analysis for a book project, but once a project is acquired, a real budget is needed. A production manager can provide the costs for paper, cover design, typesetting, printing, binding, ebook development, and shipping for the book project. That budget will include a breakdown on the costs for internal work, third-party work for all formats being produced as well as the printing and binding costs for a print version. This will need to come from a production manager who can gather estimates from different printers and work out the best option for getting the work done. Keep in mind the best option doesn't always mean the least expensive. A heavily illustrated cookbook might have a higher production cost when sent out to a freelance design studio, but the design-intensive nature requires a specialized designer.

One of the largest costs for content production in terms of planning both the budget and schedule is the actual work that takes place after the delivery of the copy edited typescript. This work includes the internal work of typesetting/composition/interior design for both print and digital formats, indexing, proofing, and quality control/validation of digital formats, and the external work of printing, binding, and packaging the final book product. Every publisher will need to create their own means of managing this part of the process as the variables that go into the production process are so broad that there isn't space here to start to cover the differences in design, paper, printing, binding, and ebook development for all publishers. The workflows will range from those of small publishers that have one person who schedules freelancers for production work to conglomerates who have specialized departments where in-house designers and ebook developers may only work on specific formats, for example, illustrated children's ebooks. Adrian Bullock's *Book Production* (2012), BookNet Canada's Tech Forum archive (https://bnctechforum.ca/), and sites such as CreativePro.com are all excellent resources to help publishers develop and evolve a production department centered around a house's specific needs.

Budget

Production managers are essential team members for the creation of a budget for a book project as they are the ones who have the tacit knowledge of the options available for various book components and the availability for each project. Production managers will be able to answer questions on paper for the book including what paper will best match the budget for the project and how it compares to the standard stock used in a house's books. Paper management often means knowing what paper is used at which printer and how to get special stock when needed. As paper is the foundation for the physical book, having the right weight, bulk, tooth, and color will provide the setting for the reading experience. Both Adrian Bullock in *Book Production* (2012, 107–116) and Marshall Lee in *Bookmaking* (2004, 99–106) provide extensive information on the topic in their respective books. In addition to what paper stock is available for the book block, production managers can provide the costs for the case, binding, adhesives, endpapers, dust jacket, and any special treatments (embossing, foils, spot gloss, lay flat binding) for the dust jacket and cover. This is the list of raw materials that go into the creation of a physical book. These costs along with the printing and binding will recur in a way that accrues with every reprint and will be variable depending on the size of that reprint. The production manager can also provide the budget for the fixed, or non-recurring, costs of typesetting, composition, and corrections.

There is also the cost of developing the ebook, which, depending on the structure of the publishing house, may happen in-house as part of the book production process or outsourced to ebook developers. While print and digital books will share a lot of the same costs in terms of development and design, publishers **do** need to budget for ebook development. Even in a workflow that is completely done through XML, there will be costs associated with ebook design. The more complex the print design the more work needed for the ebook. The standard work of fiction and non-fiction may not need that much work to convert a print design to one that can reflow on different sizes of screens where readers can alter the size of the font and spacing between the lines, but some hand coding is often required to ensure chapters start on new pages, endnotes are linked, and intertextual references are revised. Intertextual references are particularly problematic in ebooks. Any reference to a specific location in a print book ("as mentioned on page 16") becomes meaningless in a format where the contents of a page changes across devices. Publishers need to either create links for these intertextual references in the ebook, which takes time and cost in terms of having someone link the text and check the links or they can develop guidelines for the authors on how to write intertextual references that allow for the reader to search the index or table of contents for the reference ("as I mentioned in the section on project planning for content creators"). As the book gets more complicated, a publisher may need to allow for a separate ebook design from the print. This is occasionally necessary for poetry and heavily illustrated books that have images that bleed across pages or off the side of the page. Ebooks are not simply PDFs of the print book. They are the book translated into semantic HTML that is packaged to display on specific software. One example of how different the two formats can be is illustrated in the print and digital versions of Mark Danielewski's *Only Revolutions* (2006). The print version of the book is "an uneasy hybrid between an artist's book and a prose poem.... A mathematically calculated 360-page codex" that "has no front and back" as Sam and Hailey, the dual protagonists, each get to tell their story from opposite ends of the printed book requiring the reader to flip the book in order to read each narrative (Starre 2015, 163). Penguin Random House's digital version of the book has these narratives running in parallel on the screen changing the way the reader engages with the text and also completely reimaging how the text is laid out from the print edition. This may be an extreme example, but it does highlight the major issues of reflowing text and dealing with references that all publishers need to deal with when managing print and digital formats.

Production departments will also need to be part of the conversation on cover designs so they can advise on what materials and treatments are available in terms of budget and schedule. Some designers love the feeling of unvarnished paper for a dust jacket as it gives some tooth to the dust jacket.[2] While the aesthetic is appealing, it readily rips in transit and shows fingerprints or dirt when customers handle it in a bookstore. One solution is to add a UV coating to the back of the dust jacket for durability without removing the feel of raw paper from the cover. The solution raises the cost, but it offers a tactile aspect to the cover and mitigates the return of damaged books that is common with untreated covers.

Scheduling

The production schedule will outline what happens between the receipt of a typescript and delivering the finished book to a warehouse. A book's production schedule needs to plan for the layout of the text as well as the design of the components that will organize the manuscript into both a bound and digital object. This organization includes the input of the text into a design template in a desktop publishing program, checking the files, and revising the design across chapters to ensure a cohesive design. Depending on the type of house, the steps in the schedule can shift around. The typescript sent by editors in trade and academic houses may be considered the final version of the work in their process but

> educational publishing tends to involve a high number of revisions fairly late into the development cycle. Where content would already be set in a trade or academic title, in educational texts, content is often revised and re-revised in a fourth or fifth pass of the material—long after the design is set.
> (Comerford 2018)

The publisher will need to design schedules that make sense for their workflows, but at the very least the schedule needs to include time for:

- Proofing the design for typos and inconsistent designs,
- Creating, approving, and revising a cover,
- Development of general ebooks files as well as those specific to Amazon and Apple,
- Development of other digital formats for online repositories.

Once the files are complete, the rest of the schedule relies on getting the files to the printers and having time on press. Press time has become more and more precious due to active mergers and acquisitions between printers, the increase of total title output by publishers over the last decade, and the reliance of multi-national trade publishers on blockbuster titles. Barack Obama's memoir, *A Promised Land*, for example, caused delays across the industry when it was released in September 2020. The initial US print run was 3 million copies, which was more than domestic printers could handle. Crown, the book's publisher, ended up printing a third of the initial print run in Germany (Harris 2020). The other publishers of the translations of the memoir would also gobble up press time around the world during the main period for printing titles geared towards the coming winter holidays, the most active time of year for book buying in the United States and Europe. The publication of this memoir at the end of the year added days if not weeks to the schedules of those books being printed in the United States and Europe and forced production editors around the world to search for printers that had any openings to best accommodate their books' schedules.

The general timeframe for a production schedule is often around nine months. A simple breakdown of the tasks and the standard time for the work to be done during a normal year could look like:

- Edited manuscript to production marks the production start date,
- Page design: three weeks,
- Proofreading: two weeks,
- Proofed pages with queries for author approval: two weeks,
- Book cover layout: one week (concurrent with author approval of proofed pages),
- Indexing: two weeks,
- Final book files created and checked for errors: one week,
- Files sent to printer,
- Sample print pages from printer for quality control: five days from date when files sent to printer,
- Sample cover to designer for quality control: two days,
- Print books printed and bound: six weeks,
- Ebooks generated from print page designs: two weeks,
- Ebooks checked for valid code, design errors and accessibility issues: three weeks,
- Shipping of print books to warehouse: three weeks,
- Upload of ebooks to online platforms: one day, and
- Shipping of print books from warehouses to retailers / publication date: four weeks.

Other examples of production schedule formats can be found in Giles Clark and Angus Phillips's *Inside Book Publishing* where they provide a month-by-month schedule for a book (2020, 193) and Thomas Woll's *Publishing for Profit*, which offers a blank production schedule template (2014, 169). Joe Biel also offers sample production schedules for nine titles from his Microcosm publishing house in his book, *A People's Guide to Publishing* (2018, 256–260).

As book production work is a well-covered topic in the literature available about book publishing, I would like to focus on two areas of production that often get ignored in the discussion of managing production schedules: promotional reading copies and ebooks. Promotion reading copies include Advanced Reading Copies (ARCs), Book Layout and Designs (BLADs), and galleys. While each term refers to samples generated at a specific moment in the production process, these pre-print versions are also now part of the sales and marketing activities for a title.

Galleys, or uncorrected proofs, are copies of the designed books that are produced after the book is typeset but not checked. Galleys were originally samples of the hand-set pages that the compositor would send to proofreaders for review. An ARC is a designed and nearly complete version of a forthcoming book that is sent out to build hype and generate reviews. It will often feature the final cover design for the book, unlike galleys which are often bound in colored stock with essential information (author, title, ISBN, release date, publicity contact) printed on the cover. A BLAD is a sample for a heavily illustrated book and is often only a signature of the book that showcases the book's interior design. In all three cases these will need to be generated by the production department and, if printed versions are needed, sent to the printer before the finished book is complete. This means that in addition to the first edition of a book, the production department will need to schedule and budget for the creation of one or more pre-print editions in digital and print format printer. In the case of an important or major title for the publisher, the quantity of ARCs may be the equivalent of a reprint or the first printing of a more specialized title. A large trade publishers may print thousands of ARCs to be sent out to reviewers and as promotional giveaways on web sites like GoodReads and at conferences such as Frankfurter Buchmesse and the London Book Fair.

One change to the industry due to the global pandemic that affects the creation of ARCS is the move towards digital ARCs for reviews and giveaways. The lockdowns and supply chain breakdowns that were a result of the global response to the COVID-19 pandemic meant that most publishers switched to making digital ARCs the primary means to review books. The use of digital galleys, often in the form of PDFs generated from the book's print files, was available before the pandemic, but some publishers were hesitant to use the format due to piracy concerns and several book reviewers were accustomed to using print copies or found the digital rights management put in place on sites such as NetGalley and Edelweiss too onerous. The pandemic forced reviewers to use digital copies which not only reduce production costs but also reduce the number of copies of the non-recyclable bound book that often get thrown away with the arrival of the first edition.

If galleys are free copies produced before the printed copies meant for sale in the market, ebooks tend to be the copies that are produced after the files for the printed copies for the market are produced. Too many production people I've met at conferences have told me about how ebook production is often added on to the production schedule. One large US publishing house would give its ebooks division the time it took to print and bind the physical books to create, proof, correct, add accessibility, and upload the different ebook files to vendors. Theoretically, this makes sense. The ebook doesn't need a new design and should be able to use the print design, but practically there are several issues that arise. The print designers may have designed the interiors in a way that does not work for ebooks—overrides, unique attributes for text not recorded as a specific style, footnotes, and images are particularly problematic. Print is also not particularly accessible and therefore print designers often do not think about accessible features (alt text form images, semantic structures, rich metadata) when creating their files. Depending on the complexity of the interior, an ebook, such as a book of poetry with long lines or multiple line breaks, may require a complete redesign for the digital marketplace or a comprehensive reformatting for accessibility, something that often cannot happen in the time it takes to print and ship physical copies.

Development of the Project

As outlined in the discussion on scheduling above, the production department will do most of the work to convert a typescript into a book. This work will primarily be an iterative process of laying out text for page and screen followed by visual scanning of how the text displays followed by rounds of modification to improve the appearance of the text and the testing of the text at different font sizes on different size screens to ensure a similar reading experience for all readers.

Designing text on the page brings a host of challenges for the designer as they transfer edited text into a design meant for page and screen. For those professionals looking for guidance on page layouts and type on the page should invest in Robert Bringhurst's *The Elements of Typographic Style* (2019), Ellen Lupton's *Thinking with Type* (2014), and *Book Design Made Simple* by Fiona Raven and Glenna Collett (2017). Even those publishers who use templates for their books need to do more than import the typescript into a program such as InDesign and have it come out perfectly designed. The unpredictability of narrative and the variation in language means that line lengths and paragraphs will change throughout a text which leads to a host of issues when laying both the print and digital. A clean and readable design is one that balances every line on a page or screen to ensure the saccades and fixations of the eye, as it moves across a line of text, isn't tripped up by rivers of white space flowing through lines of text or ragged right margins that distract the eye from following the path of the text.

In tandem with the interior design, a cover designer will need to create different cover treatments, often between five to seven designs, that will be evaluated by the sales department, the commissioning editor, the marketing department, and perhaps the author. Unlike the interior design which needs to provide a consistent user experience across dozens of pages, the cover is a marketing tool to attract readers while on a bookstore shelf or an online retailer. The front cover attracts readers to the book and the flap copy provides a clue as to the meanings within the book and compels a potential reader to open the book (Graff 1989, 7).

The development of the book project will require the definition of the book's physical aspects. The main physical component is the paper to be used that was determined in the planning phase. In addition, there will also be decisions around the types of binding used. In both these issues the question of material should be addressed in terms of budget, but also environmental impact. Bright white paper requires heavy bleaching of the paper. The glue for perfect binding—often either PUR (polyurethane reactive) or EVA (ethylene-vinyl acetate)—have become more eco-efficient, but there are still significant issues in the energy costs for using and recycling for both types of glue binding, making them ongoing environmental concerns for printers (Pasanec Preprotić 2023).

Alongside the development of physical books is the creation of ebooks for different online distributors. Most ebook distributors use the EPUB format, but Amazon still uses a proprietary format for its Kindle platform. Publishers developing ebooks for the marketplace will need to create and test their titles for both formats across screens that range from smartphone to laptop. The differences between Amazon's format and EPUB will require the production department to decide if it will create and test the two formats separately or create an EPUB file and test and revise for Amazon. Both methods will generate files that will need to be revised and re-uploaded when typos or corrupt style is discovered. Depending on the complexity of the interior additional formats may be needed as smaller smartphone screens and support for interactivity across different devices can create unintended design issues. Of course, a publisher can also outsource this whole process to a company focused on ebook development, if the book's budget allows for those costs.

For several major trade publishers, the development of ebooks has become an afterthought to print production resulting in inferior or just boring digital products. The stagnation of ebook sales in 2016 after annual double-digit growth encouraged trade publishers to do the minimal amount of work on their ebooks and focus their attention and resources to their "preordained successes" (Alter 2020). This cooling of ebook sales in the trade market coincided with an opposite development for academic and professional books around the same time. In dealing with a publishing industry that increased its output several-fold over the last two decades, public and academic libraries have turned to the acquisition of ebook collections through apps offered by companies such as Gale, Hoopla, Libby, Bibliotheca, and Axis 360 to offer their patrons a selection of titles they could never support in terms of the purchase and storage of physical copies. The ongoing growth of these digital lending services saw explosive growth in 2020 during several months of lockdown. Overdrive reported a 33 percent increase over 2019 in lending across their global platforms (Overdrive 2021). And this move towards digital in the library space means a larger need for digital copies from publishers. According to a 2021 *New Yorker* article, The New York Public Library had purchased nearly one thousand licenses for the ebook and digital audiobook for Barack Obama's *A Promised Land* and only 226 hardcover copies. Hidden in the purchase of these quantities is the price differential where the digital rights were equivalent to 1,154 hardcover copies or "about as much as three thousand copies of the consumer ebook" (Gross 2021). This increase in the use of ebooks in libraries along with the continued domination of Amazon's Kindle marketplace in the global ebook space means for some publishers, especially those focused on genre fiction, young adult readers, academic and STEM titles, ebook development needs to be a well-considered aspect in the development phase of a book project.

Quality Control

After the creation of the print and digital product, it is primarily up to the production department to perform the testing and quality control of the final book products. Quality control in publishing can be broken down into three distinct areas: printed material, covers, and digital material. Each will require the person doing the checking to employ a different evaluative process.

Printed Books

Misspelling and typos should have been caught in the development phase, but there is often a chance that the production department can miss errors in the final product created during the printing process. While errors in printing can happen in the printing and binding process and can include easily visible errors such as printing on wrinkled paper or applying covers at an angle, the move to a digital workflow has also introduced the added layer of compositional errors. In pre-digital production processes

> the composed document was photographed to produce film, [so] it was not so important how we got to a document that was ready to print. The compositor could take shortcuts, and as long as the camera-ready looked correct, it didn't matter.
>
> (Beebe and Meyers 2000)

With books now being created as digital files, the elements a book designer creates now need to be checked against specifications and quality control guidelines. Are the images "in CMYK? Are the crops and traps correct? Is the bleed accurate? Any lack of precision will affect the quality of the final product" (Beebe 2000). This need for quality control on a file level will become even more important with digital products where the textual container is no longer a fixed format, but itself a digital file meant to be displayed across a variety of screen sizes. In terms of print format, a corrupt file of the book design can also result in printing errors where multiple signatures of the same text are printed and bound together, or accented characters are not correctly coded resulting in the appearance of the Unicode replacement character (a question mark in a diamond) or a blank square. These errors are not always visible and require someone at the printing press or the publishing house, or ideally both, to preflight the files and to check sample copies of the print book to ensure that the books are acceptable for sale. Of course, when the errors affect only a small batch in the print run, they may make it through the press inspection and make their way to the bookstore. In one instance, a publishing house I was working for discovered that one of its paperback reprints had a misprint where the last half of the book was just the last two signatures of the index repeated over and over. The Managing Editor stopped any shipments from the warehouse until all copies could be inspected. The warehouse found misprinted copies in only two cartons of the book. The rest of the print run was printed correctly, and the copies released to retailers who had ordered them. A few spoiled copies are to be expected, but a means of identifying and removing those copies as waste needs to be part of the QC process alongside the process for spot checks.

In addition to the interiors, a quality check of the printed cover at the press is the last chance to catch (and pay for) any mistakes that were missed in the proofing and checking during development. The QC process should include a check of the bar code, the price, and the ISBN on the back cover and a check that the title and author's name are properly spelled on the front. The assumption that someone had already checked these will allow these mistakes to make it into stores. The designer or art director will also need to examine the cover sample to ensure that the design elements are printed as intended. Having a physical cover to check is necessary for cover that might have special treatments. A spot gloss that is a little off from embossed text will catch the light in a way that will be noticeable on the bookshelf. The last step in the quality control should be to check the spine to make sure it reflects the estimated spine width for the book. The paper used in the interior can change from the initial specs given to the cover designer to what goes on press. Confirming that a cover's spine width matches the expected width of the printed book will ensure a spine that doesn't look off center.

Digital Books

The methods of checking and verifying ebook and digital files are far more involved than print. Digital products require a longer inspection to ensure that the files work across all potential devices and that the files meet the specifications of retailers. Performing quality control (QC) is a major responsibility that can ensure a book's performance in different environments. Many mishaps, including an infamous one involving the US publisher's Kindle version of JK Rowling's *The Casual Vacancy* (BBC 2012), are clear indications to the market of a publisher's lack of a QC process. In order to prevent these disasters, a production department needs to check ebooks for both the usability and accessibility of the ebook for the reader as well as the validity of the internal markup.

Digital books benefit from a quality assurance check throughout the development phase over a single QC check after the files are complete. Those involved in ebook development know that a Quality Assurance (QA) check requires developers to compile the ebook, convert it into the different formats, and check for errors across different devices. Once the errors have been noted, the files will need to be fixed, recompiled, and then rechecked across different devices as minor errors often appear only after a major error is fixed. The more complicated the layout or the less structured the markup, the more needed the QA cycles.

QA challenges for digital books can be separated into one of three categories:

- **Retailer Requirements**. Retailers often have explicit requirements for files being delivered to them electronically that can be as specific as file-naming conventions and file size. These requirements are often outlined in documents they provide on their website. Those performing the QA need to check that the files conform to the requirements before submitting the books for sale as retailers often use an automated process that rejects files that do not conform

to the requirements without offering any indication as to why the files failed to be accepted.
- **The Device Ecosystem**. Barnes & Noble launched fifteen models of its Nook e-reader in the first decade of its existence and readers are able to use the early Nooks as digital libraries even if the company no longer supports those models. While publishers need to plan for the future and leverage emerging technologies, they must also be aware of that past: smaller screens, less processing power, and rendering engines that do not fully support the entire CSS specification. Production must act similar to website developers in deciding how to support older devices. They need to also define when support will end for legacy e-readers.
- **User Preferences**. Designing the best book possible for digital consumption requires publishers to accept a loss of control. Technology has empowered the user with choice. When text is delivered to an electronic reader or smartphone, publishers have limited control over how the text is ultimately presented. User settings on e-readers allow every reader to manipulate typography and layout for their needs and not necessarily what the publisher intended. Having a variety of devices and reviewing the books on those devices will get the publishers closer to seeing how readers will engage with the text.

Release

Once the quality of the designs in each format are checked, those involved in content production play a supportive position when the book is released. Production departments may help with the management and revision of metadata for the print or ebooks within their vendors' systems or respond to questions about the design of the cover and text, but most of the work for a book's release will be handled by the sales, marketing, and promotional staff after the print books leave the printers and the digital versions have been uploaded to online distributors.

Closing

Those involved in content production will be involved in the maintenance of the book project as they will need to manage the revisions of files to correct any typos or design errors for the different formats and to update information such as the copyright info and URLs in the digital production files. The production manager for a book will also need to work with those in sales to determine subsequent printings, reprints, including the conversion to POD, and backlist management.

A paperback edition is often handled like a new project by trade publishers, but one with a much smaller scope, shorter timeframe, and less cost. There's little work for the content creators to do other than corrections and updates. Maybe a new introduction as it will be the dominant print format or if the edition is aligned to a publishing or cultural anniversary. Publishers of work related to William Shakespeare might decide to add new essays to their reprints in 2023 as it marks the four-hundredth anniversary of the publication of Shakespeare's First Folio. Even without any new content, the work needed in terms of production will often be enough to require it to be handled as a new project.

The maintenance of ebooks will be handled separately from print. The digital nature of ebooks and their distribution makes it easier for readers to find and report errors in an ebook. The same digital nature allows publishers to correct these errors and upload revisions on a regular basis to the retailer who can distribute those corrections to customers who have already purchased the ebook. In the testing and quality control phase, the publisher will check the different ebook versions locally before uploading the files to the online distributors, but often those quality checks are done on programs that are operating as emulators of the online distributors. The actual display of the files once they have been processed by the distributors and put up for sale might be slightly different in their display. Depending on the complexity of the design, this may require the ebook designer to modify stylesheets or HTML code and re-upload the files. Maintenance of ebooks is an ongoing issue as the specifications evolve. Similar to the way a backlist manager handles switching between offset and POD as the book's sales decline, publishers will need to have an ebook backlist manager to update policies that come from retailers and the World Wide Web Consortium (W3C) as, in the past, updates have included changes to the metadata fields for authors and series and Apple's introduction of retina displays that required publishers on the Apple Books platform to resubmit all their ebooks with higher resolution covers and images. The ebook manager will also need to deal with the more mundane work that Theresa Elsey, the then digital managing editor for the trade division of Houghton Mifflin Harcourt, described in her 2016 BookNet Canada talk "When Nothing Ever Goes Out Of Print: Maintaining Backlist Ebooks." In this presentation Elsey describes how the publisher's ebook production group managed around 1,500 titles annually, with only 450 new ebook releases. The other 1,050 titles were backlist titles that often require corrections to the text or updates to the formatting. Elsey explains that the reasons for the continual maintenance of ebooks is due to technical updates, accessibility revisions, and fixing aesthetics. The technical needs were such that the ebook group had a schedule to check and update all ebooks every three years. It is clear that the maintenance of ebooks, similar to the maintenance of print books, will need to become part of a publisher's production department, ideally with a dedicated backlist ebook manager. This position should not only manage updates to ebooks at retailers but maintain the archive of all versions of available ebooks along with any production notes from the designers in the publisher's online repository.

Content Production and the Agile Method

Now that I have outlined the work production departments do on book projects in a linear life cycle, it is also valuable to examine how this department integrates into an Agile model.

The biggest difference for a production department between a linear and iterative book project is the number of meetings about that project. For a department that focuses on developing finished books out of manuscripts without having to respond to the other departments or authors, Agile's dependence on daily standup meetings to report progress may be the most problematic part for print production people. These meetings are representative of the goals within the Agile method, notably continuous satisfaction of customers, changing requirements and delivering work frequently that will cause the most problems for those in book production. The early and continuous satisfaction of customers is foreign to book production as the standard print or ebook will be designed and created with little input from authors or customers. The idea of addressing change requirements throughout the production process can feel like a call for bespoke book designs where authors and editors can add new content such as chapters and illustrations throughout the process and booksellers and readers can request formatting changes to meet their needs. A production department could interpret their role in an Agile project as one where they need to respond to requests from content creators and content distributors as they arise, but most Agile frameworks define this work as part of the requirements and planning phases where a response isn't necessary. Instead, the changes that are requested would be recorded as new user stories that would become part of future iterations.[3] Lastly, there's this idea of frequent delivery. In terms of a print book project, a print product gets designed once and it takes several months to develop the product for market. The Agile model of a weekly or monthly delivery of a product may not feel possible, yet most of these principles are, in fact, already part of the digital workspace in a contemporary book publisher, including in production departments.

Customer satisfaction and getting input from stakeholders already happens in traditional books when sample designs or proofs are set out. Change has always been part of a production department as titles can be late in arriving or printers can modify printing schedules because of a delay in paper, repairs, or lack of personnel to run the machines.

That leaves the frequent delivery of the product. This principle does require a reimagining of the development process. For book publishers, the product is a finished book that is created and distributed. The idea of an MVP and iterative production does not align with traditional book production. But continual iteration has crept in to how the industry thinks about books. The clearest model is the hardcover/paperback/digital/audio production cycle where the text of the book remains the MVP as the formats change. Each iteration/format may add more to the text. A paperback can add a reader's guide, while ebooks add full-color images, and audiobooks perform the text. Frequent delivery means changing from the "print then other model" and identifying the best means of delivery for each title. Publishers need to think about where the simultaneous release of HC, PB, digital, and audio makes sense or where releasing digital versions of individual chapters[4] or even the whole book digitally before the print benefits the book project.

The Scrum Master

In the chapter on content creation, I outlined how a sponsoring editor can be seen as a product owner. The natural location for the Scrum Master who needs to help their team respond to the needs of the project owner would be someone from the production department. The implementation and build of the project will most likely happen in production, therefore, Scrum Masters need to manage the production staff who will compile, if not create, the elements of a book project as well as do the quality testing.

The biggest changes for a production department at a publishing house that is working on Agile-type projects will be adapting to the iterative nature of the life cycle and the regular occurrence of meetings that goes along with the iteration. In an Agile mindset, the product that is released in the first iteration will be both a fully realized product that is also a step towards an unknown end-product. It is the difference between creating a French-language workbook that expands upon the lessons from a French-language textbook and an interactive language app that will eventually adjust examples according to the user's ability. Products developed iteratively are not necessarily replacements for the products of a linear life cycle, but additions to those projects. In other words, the publisher will need to offer a textbook, workbook, and app that expands the reader base, and the Scrum Master will need to lead the way in helping departments understand that a product release no longer leads to the close of a project or the release of the team back to their departments.

This is a fundamental change in a publisher's understanding of content delivery These publishing projects can be considered as ventures that Peter Thiel has defined as going from "zero to one" instead of "one to n." Thiel explains this kind of product development as one that identifies an unmet need in the world and responds to it instead of focusing on improving upon a known market. The interactive language app above could be seen as a zero-to-one venture if it begins to focus on providing personalized language learning in an educational system that was built to teach several students of varying abilities in the same space through exercise and rote learning of written text. This venture into unknown needs means project teams will need support to make and fix mistakes over several releases based on feedback from the market, a task that can be difficult with the functional mindset that still dominates most of book publishing.

Accessibility

One of the most important ongoing changes for today's production department is in how their company is dealing with the issue of accessibility. Digital content has the ability to open up a publisher's entire catalogue to readers who have not always had access to a publisher's print books as the readers do not have the ability to hold a book or read printed text. Accessible audio and ebooks open a publisher's content to more readers. How many more? The World Health Organization asserts that 2.2 billion people across the world live with some kind of visual impairment (2022). In addition to visual impairments, there are also around 16 million people, or 2–3 percent of any given population, that have a diagnosed cognitive disability that impairs memory, decision-making, or concentration (Deary et al. 2009). For book publishers, it is long past time to acknowledge that print books have alienated a portion of their readership because of the physical demands inherent in a bound book. The availability of variable font sizes and audio versions—either a professionally produced audiobook or that ability for the digital text to be "read" by a digital assistant—opens content to a readership that, conservatively, has only had access to about 10 percent of all published information (World Blind Union 2023).

Admittedly, the topic of accessibility can be overwhelming. To simplify the discussion, I would define accessibility as the following: a collection of the thoughtful strategies and practices to bring content to readers of all abilities. This collection can be seen as a two-fold approach to accessibility to help publishers better organize their efforts while adhering to a budget that is made for a book project without any consideration for the cost of making the book accessible.

The first approach is the simple idea that publishers need to offer content to readers through as many platforms as possible: print, audio, ebooks, PDF, web page, and others. A well-designed workflow with clearly delegated tasks on to achieve this has been part of the publishing conference for the better part of a decade. The digital-first movement that uses some kind of valid mark up (HTML, XML, LaTeX) for the typescript and finished book will get most books very close to being accessible, provided the markup is used thoughtfully to create semantic text, or text where "linguistic informational content…is encod[ed] in a form that humans as well as computers understand (van der Weel 2011, 52). When publishers take words beyond print and digitize content thoughtfully, they are making their content accessible to others *de facto*. The second approach builds upon the inherent semantic structure and asks how can a publishing house make the book, not just the text, easier to understand, annotate, navigate, and consume?

This is the second approach to accessibility that provides publishers with open standards and guidelines towards making thoughtful, accessible content. Accessibility, as a rule, promotes a better user experience for everyone if it is thoughtful and courteous. Thoughtful accessibility practices can be part of the production workflow and organizations including the DAISY Consortium, WCAG, and A11Y offer a variety of tools to help make accessibility part of a book project's workflow.

Box 7.1 Basic Steps Towards Accessibility in the Production Process

An easy trap to fall into when it comes to making content accessible in the production process to address accessibility as a checklist. But with accessibility, not every title will need to check the same boxes. Some titles won't have images. Others will have multimedia videos that need transcripts as part of the digital product. Accessibility is more than just checklists. For those searching for a starting point, I would suggest beginning to develop the following actions as part of your book project.

- **Confirm semantic markup.** Making sure that the marked-up text is properly coded in terms of semantic markup is a major step in making text accessible. Ensuring that every chapter opener and paragraph is

marked as such will give screen readers the same structure that designers give text on a page.
- **Alternative text for images.** In HTML, the image element requires an alt text attribute to give context to the image. Every publisher should have guidelines on how to best describe an image. Routledge, for example, provides a best practice guide to authors as part of the guidelines for management subscription, ensuring that images come in from the author in an accessible format.
- **Color contrasts.** E-Ink devices give readers plenty of shades of grey, so a reader on these devices cannot rely on a color to understand what they are reading. Publishers should also check that images are discernable in grayscale, especially when text appears within the image.
- **Eliminate any intertextual context.** Digital text displays on a variety of screen sizes so one person's page seven may be another person's page fifteen. Intertextual references will be confusing if they state page numbers. Replace references such as "on page 606" with "in Chapter 27." Non-paginated positioning will allow content to remain evergreen as the screen size and how much text fits on a page changes.
- **QA should focus on reading modes, text sizing, and device orientation.** Laura Brady, who works as manager of the Cross-Media Department at House of Anansi Press in Toronto and is also one of the main people responsible for developing Ebookcraft's programming, offered the following advice: "You need to approach ebooks like a mischievous child, try to stretch, poke, maul and break them" (Brady 2019). Act like an ebook user and bump up font sizes or switch the display to scroll rather than the swipe function. It also helps to have informal interviews with focus groups of readers to observe how they interact with your products.
- **Explore assistive technologies—and take notes.** Becoming familiar with the assistive technologies that readers use and testing ebooks on those technologies will give publishers an idea of what the reading experience is like for low-vision and blind readers. However, keep in mind that fully abled publishing professionals will experience these assistive technologies differently from someone who is blind or has low vision.

Accessibility should be seen as an aspect of the book that goes beyond technology, but it is an aspect that is still heavily reliant on technology. Unfortunately, the industry isn't thinking about technology for the sake of accessibility. Publishers and authors brought lawsuits against Amazon when it attempted to provide both text-to-speech (allowing low-vision readers the ability to hear the text on the screen) and speech-to-text features (translating the audio into a transcript), keeping accessibility features for digital text as separate formats (Schofield 2009, Lee 2019). Of course, those who are working on making publishing more accessible will always hope for what Deborah Kaplan, the owner of Suberic Networks, a software company focused on accessibility testing and remediation, identifies as the single, accessible, standards-compliant, and feature-rich version [of a book] that is readable on myriad platforms. I hope publishing starts allocating money to make the content accessible—not just the simple text, but also the illustrations, the math, the picture books, and the rich features and multimedia of digital-only or digital-enhanced publications.

(Kaplan 2018)

In order to get to this kind of full accessibility, book publishers themselves will need to rethink how they approach the development of a book project and envision the products they offer for that project.

Notes

1 Workflow diagrams for this chapter can be downloaded at https://www.routledge.com/9781032516721
2 The hardcover of the US edition of *Beautiful Children* by Charles Bock is one cover that uses this treatment. The dust jacket for the first edition is undyed raw paper with a title that is embossed with holographic foil and a spot gloss. The raw paper mars easily and attracts dust so that it quickly looks like a used book after a few weeks on a retail bookshelf.
3 It is important to note that while production departments working on an Agile book project may understand that any changes will become part of the epics or user stories for the next iteration, those making the requests might not understand this fundamental principle of an Agile framework. It's not uncommon for content creators outside the Agile team to see this environment as a way to enact changes to the scope of a book in the middle of the development process. There may be new content from authors or content creators that "cannot wait for the next iteration." This is where the reliance on a Scrum Master becomes important. A Scrum Master's role is to protect the team from these outside intrusions. It's also why granting a Scrum Master same standing in the organization as a Managing Editor will protect the team from watching their project become unwieldy.
4 Both the simultaneous release and individual chapter models are common in academic and professional publishing. See the case study on De Gruyter in Chapter 5 or the website for this book published by Routledge. Both offer readers different ways to engage with a book as the publishers understand different audiences have different needs.

References

Alter, Alexandra. 2020. "Best Sellers Sell the Best Because They're Best Sellers." *The New York Times.* https://www.nytimes.com/2020/09/19/books/penguin-random-house-madeline-mcintosh.html. Last accessed 5 September 2023.
BBC. 2012. "JK Rowling's The Casual Vacancy Ebook Suffers Glitches." *BBC.* https://www.bbc.com/news/technology-19759117. Last accessed 5 September 2023.
Beebe, Linda and Barbara Meyers. 2000. "Reprint: Digital Workflow: Managing the Process Electronically." *Journal of Electronic Publishing*, 5(4). https://doi.org/10.3998/3336451.0005.403.
Biel, Joe. 2018. *A People's Guide to Publishing.* Portland, OR: Microcosm Publishing.
Brady, Laura. 2019. "Accessible Ebook Publishing in Canada: The Business Case." *Inclusive Publishing, A DAISY Consortium Initiative.* https://inclusivepublishing.org/blog/accessible-ebook-publishing-the-business-case. Last accessed 5 September 2023.

Bullock, Adrian. 2012. *Book Production*. London: Routledge.
Clark, Giles and Angus Phillips. 2020. *Inside Book Publishing*. 6th ed. Abingdon, Oxon: Routledge.
Comerford, Rachel. 2018. Personal Interview.
Deary, Ian J., Janie Corley, Alan J. Gow, Sarah E. Harris, Lorna M. Houlihan, Riccardo E. Marioni, Lars Penke, Snorri B. Rafnsson, and John M. Starr. 2009. "Age-associated Cognitive Decline." *British Medical Bulletin*, 92(1), 135–152. DOI: doi:10.1093/bmb/ldp033.
Elsey, Theresa. 2016. "When Nothing Ever Goes Out Of Print: Maintaining Backlist Ebooks." *Ebookcraft 2016 BookNet Canada*. https://www.youtube.com/watch?v=x9muetf6ymU. Last accessed 5 September 2023.
Graff, Gerald. 1989. "Narrative and the Unofficial Interpretive Culture." In *Reading Narrative: Form, Ethics, Ideology*, edited by James Phelan. 3–11. Columbus: Ohio State University Press.
Gross, Daniel A. 2021. "The Surprisingly Big Business of Library Ebooks." *The New Yorker*. https://www.newyorker.com/news/annals-of-communications/an-app-called-libby-and-the-surprisingly-big-business-of-library-e-books. Last accessed 5 September 2023.
Harris. Elizabeth A. 2020. "Obama's Memoir 'A Promised Land' Coming in November." *New York Times*. https://www.nytimes.com/2020/09/17/books/obama-memoir-a-promised-land.html. Last accessed 5 September 2023.
Kaplan, Debra. 2018. Personal interview.
Lee, Marshall. 2004. *Bookmaking: Editing Design Production*. 3rd ed. New York: Norton.
Lee, Timothy B. 2019. "Book Publishers Sue Audible to Stop New Speech-to-Text Feature." *Ars Technica*. https://arstechnica.com/tech-policy/2019/08/book-publishers-sue-audible-to-stop-new-speech-to-text-feature. Last accessed 5 September 2023.
Overdrive.com. 2021. "33% Growth for Digital Books from Public Libraries and Schools in 2020 Sets Records." https://company.overdrive.com/2021/01/07/33-growth-for-digital-books-from-public-libraries-and-schools-in-2020-sets-records/. Last accessed 5 September 2023.
Pasanec Preprotić, Suzana, Marina Vukoje, Gorana Petković, and Mirela Rožić. 2023. "Novel Approaches to Enhancing Sustainable Adhesive System Solutions in Contemporary Book Binding: An Overview." *Heritage*, 6(1), 628–646. https://doi.org/10.3390/heritage6010033.
Schofield, Jack. 2009. "Amazon Caves to Authors Guild Over Kindle's Text-to-Speech Reading." *The Guardian*. https://www.theguardian.com/technology/blog/2009/mar/01/authors-guild-blocks-kindle-voice. Last accessed 5 September 2023.
Starre, Alexander. 2015. *Metamedia: American Book Fictions and Literary Print Culture After Digitization*. Iowa City: University of Iowa Press.
Thiel, Paul and Blake Masters. 2014. *Zero to One: Notes on Startups or How to Build the Future*. 1st ed. New York: Crown Business.
van der Weel, Adrian. 2011. *Changing Our Textual Minds: Towards a Digital Order of Knowledge*. Manchester: Manchester University Press.
Woll, Thomas. 2014. *Publishing for Profit*. Revised and expanded 5th ed. Chicago: Chicago Review Press.
World Blind Union. 2023. "Marrahesh Treaty." https://worldblindunion.org/programs/marrakesh-treaty. Last accessed 5 September 2023.
World Health Organization. 2022. "Blindness and Vision Impairment." https://www.who.int/news-room/fact-sheets/detail/blindness-and-visual-impairment. Last accessed 5 September 2023.

8 Content Distribution Project Management[1]

Up to this point in the book, the discussion on a book project has primarily focused on converting an author's manuscript into a finished book that can be sold in the marketplace. The initiation, planning, development, and testing stages are all centered around moving towards a book that is ready to be released to booksellers and readers. The release of a book is the main objective of the book project from the point of view of those involved with content creation and content production. But subsequent to the release of different formats into the marketplace, the work of making the title both visible and discoverable becomes the second part of a book project. The media attention, marketing ads, bookstore displays, and promotional content in the media are the means for publishing companies to make a book visible in the marketplace. Publishing houses also work on making the book discoverable through developing rich metadata and propagating it to online retailers and search engines. Both of these aspects, covered in the second half of this chapter, begin in the planning stages of a book project as it can take some time to create and revise as the book project progresses through its middle phases (Steiner 2018, 121).

Even before the book files are sent to the printers those involved in distribution have started the processes for navigating the retail landscape. This landscape includes chain and independent bookstores as well as museums, supermarkets, big box retailers, and special events including conferences and author readings. With each space comes a different set of needs. Chain and independent bookstores want better discounts and more liberal return policies, giant retailers such as supermarkets and WH Smith want low retail prices. Special events need promotional material beyond the book to attract a crowd. It will be up to those involved in book distribution to respond to the landscape's needs to try and give a publisher's new titles the greatest chance of survival in the marketplace.

The Distribution Workflow

To help the sales force with their tasks, specialists in promotion and marketing work to build the hype for titles before, during, and after a book's release. This could involve promotional material for bookstores including bookmarks, posters, or shelf talkers, placards affixed to the shelf to draw attention to a book, that are sent to bookstores to promote a title. Hype is also generated through having authors appear on television talk shows, podcasts, and radio programs as well as platforms on social media and through live events that can include readings, signings, book festivals, and pop culture conferences (Helgason 2014, 16). The marketing campaigns for a book ramp up in the weeks preceding the book's release, but they are often the result of months of involvement in the creation of promotional material.

For our discussion of book project management, the work of distribution will be split into three distinct workflows. There is the promotional workflow that builds the hype across online and media channels by placing the authors in the media as experts. This promotional work may also include negotiating for the placement of an author's essay or interview in the media at the right time to raise the general reading public's awareness of the author and their book and pushing promotional material (posters, postcards, bookmarks, t-shirts, etc.) out to bookstores and on social media. The second workflow is that of marketing, which creates the online and print ads for books that appear in magazines and web publications. While the marketing team develops the marketing plan for new titles, the sales force manages the third workflow within content distribution which focused on solidifying orders with retailers and managing any licensing or sales with non-retail organizations or foreign publishers who might be interested in the book.

The sales workflow also includes book returns. Unique to book publishing is the idea that retailers can return inventory for full credit. The difference in return policies for the different formats a publisher creates (hardcover, softback, mass market, digital) with different retailers will often require subprocesses for each retailer within the returns workflow. An illustration on the differences in how returns happen between bookstores can be seen in a comparison between a bookstore attached to a college or university and the small independent bookstore. Whereas an independent bookstore will watch the sales on each of their titles and return the slow-moving titles within six weeks of arriving at the store (Done, Warner, and Noorda 2022), university bookstores will often purge all copies of required textbooks a month after the start of classes.[2] Instead of returning one or two copies of a book they may return dozens of copies of a book that were not purchased during the initial days of the semester. The difference in the continual returns from trade bookstores and the wholesale return of all titles from a university bookstore at the same time require different resources in both the warehousing and finance departments. The timing will also affect the scheduling of reprints and new editions. For trade books that had a lot of buzz pre-publication but failed to find a readership, the publisher may be able to strip and rebind the hardcover returns as paperbacks, provided the stores that ordered them return copies in good condition within a few months of publication. Textbooks, on the other hand, may lose all their value after the start of the semester if a publisher has already planned for a new edition for the next academic year, forcing college bookstores to return and reorder the new edition.

Distribution Project Management

The work done on a book project by those in content distribution often blurs together for those not working directly with the marketing or promotion departments. Content distribution can be seen as the detailed work for a book project's "last mile," the final work to get the book into a reader's hands. There often isn't a clear endpoint for the distribution work as the management of a title's visibility starts before a book's release and depending on its reception can continue for weeks or months afterwards. This chapter will focus on the work that leads up to the release of the book, but I do so with the awareness that social media has changed the relationship between readers and books so now backlist titles can become bestsellers titles for a publisher and disrupt their seasonal plans for new book releases.

A publishing house with a culture that touts the importance of content creation over marketing and sales fails to recognize how the two are equal partners in the media environment. In the current marketplace where more media than ever competes for attention from potential readers, the mantra of "marketing is everything" (McKenna 1991) should be the guiding focus of every publishing house. The acquisitions of a new book by an author with a strong track record or an important book on a core topic for the publisher requires a press release about the acquisition to be sent out for inclusion in reports of new book deals in industry publications including *The Bookseller, Publishers Weekly,* and *Publishers Lunch.* These deal notifications are the first chance to build awareness of the book for a publisher. Likewise, the interest in book titles from social media and blogs can quickly build the buzz for a book. Look at the current phenomenon of Colleen Hoover's global bestsellerdom due to BookTok. Hoover, an American author who was self-publishing her titles, now has bestselling paperback reprints from Simon & Schuster in both the United States and the United Kingdom due to a fixation on her books by TikTok users (Mechling 2022). Simon & Schuster UK currently lists eighteen titles, most of which were released as paperback reprints and landed on the UK bestseller lists thanks to her insatiable readers.[3] To help provide some context on how the department involved in content distribution drives this last part of the book project I outline how each of the three areas engage in the different phases of a linear PLC before looking at how those involved in distribution contribute to an interactive project.

Marketing

Initiation of the Project

Marketing staff need to be part of the book project starting with the initiation phase. Their role in the early stage of evaluating the book proposal is to provide insight into the potential audience. When a commissioning or acquiring editor brings a proposal to an editorial board meeting or signals an interest in acquiring a title, the marketing department should provide feedback on the potential readership for the book and what kind of interest there might be from the media and bookstores based on their subject expertise (Feather 2003, 120). Not every book will get to sit face out on a shelf in a bookstore, but the marketing department can identify those books that have a good chance of being adopted by bookstores. The marketing department's involvement with the book project begins with the book proposal where a marketer can formulate a plan for the outreach, positioning, and ads for the title. In addition to providing an outline of a marketing plan, marketing also needs to work with the editorial department at the contract stage to include its author questionnaire that will provide further definition to the marketing and publicity plans for the title.

Project Planning

In the planning phase, marketing and promotion need to be in conversation with the editorial and production departments on schedule and budget. In terms of budget, marketing needs to know the type of advance for the book and what kind of book this will be for the press. If the book is likely to be one of the house's key titles for the season, they may need to earmark money for that title and plan for a larger marketing campaign over a title that might not be seen as having as much potential. Advances are often, but not always, a good indicator of potential. If the house has paid a large advance, they need to recoup those costs through sales. Spending money to raise awareness of a title in the marketplace through shelf talkers and ads or using co-op to get better placement in a chain bookstore is one of the core methods a publishing house believes will sell more books.

One alternative to buying awareness in the bookstore is to try and create an award-winning book. There are certain names in the industry—Nobel, Booker, Pulitzer, Neustadt, Hugo, Costa, Newbery—that can help propel an author into the limelight and bestseller list. Outside of major literary awards such as the ones mentioned above or the country-specific awards like the Women's Prize for Fiction in the UK, Le Prix Goncourt in France, or the National Book Awards in America, there are hundreds of smaller awards for books offered by organizations and festivals around the world that can generate hype for a book within the audiences associated with those awards. For example, the Jhalak Prize recognizes writers of color in the United Kingdom and the Lambda Literary Awards recognizes several categories for LGBTQ writers. The expansion of publisher booths at cultural festivals, which can include book festivals such as the Hay Festival in Wales to media events like the San Diego Comic Con in California, has created what scholar David Carter had called "the public life of literature" where the goal is not just to raise the awareness of a title but to make it a part of a larger cultural discussion (quoted in Murray 2018, 83). This public life can include keynotes from the author, booth signings, or even a scavenger hunt like the one that several publishers were involved with at the 2018 San Diego Comic Con around the media property, *Buffy, the Vampire Slayer*. This public space is outside the confines of the literary world of journals and bookstores but can also be outside a physical space entirely. In *The Digital Literary Sphere*, Simone Murray devotes an entire chapter to the rise of online literary festivals, exploring their recent history and how they help to build community in ways similar to social media. In recent years these festivals have also started to focus on the importance of audience over engagement between content creators (2018, 81–110). While Murray is more interested in the cultural significance of these festivals as it applies to literature, she also provides a sense of how publishers can use the competition between festivals as well as within them to provide inexpensive marketing opportunities for titles.

As a marketing department's annual budget is based on the publisher's revenues and not the performance of individual titles, the department's allocation of money to different titles is done with an awareness of the whole fiscal year. This means that titles published in the early part of the fiscal year compete for marketing resources with titles that may not yet be acquired. It is up to the marketing managers to determine the needed budget for a title against what might be needed against future titles. This may mean that a title acquired earlier in the year might see a quarter-page ad in an academic journal and finished copies sent out for review versus a title publishing later in the year that gets a bigger budget that includes an ad in a bookstore's newsletter along with ARCs of the book and a trip for the author to a book fair for signings. The second marketing budget is three to five times larger than the first one and is probably based on both the need to recoup the author's advance in sales and the timing for publication. Ensuring that title budgets are aligned with both the advance for the book and the department's total budget is a balancing act that plays out in every book project's budget.

More important than the marketing budget—a part of the book project that may and often does change between the planning and release phase—is the development of a book's release schedule. The delivery date of a manuscript is an indication of when a book project can start, but sales and marketing will need to advise on the best on-sale date for a title. The planning of a book project's on-sale date needs to be well attuned to their marketplace and align to the appropriate time of year. Fiction titles will often see an uptick in sales around the summer and winter holidays. Textbooks rely on the start of the fall and spring semesters for most of their annual sales, but they also need to be reviewed by professors at the start of a term for future adoptions making January and February the optimal time for releasing academic and educational titles that will see adoption with schools and universities. Health and diet titles are often released around the New Year's celebrations in order to appeal to readers who have made "new year, new you" resolutions. Different countries may also have dedicated months to celebrate specific causes. In the United States February is Black History Month, followed by Women's History Month in March. Both of which provide marketing opportunities for relevant titles. In some cases, such as National Poetry Month which is celebrated in April in the US and October in the UK, publishers may need to decide where to publish first. Releasing a book of poetry for the October celebration in the United Kingdom can mean extra time for marketing and publicity in the US, but it also means releasing the book during the busiest time for new publications in the year. Conversely, the global publisher who has a forthcoming book of poetry may release it first in the US for the April celebration to give the UK imprint a summer to build hype for the title.

Development of the Project and Quality Control

The third phase of a book project focuses on the development of the product. While there are some cases where concerns over marketing have played into the development of a book's content,[4] book marketing departments often have little direct involvement with that phase. They may exercise some control over the cover design, but their main activity is to decide on the optimal time and to provide print and digital promotional copies to raise awareness of the title before its release.

Involvement with the development phase provides a timeframe for those working on the sales and marketing of a book to schedule their own work. Knowing when the author will complete their manuscripts will indicate when the author may be free to begin the publicity for a book or can be involved in additional content marketing for the book. Content marketing could involve writing an opinion piece for a newspaper or magazine around a topic from the book or doing a video presentation at a conference to raise interest in the book. One popular venue for this kind of marketing is the TED (technology, entertainment, and design) or TEDx conferences. These TED Talks are often livestreamed and made available on the TED sites and YouTube for free. What makes TED different than the promotional work for the book in other markets is that TED explicitly forbids their speakers from using the talk to "pitch their products or services, plug their books, or ask for funding" (TEDx content guidelines) meaning that all the talks at TED are not explicitly promotions for a speaker's book even if they do generate buzz for it.

The biggest task for marketing when it comes to the development cycle may be the creation of keywords and other metadata if that was not done in the planning phase. Some publishers will wait until closer to release to create a title's metadata as the title and information will be less likely to change to reflect the manuscript. Keywords and other metadata are the primary way for a publisher to create a presence for the book on online retailers and search engines. I will address metadata later in this chapter, but some of the important metadata—title, author, sales info as well as a description—needs to be added to a publisher's website as soon as possible. Richer information that echoes the main points from an AI sheet and catalog copy can be added in the development phase, but waiting until the book's release date dampens the potential hype generated from content marketing and limits any searches people might do on Google or digital bookstores between a book's acquisition and publication. Having good metadata on a publisher's site will boost the findability of the book for pre-publication orders and help generate media interest in the author.

Release

The book's release will be the final milestone for the production departments but it often signals the start for focused work of a marketing department. After finished copies are available, marketing can focus on raising awareness of the title in the marketplace. In parallel to the production work on the book, the marketing department should be working through its own marketing schedule. The creation and delivery of promotional material including shelf talkers, posters, and bookmarks will need to be printed and distributed to stores around the same time as the finished books. Send them too early and bookstores might forget about using them when the book is published. Send them too late and the publisher risks missing the peak of interest in the book. The best-case scenario for promotional material is for bookstores to host launch parties. Simon & Schuster promoted Colleen Hoover's recent novel, *It Starts With Us*, with "kits of temporary tattoos and murals" to retailers who hosted midnight pajama parties for the book's release (Mechling 2022). Other publishers have created postcard campaigns with recipes for a book protagonist's favorite meal or, in the case of Joshua Ferris's first novel, *Then We Came to the End* (2007), a desk-set that included a branded notepad and pencils.

Low-cost or free ebooks are also a tool for generating hype on forthcoming titles. The history of free ebooks promotion has a history in the genres of fantasy, young adult, science fiction and romance going back to the early days of the Internet. The publisher Baen has hosted a free library since 2000 and Harlequin offered free digital editions in 2006 to their readers. In both cases a free ebook raises the awareness of new titles with readers and helps to promote the main series. Receiving a free copy of a title in Kate Hardy's *Paddington Children's Hospital* series from Harlequin can encourage the reader to purchase another of the eleven titles in the series. It can also lead a reader to discover the medical romance genre, which currently has over 1,200 titles available on Harlequin's website. The loss of a sale on a single ebook for some of these series is minor compared to the value of the series as a whole. For example, R.L Stine's *Fear Street* has 163 volumes and Kaoru Kurimono and You Godai's *The Guin Saga* currently offers readers 147 books to go along with the anime series based on the books. Giving away a single copy of one title can lead to the sales of dozens of books that make up the rest of the series. For those publishers who are hesitant to use an ebook as promotion over concerns of sharing or piracy, there is the option to release sample chapters to online publications that can be paired with guest columns or interviews from the author.

The modern marketer looking for a more innovative way to raise awareness online may think about marketing that is native to the Internet. Offering digital ARCs through Goodreads or companies like NetGalley and Edelweiss is one avenue that publishers around the globe have found as a way to engage readers for both print and ebooks, but there are more non-traditional means for a marketing department to create hype for new titles.

The HumbleBundle, a pay-what-you-want site that started in 2010, can generate new readers who would never have picked up an author or series for full retail. The site has taken the pay-what-you-want model HumbleBundle pioneered for video games and applied it to books. Instead of one or two titles, the service offers a bundle organized into different tiers. Users can pay what they want, but if they pay over a certain amount they will get titles in the higher tiers. The company also gamifies sales by limiting the sale to only a few days and having offers that remain locked until a certain number of subscribers pledge money. The other innovation in the service is that the company partners with different charities for each bundle—the humble part. Purchasers not only get to decide how much money they are willing to spend, but they also get to choose how that money is split between the creators, the company, and the charity. For publishers that have older titles experiencing flat or decreasing sales, a bundle can help target an audience that might be looking to buy a large collection or willing to purchase some interesting books just to support a good cause. HumbleBundle has offered sci-fi and fantasy bundles that have included digital titles from Neil Gaiman, Cory Doctorow, Suzanne Collins, as well as bundles on cooking, entrepreneurship, and wellness from publishers such as Wiley, Scholastic, and Open Road. The service also offers similar bundles for graphic content from major independent comic publishers. Marketers can also explore StoryBundle, a similar site that is focused only on ebooks.

Closing

Once the book is released out into the work and all editions are available, marketers should focus on archiving their material and writing up a summary of the work that was done for the title's release. This overlooked step for the closing of most projects will provide marketing with an easy way to access this information for future titles. The book project may be part of a series that can use the same templates. Any market research and metadata can inform future projects and multimedia versions. Movie tie-in editions and anniversary editions will benefit from the shared knowledge of what's happened previously.

Promotion

The major difference between book promotion and marketing is that the publicity department's focus is as much about developing buzz among booksellers, readers, and other publications for the author and topic in the months preceding a book's publication as it is in helping to create hype or raise awareness from within the publishing house in conjunction with the marketing department (Helgason 2014, 16). This shift in focus from internal creations such as bookmarks and shelf talkers to getting others to talk about the book is important to recognize when developing a book project team. Press officers and publicists will focus on building promotion for a house's forthcoming title by engaging with potential audiences where they consume their media. A publicist will need to understand not only their readership, but also the spaces where those readers hang out and what the readers' expectations are in terms of social media interactions. Promoting a young adult paranormal novel with memes and videos in online spaces like Reddit, Instagram, and Tiktok will work to raise awareness of the title, but the same method cannot work for a business title aimed at corporate executives. The memes and videos may, in fact, alienate the readership who are not conversant in Internetspeak. A publicity plan where the authors adapt a chapter for an article at an established business publication or provide interviews to important Substack newsletters is a much better promotional plan. Today's publicist needs to be able to move between the different media outlets to find the right place to promote the book to ensure that there's a 360-degree plan between marketing and promotions to create awareness for the book both in the bookselling world and the audience's preferred media.

Initiation of the Project and Project Planning

In the early stages of a book project publicity will offer feedback on promotional opportunities that sell both the author and the idea of the book as precursors to the book's publication. When the editor is successful in acquiring the title, a publicist should be ready with a deal announcement for trade publications that speaks not to the potential audience but booksellers and reviewers. These announcements should be considered the first piece of publicity for the book. A good deal announcement provides a working title and a pitch alongside information about the author, agent, and publisher. Not only does this announcement start to build buzz, but it helps a subsidiary rights department generate interest in the title from audio and translation publishers.

Development of the Project and Quality Control

Once a manuscript has been accepted by the editor, the publicity department will determine if it needs to use the manuscript to create a galley or sampler for the book. This determination will depend on both the budget for the book and the time between acceptance and the on-sale date. If a book needs a longer lead time for reviews—literary fiction or academic monographs that will be reviewed in quarterly journals, for example—the creation of a galley or sampler may be necessary. Unlike an ARC, which is printed closer to publication, the galley provides reviewers early access to the text so they have time to write a longer review early in a book's life cycle that could be used as potential blurbs on the jacket copy. Samplers provide selections from heavily designed books such as cookbooks and reference work that offer an indication of the book's content and final design. For trade anthologies that focus on the "best" writing of the year, samplers can also be used to announce selections that will appear in the collection.

Once the book is in the process of being designed, the publicist has the opportunity to promote the book release with an ARC. The ideal time to create an ARC is when the designed files are ready to be proofed. At this point in the book project, the book's release is quickly approaching but there is still time to print and distribute advanced reading copies for those publications that publish reviews more regularly or at conferences and festivals that happen far enough away from the publication date that these copies draw attention to the hardcover's release. In a traditional publishing schedule, the creation of the final files is far enough away from the release date to give the publicist time to print ARCs, send out ARCs, and have reviewers post their review around the book's release. The timing for when to release promotional copies will often depend on the book's subject, audience, and release date. A release date for a trade book in late October may benefit from having early promotional copies that won't get lost in the glut of promotional material released in early fall for the holiday sales season, but if it is too early it may hit during the European summer holidays and get ignored. Likewise, academic and professional publishers who are creating ARCs for their titles may need to time their creation around key academic conferences. As printed and bound ARCs are often mini print runs, the decision on when these print copies will be created needs to be decided in the planning phase in conjunction with the production department which can schedule time with a printer. If printing for a conference or book fair, there's also the added logistics of storing and shipping copies from warehouses or offices to the conference. It is not uncommon for publicity and marketing to work with the sales team to prepare promotional material including catalogs and rights guides several months prior to the start of major conferences and book fairs.

Release

Outside the preparation of promotional copies and any other promotional material that the marketing department has created, the other focus for a publicity department during production work is to arrange interviews and readings for the author. These press events will need a budget for transportation, hotels, per diems, and so on, and should be scheduled so as not to overload the author. In pre-COVID days when media appearances and book tours were in-person, a publicist would try to arrange interviews with media and bookstore readings on the same day in the same town and subsequent events in towns nearby on the following days. In-demand authors would spend their mornings talking with local media or podcasters before reading at a bookstore in the evening. There is an art to the live author tour that requires publicists to approach it as its own project with a unique budget, schedule, and set of risks. When touring a celebrity known in another field there is the concern that the fans arrive with CDs, DVDs, or other media for their signature and not the book that is at the heart of this tour. One solution that has become common for bookstore events in the past few years is to charge for tickets to the event but include the book as part of the cost. This limits the crowd size to those who are willing to purchase tickets, but it also ensures sales of books at the venue.

The COVID pandemic changed the author's book tour but it did so in a way that aligned with changes that were already occurring in some sectors of the industry before any lockdowns were declared. The inclusion of a camera and microphone on nearly every computer, handheld tablet, and cell phone made it so that an author could be a talking head or disembodied voice on podcasts and talk shows without having to leave their country or even their house. The online promotion of books allows publicists and authors to remotely promote to a larger audience that often also has the chance to time-shift the talk.

The author Jenny Lawson's book tour for *Broken* was forced online due to the pandemic. This resulted in a series of online events at bookstores and libraries that were both offered as a timed broadcast for those who registered for the event and more general readings that appeared on YouTube. One such reading is Lawson's event at the Richland Library, South Carolina, in November 2020 which is available on YouTube to a much larger audience than those patrons in Richland who could attend the event in the middle of the epidemic. Another benefit of shifting the reading online was that the events could include multiple authors in conversations without the cost of transporting them to the location. When Lawson took her book tour online in 2021, she was joined at a few readings by Neil Gaiman who was stuck in Scotland. While these video readings have shown publishers a new way to reduce travel overheads for promotional events, they have also shown that online recordings appeal to a wider audience who may not be able to attend the traditional book event due to geographic location or accessibility issues.

Publicists can also use parts of these events and other recorded videos to promote titles over social media. One example of a multimedia promotion that can be used by a publicist is the unboxing video. Here the author records themselves as they unbox the first copies of their new book. This can begin a whole series of reaction videos from fans on the original unboxing and around their own reception of a pre-ordered copy. The popularity of unboxing videos started with YouTubers opening new tech including the original iPhone, but it quickly became ubiquitous on streaming platforms for a variety of products. These videos offer fans access to the author during a moment of high emotion. What were previously private moments are turned into online clips that can build the buzz for a book in the days leading up to its release.

In early February of 2018, Tomi Adeyemi tweeted a video of her unboxing copies of her first novel, *Children of Blood and Bone*. The video, since deleted from social media, ended up being reposted several thousand times across social media and was picked up by mainstream media. The video was shown on morning shows and became buzz for Adeyemi's first book. The modern publicist understands how social media can generate a large amount of buzz for a book quickly and the publicist will have no control over whether that buzz is positive or negative. In the Adeyemi example, it was positive because viewers could see a very real and honest reaction but the virality of that video was not the author's doing. Author Jenny Elder-Moke notes in an article on how authors can use TikTok, "we all know how little authors can actually impact their sales in a significant way via social media" (O'Sullivan 2022), especially when they feel the need to add perfunctory videos of them trying to sell a book amongst the millions of videos of book unboxings, author readings, Q&As, video essays, and arrangements of books on a bookcase that users post as part of what has been called BookTube, Bookstagram, and BookTok depending on the ascending social media. In addition, sites like X, formerly known as Twitter, have provided both authors and publishers a public forum to connect with readers and one another to host events such as pitch slams, where authors could submit elevator pitches to literary agents and editors for their books. The site was also where the #publishingpaidme hashtag attempted to raise the awareness about the racial and gendered biases inherent in advances from publishers. As of the writing of this manuscript, the current fixation on social media for book publishing is BookTok, TikTok videos showcasing books and book-buying culture. BookTok is credited with helping to make backlist titles from Colleen Hoover and Sarah Maas bestsellers years after their initial publication date and has even been credited by the UK publisher Sphere for their discovery of Ali Hazelwood's *The Love Hypothesis* which would go on to sell a million plus copies for the press (Peirson-Hagge 2022). Social media offers the publicist a new way to engage with readers provided those working with social media understand the fractured landscape where tribes of readers gather together on a preferred platform, be it TikTok, X, WhatsApp, Facebook, Instagram, Tumblr, Reddit, Mastodon, or whatever new platform may emerge between the writing and publication of this book. These platforms are not all the same and the savvy publicist needs to understand the different etiquettes across the platforms and their communities in order to help raise a title's visibility.

Closing

In the first decade of the twenty-first century, one could find in a house a number of file cabinets near the publicity department that were filled with publicity plans, promotional materials, and photocopies of reviews. These cabinets contained the history of the work done to make these books visible. Publicity plans, travel arrangements, reviews, and the promotional material created for a book are still an important part of a book's archive, but today that material will be stored in an online folder along with digital video and audio from media appearances, podcasts, and readings that can be pulled up by the department and quickly shared by the publicist to other media in an attempt to book them on a show. While the cabinets took up valuable real estate in the office, their new digital archives also come with a cost. The storage of audio and video necessary for today's publicity archive are significantly larger than the digitized version of the text documents from those cabinets. In order for publicists to successfully capture the work they did for a title the publisher will need to invest in a DAM or MAM that can support the needs of the publicity department as well as that of the editorial and production department.

Sales

Initiation of the Project

It should be clear from the previous two sections on marketing and promotion that those in book distribution need to be involved in the earlier stages of a book project's life cycle even if they are not the team members creating the deliverables or moving the project forward. They will have more of an advisory role up at the start of a book life cycle, but one that will prepare the house for the work that comes with a book's release. Depending on the size of the publishing house the presence of those in marketing, publicity and sales at an editorial meeting could be one or two representatives sitting in and providing feedback on the proposal to representatives from all three departments outlining the prospects of the proposal in terms of media attention and potential for translations and non-traditional sales opportunities.

The feedback from those involved in distribution will help editors understand how the publishing house will position their titles in the marketplace. Not every book is as easy to position as a fiction title by an author such as Jo Nesbø, Elena Ferrante, or Stephen King, where a bookstore knows what to expect from new titles. Editors, by nature and by training, will often acquire titles that do not fit nicely into the prescribed categories of bookstores and requires more work by the sales department to help retailers understand the book and its audience. As a young editor I acquired the reprint rights for a natural history on eels and their importance in European and American culinary history. I found the writing about the creatures compelling and it fit with both the science and cookery titles the house published. The editorial board agreed. The sales and marketing departments needed to decide on how to sell the book: Would it be a single subject science book with recipes? Or a culinary history with some science? By sales conference, the book was positioned as a single subject history that downplayed the culinary history. This positioning reflected the first impression of the book by the sales reps in the meeting who understood how to make the book make sense to booksellers in catalog copy and the two-sentence pitch a sales rep may have with a book buyer.

The ease in which a sales or marketing manager can position a book will affect how the house deals with the project in the planning and release phases. If the book reflects a popular trend in the marketplace, sales will have a clear path forward and will be able to use comp titles to sell it. It also means that there will be certain expectations on the book's design and length where marketing and sales may advise on the book's development. After the Harry Potter series became a phenomenon, publishers were quick to release other series about supernatural schools aimed at middle grade readers that were often thick chapter books with lightning bolts and hats on their covers. A more recent example can be seen in the oversized adult coloring books that appeared in 2015 from nearly every publisher. The books were 64–100 pages and often promoted stress relief and calmness on their covers.[5] For those books covering subjects new to the marketplace and publisher, those working on distribution will need to be involved in the book project from the beginning to create a sales plan that includes bespoke marketing and promotional ideas to introduce the subject into the market.

Project Planning

The sales department will also work in conjunction with the marketing team on schedule and budget. Like the marketing department, the sales department will need to know what the expectations are for the title. Is it one of the main seasonal titles that will have a big marketing push? Does the author have a strong media presence that could mean more sales to fans? Instead of controlling the planning of the book project, the sales department will provide feedback and confer with the other departments on the right way to release the title.

As mentioned above, a book's on-sale date will depend on the subject matter and the audience for the book. Sales and marketing professionals will often know what is of interest to booksellers throughout the year. While the production department may have fifty-two weeks in a year to prepare new titles for release, sales and marketing know that some weeks are more important than others. Book release slots in late September and October are needed for any of the big fall or holiday titles and releases in late spring are for titles that are often classified as light fiction for vacation reads. In the world of sales not every week is the same and the publishing house needs to be strategic in terms of when it releases its titles throughout the year. Sales will also need to push for books tied to historical events to release on dates around important historical events such as the 400th anniversary of the publication of Shakespeare's First Folio in 2023 or the 700th anniversary of the death of Marco Polo in 2024.

A recent example of how a sales department manages on-sale dates around important historical events can be seen with the publication of *Spare* by Prince Harry. The book was originally scheduled for a late 2022 release for holiday book buying but was delayed after the passing of Queen Elizabeth II on 8 September. The book provides an informative case study on how closely publishers manage release dates for their titles. Not only did Transworld and Penguin Random House, the UK and US publishers delay the publication of the book in respect to the Queen, they also used that delay to update the book. In pushing the title back to a January release, they had to fill the space (and expected revenues) from the hole created in the publishing schedule. While the change in publication date to the midway point between the passing of Queen Elizabeth II and the May coronation of King Charles III helped boost sales of the book, it was a risk the publishers took over two fiscal quarters and relied on the name recognition overcoming the traditionally slow sales of January.

On a much smaller and more common scale, academic books will often release early in the year so that universities and professors have time to review the book as a possible adoption for Fall classes. Fall adoptions at universities are usually needed by the end of the spring semester and the publishers know they will need to release titles early in the year if they hope to see orders for the Fall before university bookstores place their orders in the summer. While they have little control over the timing of production, sales departments do need to advise on the on-sale date for the release of the book as the right release date can mean strong sales in the initial weeks of publication.

Development of the Project and Quality Control

Around the time a book is in production, the publishing house will include it in its seasonal sales conference that provides the key information on the title for sales reps in the form of an Advance Information (AI) sheet or Title Information (TI or TIP) sheet that includes the sales handle for the book, key metadata (author, title, price, on-sale date, number of pages, territory) and rich information about the book and the sales and marketing plans for the title that were generated from the publisher's ONIX feed for the book or from one of the publisher's databases. ARCs and promotional material may catch the eye, but the bookseller can only spend a few minutes at most assessing most titles. An AI sheet with relevant information and strong marketing plans will often be the key means for a bookstore to decide on the number of copies to order.

In addition to the info sheets and sales conferences that often happen during the development and quality control phases of book projects in a current publishing season, sales departments will also include these titles in a seasonal sales catalogue. These catalogs will include some basic title information and cover designs for a publisher's forthcoming titles and are sent to retailers to promote new titles as well as paperback reprints, reissues, and backlist titles of interest. In the pre-digital days these book catalogs could be anything from a simple staple-bound pamphlet with titles listed in multiple columns per page to a sumptuous four-color perfect bound glossy paperback where major titles would be given two-page spreads. While a small number of these catalogs continue to be printed for conferences and book buyers, the modern seasonal catalogue is now more often a PDF available from a publisher's website[6] or from a service such as the Edelweiss catalog service. Unlike the info sheets that feel disposable, the catalogs offer book buyers a brightly colored reference to a publishing house's offerings over the next few months. They often serve as a resource to help buyers evaluate what titles to carry and can serve as visual reminders about books mentioned in radio programs and podcasts.

Release

The release of the final deliverable of a book project, the book itself, is the next to last phase in the life cycle of that book project and it relies heavily on the sales team to ensure a successful end to the book project. As Thomas Woll notes in *Publishing for Profit*, the "essence of the book publishing process is to create a profit by disseminating information" (2014, 7) and there is no profit if the information cannot be found by its audience. The sales team for a book project's work during the release phase include getting book orders from retailers, making the book discoverable through the dissemination of rich metadata, licensing any translations or multimedia editions that may bring value to the project, and finding sales opportunities outside the normal retail channels.

The successful release of a book in any format comes down to two essential steps: having a means for someone to order the book and delivering that book quickly (Feather 2003, 123). This is the work of the sales department who are responsible for generating orders from retailers and distributors, known as the sell in, and then ensuring that those books are delivered to the right spot in a timely manner and are in a quality that the customer expects so that the retailer is able to sell through their stock and reorder more copies, otherwise those books would sit on a shelf until an invoice with the publisher is set to expire and the bookstore returns those copies.

It sounds easier than it is.

The ordering process for a book publisher involves communications and interpersonal contact between the sales department and the bookstores or other retailers. Sales departments are often structured around two types of book retailers: sales reps may cover a geographical location and independent bookstores within that region work with them, or key account managers will work directly with large chain stores including Waterstones, Maruzen, and Amazon. Other types of retailers that are part of the sales network for a book publisher include distributors, jobbers, and non-book retailers such as department stores and discount clubs who will buy books by the pallet instead of cartons. These non-book sales avenues are often handled by one of the key account managers or by a special sales department who are well versed in handling the differences in invoicing and ordering for retailers outside the book trade. A sales department can also include a subsidiary rights department that handles the licensing of a house's titles out to other media companies. These licenses can include deals for translations, audiobooks, movies, and television series.

Table 8.1 Different sales reps within a publishing house will need a variety of material for their clients. Reps selling to domestic bookstores may only need marketing material and information about the forthcoming book, while those who license a translation may need proposals and typescripts from the editorial department.

Type of Sales	Clients	Needed Materials
Independent Bookstore	Small bookstores.	Galleys, ARCs, AI sheet, promotional material, seasonal catalogues, EAN-13 barcode, book metadata.
Chain Bookstore	Large chains. Often one or more sales reps works directly with the chain.	Galleys, ARCs, AI sheet, marketing information, co-op, promotional material, seasonal catalogues, rich metadata feeds, EAN-13 barcode.
Other Retailers	Department stores, warehouse clubs, supermarkets, museum stores, airport bookstores, and other outlets.	ARCs, AI sheet, promotional material, metadata feeds, seasonal catalogues, EAN-13 barcode and UPC barcode (needed for retailers in United States and Canada).
Special Sales	Organizations looking to purchase large quantities of a title one time.	Deal Memo, galleys, ARCs, AI sheet, seasonal catalogues, unique ISBN for non-retail editions of books.
Library Sales	Libraries and book distributors working directly with libraries.	Galleys, ARCs, AI sheet, marketing information, seasonal catalogues, reviews, promotional material, rich metadata feeds.
International Sales	International bookstores.	Book proposal, deal memo, manuscript, galleys, ARCs, AI sheet, seasonal catalogues, marketing information, promotional material, rich metadata, EAN-13 barcode.
Subsidiary Rights	Media companies looking to license content: movie studios, audiobook publishers, magazines looking for serialized content, reprinters, and foreign publishers looking for translations.	Book proposal, deal memo, author contract, manuscript, galleys, ARCs, AI sheet, marketing information, seasonal catalogues, rights guides, promotional material.

Special Sales, Library Sales, and Subsidiary Rights

Until the changes brought on by the wide scale adoption of the Internet, book sales departments were primarily focused on selling to bookstores and not individuals. Giles Clark and Angus Phillips provide a detailed description of a sales rep's visit to the bookstore in *Inside Book Publishing* that reflects the attention a publishing house paid to the needs of a buyer at a bookstore (2020, 288–291), but the Internet, specifically social media, has renewed the need for publishers to engage in hand-selling and direct sales to readers, albeit in a completely new way. A certain market segment, mainly small publishers with limited or no distribution, has found that selling books on a merchandizing table during reading or events and linking sales pages on social media will often attract more readers than a book on a bookstore's shelf. Translation presses such as Charco Press and literary presses including Archipelago Books, and Fitzcarraldo Editions and poetry presses like Wave Books are some of the small presses that have developed several direct sales methods including bundles and seasonal subscriptions for all titles that these houses have published. For these presses the sales and marketing departments need to engage with readers on a direct level, often through social media and weekly or monthly newsletters, instead of relying on bookstores as intermediaries.

Reader engagement has drastically changed over the last thirty years. The links to purchase on Bookstagram, BookTube, and BookTok now rival what a chain like Waterstones or Amazon can sell. The development of a special sales rep to focus on reader events is essential for publishers hoping to take advantage of changes in how readers find and purchase books. These specialized sales teams expand a book's reach beyond the bookstore and provide a publisher with more opportunities to sell the book directly to a specific audience. These special sales are often working directly with a company that wants to provide a copy of a specific book—often a business title written by the CEO, or a book on a subject matter relevant to the company—to every employee. They can also be engaged with the major book clubs that host community-wide readings.

Around the same time as the founding of current social media companies, community reading programs were growing in popularity in the United States. Similar to the book clubs started by television personalities including Oprah Winfrey, Richard Madeley, and Judy Finnigan. Nancy Pearl, a librarian at the Seattle Public Library, created one of the first community-wide book clubs in 1998. The idea of having a city or community all reading the same book grew in popularity until there were around 350 such initiatives in the United States with names such as "The Big Read" and "One Book, One Community" (Cole 2006). Similar programs in the United Kingdom include Overdrive's "Together We Read" and the BBC and The Reading Agency's "The Big Jubilee Read." For a special sales department, the ability to influence one of these clubs to pick their titles can mean sales of thousands of copies to the organization as well as the increased awareness of the book and additional sales in local bookstores.

The rise of community book clubs as spaces to sell print books coincided with changes at libraries. Not only have libraries become a locus for these book clubs, but they have also had to change their acquisition model towards digital access. Faced with hundreds of thousands of titles publishers now release annually and an often small increase in their acquisitions budget, libraries have had to re-envision S.R. Ranganathan's axiom of "every book their reader" that is at the core of their work. One means of rethinking the library has been Demand-Driven Acquisitions (DDA). In DDA the library offers access to large collections of digital titles but only pay for the titles that patrons read. This allows libraries to broaden their offerings and publishers a chance to have titles used in libraries that would never have purchased the title in print. Providers such as EBSCO Information Services, Bibliotheca Odilo, StoryTel, and Libby show libraries not only what is being checked out, but also what books have the most holds placed, an indicator that more copies may need to be purchased. Books are no longer only acquired based on subject and reviews, but also the demand from patrons, which depending on the type of library can be created through several different sources. Academic libraries may find researchers asking for titles they heard about at a conference, as a citation, or from a publisher's e-mail newsletter. Patrons at public libraries may ask about books they found in a citation as well, but patron requests are now just as likely to come from watching book-themed social media.

In addition to having special sales reps licensing books to online collections, community reading programs and other non-traditional opportunities such as selling books into organizations for promotional purposes (pledge drives, give-aways), a fully staffed sales department should also include a subsidiary rights department and international sales department who can deal with the release of the title to the global marketplace. The international sales department has the difficult task of placing a publisher's books in foreign countries. This often means knowing the specialized bookstores in each country that will sell foreign language books within those countries. For English-language publishers this means knowing what bookstores in Europe will carry English-language titles and having their international sales reps develop relationships with those stores. Relationships with online retailers including Amazon, Flipkart, and Kobo are also essential for international sales. In addition, there are also bookstores that have expanded into global chains. One such company is Japan's Kinokuniya Shoten. In addition to the seventy-one stores it has throughout Japan, the bookstore also has sixteen physical stores in the United States as well as stores throughout Southeast Asia and Australia (Kinokuniya 2020). The stores outside of Japan operate as both a local and Japanese-language bookstore. In the New York City store, the main floor looks like a regular independent bookstore with English-language titles from several US publishers while the basement is a dedicated Japanese-language bookstore, and manga occupies the whole of the second floor. In terms of customers the bookstore appeals to both the regular US book buyer as well as readers interested in Japanese-language titles and customers searching for manga in both English and Japanese. For the Japanese publishers working with Kinokuniya, their sales reps will need to ensure that the titles placed with the bookstore are managed differently in their Japanese bookstores and their global stores depending on the language of the author contract in terms of global distribution.[7] For those publishers working with Kinokuniya, it may mean requiring both a local and international sales rep to sell the book to the different divisions of the bookstore.

Competing with the distribution of a publisher's native language titles in the global marketplace is the licensing of translations, which falls to another group within the sales department: the subsidiary rights department. This department often sells translation rights for a publisher's book to other publishers around the world but may also handle licensing audio versions or occasionally working with movie and television producers on treatments for future movie and television projects based on the books. The different opportunities for a subsidiary rights department as well as the legal and logistical issues these sales reps need to understand has been outlined in depth in Lynette Owen's *Selling Rights* (2024), the rare handbook focused on a publisher's sales department. While often a part of the sales team, subsidiary rights reps need to be involved in a book project from the editorial board meeting. Because of the global reach of the bookstores mentioned above, rights departments often try to license translations as early in a book project's life cycle as possible. The closer a translation can release to the original version's publication date the better. If you are a French publisher who is releasing a translation of a British cozy mystery, having that translation ready when the UK edition releases means the ability to coordinate marketing between the two countries to raise awareness for both editions of the book. It also means diverting readers from going to Amazon or Waterstones to order the English-language edition because the French one is not yet available. This rush to publication means the licensees need the manuscript as soon as possible to translate it, often right after the copy edit. Foreign publishers rarely need the interior layout or cover as they design their own for the local market.

Distribution

Depending on those involved in the creation and warehousing of print, the path of a book from production files to copies in a bookstore can be a gnarled logistical pathway that stretches around the globe. For most small publishers, printing may be done locally, and the books delivered to a distribution warehouse that sends copies out to independent bookstores, giant retail chains, and other retailers. In countries such as the United Kingdom and Japan this may take a few days as the intranational distances between the printers and a company's warehouse are not that immense. The opposite situation would be for a children's publisher who has licensed several translations and is publishing the four-color book with a printer in China. In order to reduce printing costs, the publisher may offer those publishers who licensed the book the chance to produce a co-edition. A co-edition allows several publishers to be part of the same print run. This is common in children's publishing where all publishers may use the same illustrations and only need to change the text for each edition. This will require only a change to the plates that print black and can offer significant savings to the different publishers offering the title. After the books are printed and bound, the printer can ship the different editions out to the specified port for each publishing company where the books are then loaded on a second means of transportation and delivered to its own warehouses. The transportation distances in Europe and the United Kingdom between the receiving port and a publisher's warehouse may only be a few hundred kilometers, but in the United States, printed books from China and Taiwan that arrive at a port such as San Francisco on the West Coast will need to make a 3,800 km trip by semi-trailer to warehouses in the book distribution hub of Nashville, Tennessee, before being sent out to bookstores across the country. This transportation of physical material, what Clark and Phillips call "book miles" creates an environmental impact that is often not part of the financial consideration when a publisher evaluates the cost for printing and distribution of a book (2020, 237).

The delivery process for books can also mean shipping special editions of books to organizations that might have worked with the publisher's special sale department to create branded books as promotional material for the organization, a common agreement for memoirs or biographies of the organization's founders or titles by a current chief officer. These corporate sales had helped the modern business book to become a valuable subject for publishers. A proposal from these authors could come in with a guarantee of a sale of a few thousand copies to back the author's organization, upping the print quantities before any sales kit has been created. The books often require a special branding on the cover or may leave off the UPC code as they cannot be sold and should not be part of the normal retail sales for the book. Similar licenses can be created for books by politicians or on books that approach a current topic, such as climate change, health issues, or retirement planning, that an organization feels its employees may benefit from reading about. These are often part of an employee engagement or can be part of an organization's book club.

Closing

The closing and maintenance phase for sales can take several different forms. Looking at the sales reports for titles several months out from a book's release date can also show how markets had responded to different books. Some titles that had never found traction in the local market may have found a readership in translation or as an audiobook. I have seen Japanese licenses for a book about physics involving Sherlock Holmes outsell the English-language edition to the point where royalties for the author were almost exclusively from the translation. Titles will not always perform the same in different formats and in different markets, so taking the title to analyze all markets, not only the major retailers and bookstores, may provide insights on where readers for certain titles are buying their books. Sales reps for the romance genre know that readers have been consuming texts online since the introduction of desktop computers. They also know romance readers are voracious and have gravitated to sites like Kindle Unlimited where they can pay a monthly fee to binge read their preferred subgenres and that the earnings from these online subscription services are not commensurate with the publisher's overhead. Academic sales reps know that textbook purchasing by university students has dropped precipitously due to the introduction of the rental market and online piracy. A publisher's sales reps need to have the same kind of understanding about their markets as it pertains to current and future titles so that they can provide more accurate estimates on future projects.

Book Returns

The problematic aspect of book returns is also an issue that arises in the closing of a book project. While every industry deals with returns, most do not do so at the scale of publishing. In the last two decades of the twentieth century the dominance of chain bookstores, such as Waterstones and Barnes and Noble, turned book returns from a few copies being returned from small booksellers to unopened cartons of a title that had sat in a chain bookstore's warehouse for several months. According to John Thompson, "the average publisher's returns are at thirty percent" but that rate will vary depending on the publisher's position in the marketplace; publishers with extensive backlists will see lower rates and books that don't work in the marketplace may see returns closer to 60 percent of the order. "That means that for every 100 new hardcovers shipped out, somewhere between thirty and sixty will come back to the publisher as returns" (2012, 284).

While inventory management at large retailers has attempted to decrease the return rate from where they were a decade ago, the question of print returns is still an issue for all levels and types of publishers. With every return, a publisher's warehouses will need to evaluate the quality of the returns and then restock unopened cartons from retailers and decide if loose returned copies will be part of a remainder sale or disposed of as wasted copies. This works adds to the overhead of warehousing and affects the inventory management that uses the data on warehouse stock to indicate when reprints are needed. A big return that comes in at the end of a hardcover's sale period can mean that publishers may have overestimated the new paperback's first print quantity as well as the sales on an author's royalty sheet.[8] In the digital space returns are virtually non-existent; there is no stock to return, only access to be denied or granted.

Metadata

The importance of metadata should not be understated when talking about book distribution. In an industry that has seen new books offered from traditional publishers surpass a million titles a year in the three most productive markets—600,000 in Europe, 300,000 titles in the United States, 300,000 titles in China (Federation of European Publishers 2022)—the need to make sure a title is discoverable is essential. Sales departments need to ensure that information attached to a book title is robust and descriptive. It is no longer enough to have title, author, price, format, ISBN, category code—BISAC in the United States, BIC in the United Kingdom—and publication date as the key information. Good metadata should also include abstracts, book descriptions, author bios, categories, excerpts, blurbs, table of contents, and keywords that are structured to feed into various retail and library systems.

Keywords specifically have become one of the most important aids for discoverability on online bookstores' search engines. Instead of "cookbook" or "French cuisine," publishers should try to include as many of the recipe titles and ingredients for those recipes in their list of keywords for the book. The metadata provided to an online retailer should equate to that of giving a customer access to a book's index in a physical store. Publishers should view metadata as an evolving sales element; good metadata is metadata that is updated and revised. In a personal interview with Joshua Tallent, Director of Sales and Education at Firebrand Technologies who trains publishers on keyword creation, he notes that "online metadata that is updated regularly is more likely to result in more views and more sales. Search engines take new information into consideration, and consumers can tell when a title looks kind of old. Tweaking metadata, adding new information, and changing out text that is not working can all make a big impact on your sales" (Tallent 2018).

As the number of books published globally continues to grow annually, the space for professional book reviews is rapidly shrinking. Readers now rely on online publications, social media, and Goodreads for their book discovery. Instead of the page-long reviews that appear in the *London Review of Books* or the *New York Times Book Review*, readers now rely on the ones that are around a hundred words and often personal in nature as well as the number of stars the reader gave in their ranking of books. This reliance on the personal over the professional has also expanded the number of reviews a reader has access to when searching for a book to read.

Ultimately, the number of books and reviews that a reader finds when looking for something to read may push them away from unknown authors and towards known entities. In his book *The Paradox of Choice*, Barry Schwartz, a psychologist who has studied the relationship between happiness and choice, makes the argument that the more options consumers have, the more anxious they feel about that choice. When faced with an abundance of products, customers are more likely to choose the most familiar. Schwartz demonstrates this through an experiment with several flavors of jams and jellies in a supermarket. The more flavors offered, the more likely a consumer will turn to strawberry or grape (Schwartz 2016, 19–22). In other words, when faced with thousands of new fiction titles to read, most readers will turn to the names they know: Robert Galbraith, Lee Childs, Zadie Smith, Stephen King, and others, to the point where as little as 5 percent of a publisher's list can produce up to 70 percent of its sales (Shatzkin 2013). As these authors stay on the bestseller lists they remain the authors that readers gravitate towards when searching for a new book, closing the loop on discoverability for new authors.

Rich metadata is one way to weaken this feedback loop. In two comprehensive studies on the use of descriptive copy, covers and keywords, Nielsen/ NPD found that adding this material to online databases can help a book's online sales (Tallent 2018). The inclusion of more metadata for a title provides better search results which cuts down on the number of choices that confronts a reader. Readers may have access to millions of titles, but they only want the three to five most relevant results when searching for a book, any further results become noise.

While the publishing industry continues to work on the creation of good metadata to share with retailers and libraries, there are some retailers who are moving ahead with more daring data experiments that bring analytics into the world of discoverability. Services such as Amazon's X-Ray which breaks down a book's content to show how many times a character or place is mentioned and creates a visual index to show subject and topics instead of a traditional index at the back of the book. This kind of information offers readers a new way of accessing a book but it also maps out a book in a way for companies to analyze how readers read. The flip side of X-Ray is that Kindles track reading speed, word searches, and reader highlights. They record a user's reading speed and how long a reader engages with a title before switching to another title or, in the case of tablets and smartphones, switches to another app.

This use of personal metadata keeps track of how, when, and where readers read. Some believe it is the next step in the digital reading experience. E-reading devices can already track reading speed and monitor highlights, annotations, bookmarks, and notes, why not analyze that information? Most digital devices, including smartphones and e-readers, come with GPS integration, so a reader's location can be added to the analysis as well. For a publisher this information about where, when, and how the reader reads a book could be a goldmine of trends. Imagine if publishing houses started to receive the firehouse of data about their titles, including reader reviews, common highlights, reading speed, sections where readers stopped reading, and information about the reading speed of different groups of readers. What could a publisher do with that information?

Content Distribution and the Agile Method

Those who work in the marketing, promotion, and sales departments will retain their role as the connector between user and creators in an Agile book project. They will be the ones who track responses after the release and provide a new list of requirements based on that feedback for future release cycles. As noted in a previous chapter on content creation, an acquiring editor acts as a product owner in the Agile model, but in an iterative cycle, that product owner needs the feedback on previous releases from customers to steer the next iterations in response to that feedback. For Agile book products that are developed in a publisher founded in traditional book distribution models, the marketing and sales teams will be the only departments within the organization that have access to the retailers and users for that feedback.

User Feedback

One method for gaining feedback from users of digital content is to create surveys that are broadcast out to users. Internet users should be familiar with this process as it often appears as a pop-up survey asking for feedback. These targeted surveys provide insight into the areas that frustrate or delight users that might not be captured in the user experience data from an app. The downside to this method is that only a small percentage of users fill out surveys.

Another feedback mechanism can be the pop-up request to rate the app that appears at a set time after the user has used the app. This pop-up will engage the reader to either give a positive review that will lead to a spot where they can add it to other reviews on an App Store or will send negative reviews to a customer service routine to collect the negative feedback about the app. Similar to community reviews for books described earlier in this chapter, app reviews will often include some information on what delights and frustrates users about the service. A publisher may be able to find new user stories for future iterations when evaluating these reviews. Comments on the responsiveness and other UX experiences including, "I can't get back to the main table of contents from a video" can provide important information for future user stories ("As a user I would want a link back to the TOC on all multimedia pages because it would help provide a visual way back to the main content"). Comments can also indicate the desire of users for unreleased features that may push those features into an earlier cycle. Analyzing these reviews can be time-consuming work that will often need to happen in the period between a release and the next iteration. This can lead to a delay in responding to feedback over several iterations. It may take two or three product releases to respond to user concerns. Communication on what's being done and what to expect on a future release can work to keep the user engaged with a product even when frustrated. This is why distribution may also need to be the team members responsible for the communication plans or at least work with the communication teams to include external as well as internal communications.

For those publishers who are used to working in the print to bookstore model, the focus on reviews and inclusion of space for ads within the product, common in free apps that provide textual content, is a different outlook on how readers engage with a product. The idea that the relationship between publisher and book ends at the register no longer holds true in the app world. Customer engagement is a major phase of product development and needs to be part of every release cycle. John Murray's Language Library expands the resources for their *Contatti, Façon de Parler, Pasos* or *Willkommen!*, and *Voici* or *Voilà* language courses onto a learner's handheld device to help them discover more multimedia content than what is available through the course books. Through this app John Murray extends the book beyond what is available at the time of purchase and gives users a more responsive means for language learning (John Murray Language Library 2021). Income from the purchase of the app and in-app purchases may make the products profitable,[9] but the insight that comes from tracking user interactions and seeing the engagement of users with the app will be a rich source of data that will suggest improvements on the next iteration.

The book app marketplace can provide an idea on how this would work even in digital content that is purchased and not ad supported. The release of most book apps through Apple's App Store or the Google Play Store is only the start of the engagement for the publisher with the reader. It's no longer an endpoint for the relationship. Once the reader has an app, their interactions with that app will reveal the patterns of engagement with the content. Unlike print books, this engagement can show what content readers prefer. For educational apps it can show what features (multimedia, interactive quizzes, etc.) are most or least used and, if the app is linked to internal and external resources such as Wikipedia and dictionaries, user interaction can indicate terms or text that are problematic. Unlike a book that remains a closed system to the reader, digital content is networked and the use of that content is often recorded and can provide information on the user's needs beyond what they say in reviews.

Emerging Technologies

Previous chapters have explored how work within a publishing house has changed due to new technologies. Some of the same technologies are also changing how companies engage with retailers and potential readers. Earlier in this chapter I outlined how metadata has aided in online discoverability and how social media can be used by publishers to raise awareness of their titles. Marketers need to approach social media more as users than as marketers. It's not only using Social Media optimization (SMO) to get content before a target audience. It's also about understanding who is using what platform and engaging with them as users of the platform in a way that feels native and natural instead of forced. For some publishers the right audience might not be on the largest platforms. Take Tumblr, for example. Tumblr launched as a microblogging service in 2007 and was the most popular service with teen and college-age users in 2011 but remains an obscure and often ignored space by nonusers (Tiidenberg, Hendry, and Abidin 2021). In the intervening decade since its founding, Tumblr became recognized as a community-building space for LGBT groups and fandoms of bands such as One Direction. After two changes in corporate ownership, the site has now become an online space mostly used by female-identifying Millennials, one of the largest demographics of book purchasers. While Tumblr doesn't get the same attention as sites like TikTok and Instagram in terms of book visibility, the site has the potential to attract a significant readership for the right kind of book, most likely a title focused on LGBTQ+ and social justice issues. In addition to cultivating online communities across social media platforms, today's book marketers also need to add podcasts, digital author Q&As, and online author readings to their list of promotional tools.

In terms of new avenues for book sales, two of the most exciting means for increasing a readership for a book skip the retail space and appeal directly to the readers: crowdfunding and subscriptions. These alternative distribution methods have shown promise for small houses who might not have the marketing money to rise above the hundreds of other books released every month. In these models publishers can not only sell copies of books but gather data on what interests the readers about a book or book series.

Crowdfunding

The idea is simple: an author or publisher puts up a campaign on a crowdfunding site where they identify what they want to do (write/publish a book), how much money they need to do it (US$40,000), and what their backers will get in return (a digital copy of the book). If the campaign reaches the goal set by the creator, the backers pay their pledge to the creator. If the campaign fails to reach its monetary goal, the campaign creator can cancel the campaign and move on to the next project. Unlike traditional publishing where the acquisition of a book is based on past sales and a sense of how readers will respond to the title, crowdfunding creates an environment that minimizes the risk; readers need to commit to purchasing the book before it is even made.

The model can be seen as a digital version of the direct sales methods that publishers used at the turn of the twentieth century. Instead of a mail-in order form for books, readers are now able to sign up for a title digitally. If there's not enough interest and the book never gets made, there's no cost to the reader. In cases where the idea does appeals to readers, a crowdsourced book can provide authors and publishers with the capital needed to create the product. Instead of making up the costs through sales post-production, the publisher can acquire capital from readers to pay for the costs before the book is produced. Successes include the bestselling *Good Night Stories for Rebel Girls* (2016) by Elena Favilli and Francesa Cavallo which ended up raising nearly seventeen times its original revenue goal and Ryan North's *To Be or Not To Be* (2016), an interactive retelling of Shakespeare's *Hamlet*, which raised twenty-nine times its original revenue goal from over 15,000 backers. In 2022 author Brandon Sanderson created the most successful Kickstarter campaign in the company's history when he raised over US$41 million in pledges from 185,341 backers to self-publish four of the novels he wrote during the pandemic (Harris 2022). The cost for the hardcover reward to backers was roughly US$40 per title, the same cost as a retail hardcover title. But these campaigns are not just for authors with a proven track record. Some publishers have turned to crowdfunding as the first step in all their publishing ventures.

Beehive Books was founded in 2016 by artist and designer Maëlle Doliveux, and writer and editor Josh O'Neill. Beehive publishes deluxe editions of distinctive literary and pictorial works including art books, comics, illuminated texts, and a collection of forgotten masters of the graphic arts. All their published books have started as crowdfunding projects. According to Josh O'Neill the books they publish are in "strange formats and traditional publishing is too restrictive" for this kind of variance. The press turned to Kickstarter for their books from the very start and it has been an important part of their publishing process. By using crowdfunding the press can make a publishing project profitable before a retailer orders a copy of a title. O'Neill noted that "the publisher is also getting 100% of the money (minus a small fee from Kickstarter) so the profit margin on the books is much higher than going the traditional retail route" (O'Neill 2018).

What makes crowdfunding work so well is that it balances different levels of contribution. Any campaign will have a significant number of subscribers who contribute because they want to support the idea; Kickstarter reports this group to be around 15 percent of all contributors. These backers give money but never fill out the information to get their rewards. Another group of contributors is those who see the campaign as a way to pre-order a book and provide the creator with the capital they need to produce the book. It is a low-risk endeavor that gives publishers income ahead of their production costs. The third group that needs to be mentioned is the high-end patrons. This would be the group willing to offer hundreds or thousands of dollars to get more personal rewards such as a signed copy of a book or even a dinner with the author.

One of the newer models in the crowdfunding space is serial distribution, represented by Patreon. Patreon offers a model where readers can subscribe to an author and automatically pay for everything that the author releases on the site. It's designed to create a sustained funding model. For publishing this can take the shape of a serialized novel where readers pay for access to chapters.

Crowdfunding remains under-appreciated for how much it changed artistic endeavors. Sites such as Kickstarter, Patreon, Indiegogo, GoFundeMe, and WeMakeIt, to name a few, have given writers and artists a direct line to their audience. And they have given a direct line for the audience to the artists. The publishing projects on crowdfunding sites act as a stark reminder of the value the book publishing industry brings to a book project as it exposes all the work done to create a book and market it to an audience. In *The Art of Asking*, Amanda Palmer describes the time she spends—often two to three hours—after a Dresden Doll show talking to the fans. (Palmer 2015, 101–104). She also mentions a specific reading where Neil Gaiman spent seven hours signing books for fans (Palmer 2015, 184). Media companies have had to manage their talent to strike a balance between scarcity and abundance. Too many appearances and the magic might wear off (Gaiman excluded), too few and the fans might forget about the author. Putting a value to this balance between scarcity and abundance remains difficult, but crowdfunding has helped to identify some of the breakpoints.

Digital and Print Subscriptions

Kickstarter and other crowdfunding services can be important at the start of the process as they provide the capital to start a project, but one way to increase visibility for titles is to align with a subscription service for books that can get a publisher's title in front of the right audience. Depending on your age you'll recognize this as either the Book of the Month Club model in the United States or the defunct Book Club Associates company in the United Kingdom or a twist on Patreon. These subscription services have a solid history in the print side of the industry, and it makes sense that publishers and entrepreneurs see them as an opportunity in the digital marketplace, but they have yet to find the right model. To date the most successful service has been Amazon's Kindle Unlimited. For about US$10 a month users have access to all the books in the Unlimited library. Publishers get a small royalty rate if their books are read. Because we're living in an age of big data, Amazon pro-rates the payout to publishers based on the number of pages read by the user. Other services that have attempted to operate in this space include Oyster, Entitle, Downpour, Storia, Rooster, Pigeonhole, and Scribd. Entitle closed in 2015 and Oyster was shuttered in 2016 after an acquisition by Google. Pigeonhole, Downpour, Storia, and Scribd are all still active as of the writing of this book.

These digital subscriptions are often seen as a buffet-style subscription where readers pay to access as much as they can read and retailers pro-rate payment to the author based on how much the reader has read. As interesting as these new services are and what insight they can provide publishers on their reader's engagement, that information is often not shared by the subscription service. Instead of lamenting the lack of transparency in the digital subscription model, I want to end this chapter with a new distribution model that echoes the industry's past.

In the second half of the 2010s readers were offered a new way to discover books. Instead of wading through an online retailer or trying to keep up with suggestions from social media, readers were offered the opportunity to have a service pick out titles for them based on their interest. These bespoke subscription services would curate new title offerings and send what they felt were the strongest new titles to their subscribers. This model is not new. Publishers have been offering subscriptions and direct sales campaigns for over a century, but they have often done so in the clunky world of physical interaction where readers had to make choices or be active in the management of their subscriptions. This new model, which is often called a book subscription box, follows the model set out by other companies dealing in clothing, food and makeup. The subscriber doesn't decide on the contents of the subscription box outside of genre preferences and relies on the service to choose on their behalf what gets sent out. Unlike the standard Book of the Month Club model that simplifies the purchasing process for readers but allows readers to choose the titles they want, these new boxes manage the decision process by sending a pre-determined selection of titles. They offer the chance to discover new titles without being overwhelmed by the selection of titles displayed on a digital bookstore's sales page or on the shelf of a physical bookstore. These boxes represent the rise in consumers' need for curation in a world of choice. For the publisher, these new services offer a way to get titles in front of a different readership. While this model doesn't have the same influence as social media—they aren't selling millions of copies of Colleen Hoover—they do offer a means of low-cost discoverability for titles that fit within the focus of these subscription services and will count as direct sales for a title, providing another data point in understanding what readers want.

Notes

1 Workflow diagrams for this chapter can be downloaded at https://www.routledge.com/9781032516721.
2 Both of these bookstores may turn around and re-order copies. For trade bookstores the focus is around keeping open invoices for the titles so they are never stuck with non-returnable stock. University bookstores have developed a complicated returns process that compares stock to historical orders by semester. The bookstore is rarely privy to the course decisions of academic departments, so they guess on adoptions until the next semester's schedule is set midway through the current semester.
3 The phenomenon of a publisher benefitting from online buzz for an author's previously published work is nothing new, although social media has certainly raised the bar for these books in terms of sales. *Fifty Shades of Grey* became a global phenomenon for Penguin Random House after EL James self-published with a small Australian publisher.

Authors including Anna Todd, Andy Weir, LJ Ross, and Amanda Hocking have all seen previously published work hit a bestseller list after readers discovered their work.
4 *Cathy's Book* (2008) by Sean Stewart and *The Bulgari Connection* (2001) by Fay Weldon both had deals with make-up (Stewart) and jewelry (Weldon) brands as part of their narratives.
5 The academic publisher, University of Chicago Press, was able to use this trend to release *Doodling for Academics: A Coloring and Activity Book* (2017) released for the iPad that offered "readers" the chance to color the campus as it normally looks and as it appears during parents' weekend.
6 See Carcanet's website which offers its catalogs from 2015 to the present at https://www.carcanet.co.uk/cgi-bin/scribe?showinfo=ip016.
7 Distribution of a book title is defined in the granting of rights in an author contract. A publisher needs to acquire not only the right to publish a book in one or more language, but also the right to distribute the book around the world. In some cases, such as the licensing of a book from the United Kingdom to the United States, the distribution rights may be limited only to the United States and its territories.
8 A concern that has evolved into a line on an author royalty statement where the publisher has a reserve against returns.
9 Faber and Faber and Touch Press's app on T.S. Eliot's The Waste Land app released for the iPad in June 2011 took around six weeks to earn back the development costs on the app providing an early indication that there was an audience for enhanced e-editions (Dredge 2011).

References

Carcenet Press. 2023. "Catalogues." https://www.carcanet.co.uk/cgi-bin/scribe?showinfo=ip016. Accessed 3 August 2023.

Carter, David. 1999. "Good Readers and Good Citizens: Literature, Media and the Nation." *Australian Literary Studies*, 19(2), 136–151.

Clark, Giles and Angus Phillips. 2020. *Inside Book Publishing*. 6th ed. Abingdon, Oxon: Routledge.

Cole, John Y. 2006. "One Book Projects Grow in Popularity." *Library of Congress Information Bulletin*. Washington DC: Library of Congress. https://www.loc.gov/loc/lcib/0601/cfb.html. Accessed 3 August 2023.

Done, Rachel, Rylee Warner, and Rachel Noorda. 2022. "Publishing Distribution Practices: New Insights About Eco-Friendly Publishing, Sustainable Printing and Returns, and Cost-Effective Delivery in the U.S." *Pub Res Q*, 38, 364–381. https://doi.org/10.1007/s12109-022-09882-5.

Dredge, Stuart. 2011, August 8. "The Waste Land iPad App Earns Back its Costs in Six Weeks on the App Store." *The Guardian*. https://www.theguardian.com/technology/appsblog/2011/aug/08/ipad-the-waste-land-app. Accessed 3 August 2023.

Feather, John. 2003. *Communicating Knowledge: Publishing in the 21st Century*. München: K.G. Saur.

Federation of European Publishers. 2022. "European Book Publishing Statistics 2020." https://fep-fee.eu/European-Book-Publishing-1400. Accessed 3 August 2023.

Harris, Elizabeth A. 2022. "Fantasy Author Raises US$15.4 Million in 24 Hours to Self-Publish." *New York Times*. https://www.nytimes.com/2022/03/03/books/brandon-sanderson-kickstarter.html. Accessed 3 August 2023.

Helgason, Jon. 2014. *Hype: Bestsellers and Literary Culture*. Lund: Nordic Academic Press.

John Murray Language Library. 2021. "Hachette UK App Available for Apple IOS." https://apps.apple.com/us/app/john-murray-languages-library/id1472153952. Accessed 3 August 2023.

Kinokuniya Bookstores of America Co. 2020. "Kinokuniya Worldwide." https://usa.kinokuniya.com/worldwide. Accessed 3 August 2023.

McKenna, Regis. 1991, January-February. "Marketing Is Everything." *Harvard Business Review*, 65–79.

Mechling, Lauren. 2022. "'Never seen anything like it': How Colleen Hoover's Normcore Thrillers Made her America's Bestselling Author." *The Guardian*. https://www.theguardian.com/books/2022/oct/11/colleen-hoover-author-tiktok-it-ends-with-us. Accessed 3 August 2023.

Murray, Simone. 2018. *The Digital Literary Sphere: Reading Writing and Selling Books in the Internet Era*. Baltimore: Johns Hopkins University Press.

O'Neill, Josh. 2018. Personal interview.

O'Sullivan, Joanne. 2022. "YA Authors Talk #BookTok: Boon or Burden?" *Publishers Weekly*. https://www.publishersweekly.com/pw/by-topic/childrens/childrens-industry-news/article/90616-ya-authors-talk-booktok-boon-or-burden.html. Accessed 3 August 2023.

Peirson-Hagge, Ellen. 2022. "How #BookTok is changing literature." *The New Statesman*. https://www.newstatesman.com/culture/books/2022/11/tiktok-booktok-changing-literature. Accessed 3 August 2023.

Schwartz, Barry. 2016. *The Paradox of Choice: Why More Is Less*. Revised edition 1st ed. New York: Ecco.

Shatzkin, Mike. 2013. "Finding Your Next Book, Or, the Discovery Problem." *Idealog.com*. https://www.idealog.com/blog/finding-next-book-discovery-problem. Accessed 3 August 2023.

Steiner, Ann. 2018. "The Global Book: Micropublishing, Conglomerate Production, and Digital Market Structures." *Pub Res Quarterly*, 34, 118–132. https://doi.org/10.1007/s12109-017-9558-8.

Tallent, Joshua. 2018. Personal interview.

TEDx Content Guidelines. https://pb-assets.tedcdn.com/system/baubles/files/000/008/468/original/tedx_content_guidelines_fact_check.pdf?1588684684. Accessed 3 August 2023.

Thompson, John. 2012. *Merchants of Culture*. Cambridge: Polity Press.

Tiidenberg, Katrin, Natalie Ann Hendry, and Crystal Abidin. 2021. *Tumblr*. Malden, MA: Polity.

Woll, Thomas. 2014. *Publishing for Profit: Successful Bottom-Line Management for Book Publishers*. Revised and expanded 5th ed. Chicago, IL: Chicago Review Press.

Conclusion
Final Note

Over the last decade of teaching courses on book and digital publishing I have had students working at literary magazines or in one of our book design classes pitch the idea of a book hackathon. Instead of taking the full semester to acquire, assess, design, and produce an issue of their publication or required book (our book and ebook classes require students to produce a complete and valid book/ebook from public domain sources as a final project), they want to run the whole process in a weekend similar to the app hackathons that became part of the entrepreneurial culture around smartphones. These hackathons are the latest iteration of the marketing and publicity events that publishers have been performing at book festivals and book shows for decades. At the 2009 Book Expo America conference, the Perseus Book Group ran a promotion of creating, designing, and releasing a POD, ebook, digital audio, and large print editions of a crowdsourced collection of first lines to sequels to classic works of literature called *Book: The Sequel*. Outside these industry gatherings, online POD printing services pitch the speed in which they can print and deliver copies of an author's book. The Espresso Book Machine from On Demand Books has even moved this idea into bookstores and libraries throughout the world.

What my students soon learned is that the semester-long work they needed to do couldn't be condensed into a weekend. Like any good magic trick, the key to instant publications is the prep work. Book hackathons and POD publishing relies on the creation of templates ahead of time and automating the repetitive work involved in layout and design. It also meant the removal of other processes entirely. The prep work to identify and edit the content (initiation) and create and test the needed templates (planning, development, and quality control) happened in the weeks before the hackathon (release). There was also no marketing, publicity, or sales for these books within the event. And the documentation on what they learned? That wasn't part of the weekend. It's become the final class session in my design classes, but the insights gained at the hackathons were never passed along to future editors of the magazines. In other words, the students soon came to learn that while some parts of publishing can be done quickly, the complete project of creating a book cannot be done simultaneously and the distribution process will continue for weeks after their hackathon. These hackathons became lessons on linear and iterative project management for the students outside the classroom.

DOI: 10.4324/9781003403395-13

As book publishing continues to become more and more digital—production and distribution is already completely digital at this point and the advances in AI indicate creation may soon be completely digital as well—the organizational structure of a publishing house needs to change. The industry can no longer approach its work from a functional mindset. When every step in a book project can be outsourced, the idea of keeping departments separate and limited to their function within the house make little sense. In this book I've tried to suggest how the industry can use project management principles as a model for the work of a publishing house. I've limited the discussion to that of the book project as it is the common work that is carried out across the different areas of the book publishing industry and is understood by anyone working in the industry. But what has been outlined in this book also applies to the projects that are run outside the creation of titles for a seasonal list. Mobile apps, databases, management systems, and the needed management of outsourcing agencies all follow a similar life cycle.

Doing just their part of the work to make a book is no longer enough for a publishing professional. They need to understand the holistic process of making a book across the areas of creation, production, and distribution. While books have a long history of being produced by publishers of all sizes with different needs, they all are working on the same problem: how to efficiently turn a manuscript into a book and effectively get that book to an audience. I hope this book has provided an outline on how this can be done once a house commits to viewing its work through the lens of project management. There is no cookie-cutter solution to creating a more efficient publishing house, but removing the departmental silos and developing cross-departmental teams can start to make a house more flexible. This flexibility will be essential as publishers move forward to respond to the readers' need for print, digital, serialized, and accessible texts.

Index

A

A11Y project 37, 133
acceptance criteria 55, 86
accessibility 7, 123, 132–135; and QA guidelines 73; for ebook files 27, 37, 55, 128, 130
acquisition memo *see* deal memo
Adeyemi, Tomi 147
advanced reading copies (ARC) 16, 22, 100, 123, 145
advance information (AI) sheet 19, 63, 107; in development phase 142, 150; version control of 110
Agile model 6, 14, 80–83; and content creation 111–113; and content distribution 159–161; and content production 130–132; as iterative process 92; design phase 87–88; development phase 88–92; planning phase 85–87; release phase 92; requirements phase 83–85
Amazon 39, 134; Kindle format 34, 110, 122, 126; Kindle Unlimited 156, 163; X-Ray 159
A Million Penguins (website) 93
analytics 113–114, 159
Anand, Bharat 112
Apple 110, 122, 130; app store 85, 160
Archer, Jodie 114
Archipelago Books 153
artificial intelligence 113–114, 168
assessment and redesign of publishing process 42–48
asset management 108–111
Association of Project Management (APM) 51
audiobook 11, 13, 78, 131; creation and distribution model 19–20; in libraries 126; licensing of content for 2, 152
Australia 51, 154

author 99; appearance at literary events 13, 30, 83, 137, 140, 146; as trigger in a book project 41, 66, 103; identification in swim lane diagram 38–39, 42, 44; missing deadlines 32, 71, 75; name as metadata 107, 124, 130, 150, 157; relationship with editorial department 2, 57, 62; relationship with marketing department 140–143; relationship with production department 121; relationship with publicity department 102, 138, 145; role as stakeholder 56, 68; role in the communications circuit 5, 17–25; view of publishing, 1
author advance 15; and risk assessment 32; as part of an editorial workflow 100; as part of linear PLC 103, 105–106; as part of the business case 66–67
author contract: in the linear PLC 62, 104–105; negotiations 40, 105, 114; as trigger in workflow 39, 43. 100; work-for-hire agreement 101

B

backlog documents (Agile) 85, 90, 92, 112
Baen Books 143
Barefoot World Atlas app 79–80, 85, 92
Barnes and Noble 110, 157; B&N Nook 129
Barrett, Dave 51, 54–55, 82
Beehive Books 162
bestseller list 139, 140, 158, 165
beta reader 21, 22
Biel, Joe 2, 123
binding 18, 120; budgetary constraints on 106, 118, 120–121, 125; quality control 127; strip and rebind 138
book apps 30, 87, 112, 160; as iterative projects 63, 79, 83, 92
book as linear project 64–66
book awards 102, 140

Index

book clubs 22, 152, 163; community reading programs 153
book festivals 30, 138, 140, 145, 167
Book Industry Standards Group (BISG) Workflow Committee 2, 24, 25
book interior design 2, 11; and accessibility 133; and book project scheduling 124; in development phase 125; in linear PLC 19, 62, 65, 117; as part of process management 27; in planning phase 120; and quality control 128
book layout and designs (BLAD) 123–124
book miles 156
BookNet Canada 120, 130
book packagers 4, 12, 21, 27, 101, 118
book project 13–16; and accessibility 132–135; closing phase 75–76; and communications circuits 16–20; development phase 71–72; and the distribution workflow 137–139; in the editorial department 105–108; and the editorial workflow 100–102; as an iterative project 93–94, 111–113, 130–132, 159–161; initiation phase 66–69; as linear project 64–66, 76; in the marketing department 139–144; in the production department 119–129; and the production workflow 117–119; in the publicity department 145–148; in the sales department 148–153, 155–157; mapping of its workflow 38–39, 46; planning phase 69–71; quality control phase 72–74; release phase 74; workflow 5–6, 29
book returns 7, 12, 14, 20, 138,; in the distribution workflow 137–138, 157; of award-winning titles 102; textbook 138, 164
book reviews 22, 50, 69, 102, 145, 152, 158; archive of 110, 148
Bookstagram 22, 147, 153
bookstore 7, 14, 21, 101, 107, 127; in the communications circuit 18; in the distribution workflow 138–139; readings see book tour; sales material for 152
BookTok 22, 139, 147, 153
book tour 22, 146–147
BookTube 22, 147, 153
Brady, Laura 134
Bullock, Adrian 2, 19, 107, 120
burndown chart 90–91
burnout within publishing industry 3, 52, 55
business case 55, 66–67, 103; versus requirements phase 83
Business Process Management (BPM) 25, 27–28; framing process 29–34; mapping process 24, 34–35, 46, 57–58

business value creation 50, 57, 69, 100
buzz 138, 144, 147

C
Canelo 28
Carter, David 140
change management 56, 72, 76, 111
change report 72
Charco Press 153
ChatGPT 114
children's book publishing 118, 155
Childress, Clayton 13–14
China 27, 45, 117; shipping from 156–157
choice anxiety 158
Clark, Giles 2, 123, 153, 156
closing phase: and iterative PLC 83; as part of project life cycle 54, 59–60; for book project 74–75; for content creation 108; for content distribution 144, 148, 156; for content production 129–130
co-edition 105, 155
Comerford, Rachel 118, 122
commissioning editor 2, 21, 69; and list development 103; and the project initiation phase 66, 139; as product owner 111, 159; in process mapping 27, 39, 48
communications circuit 16–25
communications plan 65, 106, 160; as part of book project 59, 70, 76
community publishing platforms 7, 79, 113
Complete Anatomy app 87, 89, 92, 93
conflict of interest 68
consequence of inaction in design process 47
content creation 5, 7, 14, 18, 99–100 ; and asset management 108–110; how to identify on a Kanban board 86; in an Agile methodology 111–114, 159; quality control 108; relationship to content distribution 137, 139; relationship to content production 7, 129; representation in swim lane diagrams 38; role in the book project 21, 94, 100–110, 119; within community publishing sites 113–114; workflow 101
content distribution 5, 7, 14, 137; aiding in discoverability 22; emerging technologies in 161–166; in an Agile methodology 159–161; relationship to content creation 139; representation in swim lane diagrams 38; role within a publishing house 6, 14, 63; role within the book project 94, 108, 137; workflow 22, 63
content management system (CMS) 42, 44, 110, 117; content production 5, 7, 14 70, and book project closing 75; in an Agile

methodology 130–132;in communications circuits 18–20; relationship to content creation 129, 131; relationship to content distribution 137, 146; representation in swim lane diagrams 38; role within book project 51–54, 120–130; workflow 4, 15, 63, 117–119
contingency plan 32–33, 71, 113
copy edit; 46, 65; in editorial workflow 101; representation in swim lane diagrams 38, **39**
course of action statement 46
COVID-19 pandemic 24,32, 124, 146
creating process maps 38–41
critical success factors (CSF) 29–30
cross-functional teams 28, 52
Crowdfunding 7, 161–163
Crown Publishing Group 122, 136
curation 81, 126, 163–164

D
Danielewski, Mark 112, 121
Darnton, Robert 16, **17**, 19, 21
Deahl, Rachel 2
deal announcement 145
deal memo 39, 57, 67, 104, *152*
definition of a project 50, 54
De Gruyter 78–79
demand-driven acquisitions 154
desktop publishing 3–4
developmental edit 21, 25, 59, 100, 107
development phase 71; and editorial department 107; and marketing department 142; and production department 125–127; and publicity department 145; and sales department 150; in an iterative project 79, 88–89, 94
digital asset management (DAM) 7, 15, 68, 110, 148
digital repository 110–111, 130
discoverability 22, 137, 151, 157–158, 164
distribution of product 155–156
distribution project management 137–138; workflow 137–139
distribution warehouses 11, 14, 35, 69, 138, 156, and book returns 157, in publishing communications circuit 20, 22
Dohle, Markus 15
Doliveux, Maëlle 162

E
Ebook Central 81, 83
ebook developer 2, 62; focus on accessibility 37; outsourcing to 27, 113, 121; QA testing 73, 128

ebook 11; and accessibility 37, 55, 73–74, 133–135; and asset management 109–110; in closing phase 75, 130; in development phase 112, 126; in planning phase 120, 121; and quality assurance guidelines 73–74; in quality control phase 108, 128–129
Edelweiss 124, 143, 151
editorial assistant 27, 42, 43; proofing of book cover 47; responsibility for coding manuscript 44
editorial department 7, 99, *152;* acquisition process 62, 63, 66; and iterative PLC 111–114; meetings 66, 67; project development 107; project initiation 103–105; project planning 105–106; quality control, release, and closing 108; and XML workflows 44
editorial project management 103–108
editorial workflow 25, 100–103
efficiency 48, 65, 68; and XML workflows 44; in publishing workflows 3, 25, 26, 43
Elder-Moke, Jenny 147
Eliot, T.S. 63, 112, 113
Elsey, Theresa 130
emerging technologies in book distribution 161–164
environmental impact of publishing industry 124, 125, 156
epics (SCRUM) 84, 85
e-reading devices 22, 73, 110, 128–129
Europe 17, 123, 146, 154; environmental impact of transportation 156; title production in 157
European Accessibility Act (EAA) 37, 55
executive dashboard 90

F
Faber 63, 112
fantasy (genre) 66, 106, 113, 143, 144
Faulkner-Wilcocks, Rachel 99
feasibility statement 67
Federation of European Publishers 27, 157
Ferris, Joshua 143
file naming convention (FNC) 74, 109–110, 128
Firebrand Technologies 65, 158
Fitzcarraldo Editions 153
flow diagram *see* network chart
framing the publishing process 30–34
France 140
freelance workers : in editorial workflow 21; in production workflow 118; in project development 72; in project planning

57, 106, 120; as part of publishing communications circuit 18; part of publishing workflow 11, 27; in workflow models 29, 35, 38
functional business orientation 14, 28, 31, 51, 52–53, 81, 132, 168
Functional Managers Versus Project Managers 52–53

G
Gaiman, Neil 147, 163
galley 124, *152*; in book production workflow 123, 124; digital 110, 124; in promotion workflow 145; as publicity deliverable 55
Gantt chart 70, **70**
Germany 27, 123
Goals and obejctives for workflows 33–34
Google 142; Gemini AI 114; Ngram Viewer 114; Play store 160

H
Hachette Book Group 44, 101
Hall, Frania 2, 53
hardcover format 42, 59; and book returns 157; as deliverable of book project 59, 67, 131; economics of printing 118
Harlequin Enterprises 143
Have, Iben 19
Hazelwood, Ali 148
Hoffman, Mary 24
Hoover, Colleen 139, 143, 148, 164
HTML: and accessibility 134; maintenance of 130; use within ebooks 121
HumbleBundle 143–144
hype 16, 124, 137, 144

I
India 45
Initiation of the book project 66–70
initiation phase 56–57; in Agile projects 82; in editorial project management 103–105; in marketing department 139; in production department 119; in publicity department 145; in sales department 148–149
Institute of Creative Technologies at De Montfort University 93
interactivity 79, 112, 126
international sales department *152*, 154
intertextual references 121, 134
interviews: importance in process mapping 35–38; in the creation of user stories 84, 95; to evaluate accessibility 134; inventory management 157

INVEST principle 84
Iron Triangle **56**
iterative project life cycle (PLC) 78–80; compared to linear PLC 62, 78; for content creation 111–114; for content distribution 159–160; for content production 130–132; design phase 87; development phase 88–89; planning phase 85–87; release phase 92; requirements phase 83–85
iterative publishing projects 93–94

J
Jacaranda Books 102
Japan 80, 154, 155
Jess, Tyehimba 102
Jockers, Matthew 114
John Murray Learning Library 63, 160

K
Kanban board 6, 78, 86–87, 90
Kaplan, Deborah 134–135
Karunatilaka, Shehan 102
key performance indicators (KPI) 14, 37, 44, 67, 95
keywords 142, 157, 158
Kickstarter 162–163
Kinokuniya Shoten 154
Klopotek 65
Kuang, R.F. 1

L
LaTeX 4, 133
Lawson, Jenny 146–147
Lean Publishing Manifesto 15
Lee, Marshall 120
Library Sales Department 152, 153
Libraries: community reading programs 153; digital acquisition models 19, 81–82, 126, 154; and Open Access 12, 53
life cycle model 5–7, 52–61
linear project life cycle (PLC) 62–64; book project as 64–66; closing phase 108–109, 129–130, 144, 148, 156–157; compared to iterative PLC 78–80; concerns about 75–76; development phase 107, 125–126, 142, 145–146, 150–151; initiation phase 103–105, 119, 139–140, 145, 148–149; planning phase 105–107, 120–125, 140–141, 145, 149–150; quality control phase 108–109, 126–129, 142, 145–146, 150–151; release phase 108–109, 129, 142–144, 146–147, 151–156; scheduling 122

literary agent 1, 40; in communications circuit 17; role as stakeholder 68; role in book project 21, 27, 101
literary festival see book festivals
Lonely Planet 94

M
Madans, Phil 44
manuscript delivery 2, 104; as trigger for book project 63, 99, 141; delay from author 32, 71, 75
mapping workflow 6, 34–43, 47, 57–58
marketing department 7, 16; in an iterative PLC 93, 159; and the marketing plan 2, 20, 42, 55; project closing 144; project development 107, 142; project initiation 139; project planning 140–141; project release 142–144; quality control 142; role in the book project 12, 15, 53, 74, 118
markup language 4–5; and accessibility 133–13; quality control in digital books 128–129
Martin, Bill 109
matrix structure 14, 28, 53
means of measurement 46
metadata 65, 157–159; and discoverability 137, 142, 161; development through artificial intelligence 113–114; use by editorial department 108; use by marketing department 142; in Open Access 53; use by production department 129, 130; use by sales department 151, 152
milestones 33–34; in an iterative PLC 84; in linear PLC 67; in project planning 35, 57, 106
minimum viable product (MVP) 79, 85, 86; and user stories 111; use in design phase 87
mission statement 30
mobile apps 11, 30; as iterative PLC 51, 112
Moretti, Franco 114
MoSCoW (Must, Should, Could, Won't) method 85, 86, 88, 92
Murray, Padmini Ray 167–19, 18, 21–22
Murray, Simone 16, 140, 141
mystery (genre) 114, 155

N
natural language processing 114
NetGalley 124, 143
network chart 57, **58**
Nixon, Cornelia 13
non-book retailers 137, 152

O
Obama, Barack 122, 126
Ohno, Taiichi 86
O'Neill, Josh 162
Online Information Exchange (ONIX) 150
open access (OA) 53, 78, 117
organizational structure 5, 25, 28, 52–53, 168
outsourcing of work: as part of publishing communications circuit 18; in a publishing workflow 26, 64, 117, 168; in workflow models 37–38, 45
Overdrive 126

P
page design and layout 27, 117, 120, 125; proofs 100, 131;
Palmer, Amanda 163
paperback; in a business case 67; and content distribution 139; in project closing 59, 108, 129; quality control of 127, 151; returns 138, 157
parallel work in assessment process 43–44, 47
pay-what-you-want monetization 143
Pearl, Nancy 153
Pearson 14, 28
Peck, Gretchen 13
Pedersen, Birgitte Stougaard 19
peer review 12, 20, 101
Penguin Random House 15, 93, 121, 150
Phillips, Angus 2, 19, 68, 123, 153, 156
planning phase 57–59; and editorial department 105–107; in an iterative PLC 85; in a linear PLC 69–71; and marketing department 140–141; and production department 120–125; and publicity department 145; and sales department 149–150
postmortem 60, 110
process maps 38–41, 47–48
Prince Harry, Duke of Sussex 150
printing and binding process 35, 118, 120, 125, 127
printing schedule 20, 105, 122, 131
print on demand (POD) model 2, 117, 129
process map 34–35; creation 38–42; workflow variations 41
process-oriented framework for book publishing 16–22
production department 2,4; and accessibility 132–135; and iterative PLC 130–133; and linear PLC 55, 118; project development 108, 125–127; project initiation 119; project planning 105, 119–124; project release

129; project closing 129–130; quality control 73, 126–129
production editor 42, 100; and the BMP model 27–29; and workflow mapping 38
production schedule 94, 106, 122–125
production workflow 7, 117–119, 133
profit and loss (P & L) statement: creation in project initiation 56–57, 104; relationship to business case 67; use in project planning 57, 106, 120
project change 56; in iterative PLC 131; limitations in linear PLC 75–76
project charter 67–68; defining project deliverables 72; for iterative PLC 83; in book project initiation 103, 104; in book project planning 69, 71
project closing *see* closing phase
project constraints 55–56, **56**, 66
project deliverables 19; and the editorial workflow 100; and the production workflow 119; as part of goals and objectives 33; defined in book project initiation 51, 148; influence on project viability 57; in iterative PLC 79–80; in WBS model 57; role in project mapping 40
project development *see* development phase
project handoff 59
project initiation *see* initiation phase
project life cycle 54–55, 60, 81–83
Project Management Institute (PMI) 50–51, 79
project management office (PMO) 14, 50–51, 52
project management theory 2, 5–7, 11–16, 27–29, 50–55 see also iterative project life cycle and linear project life cycle
project managers 2, 51, 52–53, 56, 84
project owner 84, 89, 103, 111, 132
project planning *see* planning phase
project release *see* release phase
project team 52, 54–55; development of user stories 84–85; roles in iterative PLC 81–82; role in project closing 59, 74; role in project initiation 57, 103; role in project planning 71
project viability 57, 68, 101
promotion department *see* publicity department
promotional workflow 22, 138
ProQuest 81, 83, 109
publicity department 7; project closing 148; project development and quality control 145; project initiation and planning 145; project release 146–148
publishing house culture 30, 94, 102, 103

publishing houses: development of publishing workflows 24–27; position in communications circuit 17–19; use of project management 6, 11–12, 50–54
publishing proposal form 20, 103; use in project planning 55, 106–107
Publishing workflows 15, 20, 24–27, 65, 94

Q
quality assurance (QA) 72–74, 82; and accessibility 134; for ebooks 128–129
quality control (QC): for content creation 108–109; for content distribution 142, 145–146, 150; for content production 118, 126; of digital books 128–129; of book project 63, 72–74; of printed books 127–128
quality management 72–74, 108

R
Ray Murray, Padmini 17, 21, 22
redesign process for workflows 45–48
release phase 59; for content creation 108; for content distribution 142–144, 146–148, 151–156; for content production 129; in iterative PLC 82, 92; in linear PLC 74
requirements phase 82, 83–84, 95
retrospective meeting 92
return on investment (ROI) 56–57, 67
risk assessment 31–33, 57, 105, 113
risk matrix 32–33, *32*, 71
romance (genre) 114, 143, 156
royalty payments 12, 100, 156
Running Press 101

S
sales conference 20, 68, 108, 150
sales department 7; and iterative PLC 159–161; library sales *152*, 153–154; project closing 156–157; project development 150–151; project initiation 148–149; project planning 149–150; project release 151–158; quality control 150–151; special sales *152*, 153–154; subsidiary rights 2, 44, 100, 105, 145, *152*, 153–155
schedule 2; for book project 70–71; as part of project planning 122–125
Schwartz, Barry 158
science fiction (genre) 143
scope (constraint) 55–56, 85, 105; creep 111
scope statement 31, 61, 69

Scrum 6, 89–93, 130–131; in iterative book project 78, 94
Scrum Master 84, 89, 92, 131–132
Scrum tracking 90–92
semantic markup 4, 74, 124, 133
sensitivity reader 21, 105
Shatzkin, Mike 158
Simon & Schuster 15, 110, 139, 143
softback *see* paperback
Sort of Books 102
Sphere (publisher) 148
sprint (Scrum) 83–84; backlog 90; relationship to user stories 85
Squires, Claire 17–19, **18**, 21–22, 107
stakeholders 50, 68–70, 131; and product owner in Scrum 89; as part of scope statement 31
Starre, Alexander 120
Sticky Notes 40–41
strategic plan 7, 30–31, 34
subprocesses 39, 40–41, 45, 138
subscription services 163–164
swim lane diagrams 6, 34, 38–42, 47, 117
Swoon Reads 93, 95, 114
SWOT analysis 33, *33*, 44
system as actor in project mapping, 41–42

T
Tallent, Joshua 158
Tapas Entertainment 79, 113
Thompson, John 157
D4Medical 87
Tian, Xuemei 109
timebox 86, 89
title information (TI) sheet, see advance information (AI) sheet
title list development 103–104
title list management 7, 129
Touch Press 63
Transworld publisher 150
Trello (Atlassian software) 65, 86, 103
Tumblr 148, 161
Turk, Wayne 55
typos: as part of quality control 108, 127; corrections as part of workflow 63, 117, 122

U
unboxing video 147
United Kingdom 27, 141, 153, 155

United States 27, 123, 139, 141, 156
user experience (UX) 112, 125, 133, 159
user stories 84–86; backlog 95; and content creation 111–112; and content production 131; and content distribution 160 ; management by Scrum team 89–90; as part of release phase 92; as part of repeat phase 92; use with Kanban Board 86

V
van der Weel, Adriaan 3, 17, 133
variations in project mapping, 41–42
velocity chart 90–92
version control 7, 95, 108–109

W
Wark, McKenzie 93
The Waste Land app 63, 112
waterfall model *see* linear project life cycle (PLC)
Waterstones 153, 157
Wattpad Webtoons Studio 79, 113
Wave Books 102, 153
web content accessibility guidelines (WCAG) 37, 133
Weinberger, David 93
Wiley 14, 28
Winston, Charlie 13
Woll, Thomas 15, 123, 151
work breakdown structure (WBS) 57–58, 107
workflow: analysis 5, 20, 21–22, 25–26; assessment 42–45; and BPM 6, 27–28; for book publishing 24–27; for content creation 100–103; for content distribution 137–138; for content production 117–119; framing 30–33; goals and objectives 29, 33–34, 42; mapping 34–42, 57; modeling 29–34; redesign 45–48
work-for-hire agreement 60, 101
World Health Organization 132
World Wide Web Consortium (W3C) 81, 130

X
X (formerly Twitter) 22, 147
XML 2, 110, 121, 133; workflows 15, 44

Y
young adult (genre) 114, 126, 143, 144

For Product Safety Concerns and Information please contact our EU representative GPSR@taylorandfrancis.com
Taylor & Francis Verlag GmbH, Kaufingerstraße 24, 80331 München, Germany

www.ingramcontent.com/pod-product-compliance
Lightning Source LLC
Chambersburg PA
CBHW051400290426
44108CB00015B/2090